MUSIC & SPEECH PROGRAMS FOR THE IBM PC®

No. 1596
$16.95

MUSIC & SPEECH PROGRAMS FOR THE IBM PC®

BY ROBERT J. TRAISTER

TAB BOOKS Inc.
BLUE RIDGE SUMMIT, PA. 17214

NOTICE:

IBM Personal is a registered trademark of the IBM Corporation.

FIRST EDITION
FIRST PRINTING

Library of Congress Cataloging in Publication Data

Traister, Robert J.
Music and speech programs for the IBM PC.
Includes index.
1. Speech processing systems. 2. Computer music.
3. IBM Personal Computer—Programming. I. Title.
TK7882.S65T7 1983 001.64'43 83-4853
ISBN 0-8306-0196-1
ISBN 0-8306-0596-7 (pbk.)

Contents

Acknowledgments

I wish to acknowledge and thank Frederick Computer Products in Frederick, Maryland, for supplying me with an IBM Personal computer for writing and testing the programs in this book. Special thanks also go to the Votrax Division of Federal Screw Works, Inc. for providing me with a Votrax Type-'N-Talk speech synthesizer which enabled me to include speech programs here.

Other TAB books by the author:

No. 1254 *How to Build Hidden, Limited-Space Antennas That Work*
No. 1316 *The Master Handbook of Telephones*
No. 1409 *Build a Personal Earth Station for Worldwide Satellite TV Reception*
No. 1419 *Astronomy and Telescopes: A Beginner's Handbook*
No. 1433 *Make Your Own Professional Home Video Recordings*
No. 1486 *32 Electronic Power Supply Projects*
No. 1487 *The Shortwave Listener's Antenna Handbook*
No. 1496 *The IBM Personal Computer*
No. 1506 *Making Money with Your Microcomputer*
No. 1526 *33 Games of Skill and Chance for the IBM PC®*
No. 1536 *Beginner's Guide to Reading Schematics*
No. 1556 *Graphics Programs for the IBM PC®*
No. 1566 *Cave Exploring*
No. 2097 *All About Electric and Hybrid Cars*
No. 2321 *The Joy of Flying*

Introduction

Your IBM Personal computer can produce music, sound effects, and speech. For music and sound effects, you won't need any optional accessories. You will be surprised at all that can be accomplished using the computer's built-in speaker and the wide-range tone generator. To obtain speech output, you will need an electronic speech snythesizer, and you will need to connect it to the output of the asynchronous communications adapter.

If you are a novice computerist, you will be pleased with the ready-to-run programs in all three modes that fill this book. There is nothing to fear about getting into sound effects, music, and speech. Generally, these are easy programs to write and may require no more talent than is required for writing the simple text-mode programs.

Of course, a ready-to-run program by itself may be of little or no help in learning to write similar programs on your own, but this book is not comprised solely of ready-to-run programs. Each program is accompanied by a detailed description of how the program was written and how it functions. This will help you form a solid basis in writing programs that output some form of audio information. Whether you're looking for the lovely "Intrata" by Johann Sebastian Bach, the sound of an electric generator starting up, or even a clock that will output the time verbally, this book has it all.

Additionally, several chapters are devoted to a description of the IBM Personal computer, IBM BASIC, and also to the mechanics of speech, music, and sound effects. This book may serve a dual function: First, it provides over 125 ready-to-run programs that address music, speech, and sound effects. Some even combine these three modes of operation. Second, it provides detailed information needed to write original programs on your own. Using this book, you will be able to learn from the ready-to-run programs while enjoying their interesting and quite informative outputs.

The IBM Personal computer is a very powerful and easy to operate device. Coupled with the basic knowledge needed to program in all areas, your machine will become immediately more useful and certainly an invaluable aid to furthering your computer pursuits.

To Cathy Ann . . . she knows why.

The IBM Personal Computer...

Chapter 1

IBM Corporation, the recognized leader in large computers, announced its smallest, lowest-priced computer system, the IBM Personal computer on August 12, 1981. While IBM had been studying the personal computer market for some time, the program that produced the IBM Personal computer took only thirteen months.

Even IBM was surprised by the machine's popularity. Sales of the IBM Personal computer greatly exceeded even their most optimistic expectations, and this machine is rapidly coming to the forefront in overall microcomputer sales. Why? It would be fair to say that IBM's name has stimulated immediate interest among all personal computer owners and potential owners. Of course, this can be a mixed blessing. When people think of computers, they think of IBM. Any computer bearing the IBM Corporation emblem is automatically expected to be outstanding. Following long-established traditions, IBM has developed a product commensurate with its name.

Probably the most talked-about feature of the IBM Personal computer is its 16-bit microprocessor. Most other personal computers are still built around the 8-bit microprocessor, which took the place of 4-bit microprocessors. The IBM Personal computer uses the Intel 8088 microprocessor, which is really an 8-bit microprocessor with 16-bit architecture. This means processing is done on the 16-bit level, but input/output is performed at the 8-bit level. At this point in microcomputer development, the 8088 type of microprocessor is ideal. The 8-bit input/output bus allows for two-way communication. The IBM Personal computer has the power of a 16-bit machine and is compatible with the more common 8-bit interfaces.

The basic IBM Personal computer is shown in Fig. 1-1 and consists of the system unit, an 83-key adjustable keyboard, and the IBM monochrome display monitor. The system unit contains all processing circuitry and will internally accommodate up to two 5¼-inch disk drives. The interior of the unit contains five System Expansion Slots, shown in Fig. 1-2, which allow for the insertion of memory cards and various adapters for a printer, monochrome display monitor, color/graphics monitor,

Fig. 1-1. The IBM Personal computer system consists of the system unit, keyboard, and monochrome display. (Courtesy IBM Corp.)

asynchronous communications, game control, and so forth. The system board is mounted at the bottom of the system unit enclosure and contains the microprocessor and all pertinent circuitry. In basic form, 16K of read/write memory is contained on this board in five memory chips. There are three additional rows of memory sockets that allow for on-board expansion to 64K. The system expansion slots must be used for additional memory expansion, which is handled by memory boards each containing 64K. Using the slots, storage capability may be increased to a maximum of 256K of RAM.

The IBM Personal computer contains a very powerful read-only memory (ROM). This gives the system versatile on-board capability. Whereas most personal computers may contain less than 64K of ROM, the IBM Personal computer contains 40K and thus in many ways resembles a minicomputer rather than a microcomputer.

IBM has designed its personal computer for the first-time user or for someone with advanced microcomputer experience. The machine is applicable to business and is useful for students. The 83-key adjustable keyboard is equipped with a 6-foot coiled cable and may be operated some distance from the system unit and the IBM monochrome display, which is mounted on top of the system unit enclosure.

The IBM monochrome display is driven by an adapter card, which is inserted into one of the system expansion slots (Fig. 1-2). This display has an antiglare screen, controls for brightness and contrast, and outputs green phosphor characters. Automatic flashing and underlining capabilities are provided, which can be used to call attention to important information on the screen. This is a high-resolution monochrome monitor, one of the best available. Unfortunately, this unit does not possess high-resolution graphics capabilities. Any serious graphics work will require a color/graphics monitor and a matching adapter card. This card also outputs composite video, so a modulator may be connected to the output jack in order to drive a standard television receiver. Several companies manufacture modulators that interface directly with the IBM Personal computer. IBM does not offer such a device. The IBM monochrome monitor may be used for limited graphics work. This involves calling up ASCII characters within the program, then printing these characters on the screen. Using this method of programming, bar graphs may be easily drawn, as can squares, rectangles, and other geometric designs. More programming is necessary than with those units equipped with color/graphics adapter cards and appropriate monitors. The IBM Advanced BASIC language (BASICA) is used in the color/graphics mode to easily draw circles, rectangles, lines, and so forth. With these additions, the IBM Personal computer becomes a very powerful graphics display device.

The IBM monochrome display adapter also contains printer adapter circuitry. You can, however, buy a separate printer adapter if you intend to use a monitor other than IBM's monochrome dis-

Fig. 1-2. The system expansion slots are used to insert memory cards and adapters.

play. The monochrome display/printer adapter card combination costs approximately $300, whereas the discrete printer adapter card is only $150. The IBM 80 CPS printer provides twelve type styles; is a compact impact printer, accepting form widths up to 12 inches; and is attached to the system unit by an IBM-supplied cable. The printer is powered from a separate 115-Vac source and contains an on-board printer self-test function, permitting it to be fully checked even when not connected to the system unit. Printing occurs at 80 characters per second using a long-lasting ribbon cartridge.

Most people order the IBM Personal computer with the 5¼-inch disk drive adapter and at least one disk drive. My unit contains two drives, which I have found convenient to process the large number of programs that must be stored and run when I write books on programming. Each disk has a storage capability of 160K and is used with the IBM disk operating system (DOS) program. IBM does offer an optional disk drive that stores up to 340K.

Another option is the asynchronous communications adapter, which provides the user with a channel to data processing or input/output devices which are outside of the immediate system. Such devices often are connected by telephone lines using a plug-in modem or by cable when the device is nearby. This allows the IBM Personal computer to contact other IBM Personal computers, large host computers, paper tape readers, laboratory instruments, or other machines providing the popular RS-232-C asynchronous interface. The adapter is flexible enough to match most computers and related products available in the microcomputer marketplace.

A user's program allows for the selection of 50 to 9600 bits per second (BPS); 5-, 6-, 7-, or 8-bit character format; and parity and stop bits to reflect the attached device. When communication has been established, this same program performs the read/write function and allows for interrupts to permit the program to perform data processing tasks.

Votrax Consumer Products in Troy, Michigan now makes a phoneme-based speech synthesizer, the Type-'N-Talk, which may be connected directly to the asynchronous communications adapter to give the IBM Personal computer unlimited speech capability. The synthesizer creates speech from electronic phonemes using a set of rules that describes English pronunciation. An unlimited vocabulary is inserted directly into the user's software program, in much the same manner that statements are used to activate the 80 CPS printer or monochrome display. This synthesizer sells for less than $400 and interfaces directly to the IBM Personal computer through the asynchronous communications adapter. It accepts input from the computer at 9600 baud.

BASIC language application programs that support communications require a disk-based 32K system (minimum) containing IBM DOS and BASIC extensions that include communications support.

WARRANTY AND MAINTENANCE

When considering any piece of electronic equipment, especially a highly complex machine such as the IBM Personal computer, the warranty and maintenance program established by the manufacturer is a major factor. IBM has long been known for its excellent maintenance programs; the IBM Personal computer is no exception. This machine has a warranty period of three months; service may be obtained by delivering a malfunctioning machine element (system unit, keyboard) to an IBM Product/Service Center, an IBM Customer Service Division (CSD) designated Service Location, or to an authorized IBM Personal computer dealer. Warranty service is also available by mailing a malfunctioning unit to the IBM National Support Center in Greencastle, Indiana. Proof of purchase from IBM or an authorized IBM Personal computer dealer is required to obtain warranty service.

Warranty service by IBM consists of the repair of the system unit and the replacement of the monochrome display, the matrix printer, or the keyboard. The replacement unit will be a similarly configured unit in good working order. The malfunctioning unit becomes the property of IBM.

Customers desiring warranty service from IBM must call the toll-free number for the National

Support Center and provide information including: the results of the problem determination Diagnostic Aid program, machine serial number, location, and whether the malfunctioning unit will be carried to a service location or mailed to the National Support Center.

Units taken to a service location must be picked up by the customer. For units mailed to the National Support Center, the customer may pay shipping charges to the center and must purchase insurance, or assume the risk of loss or damage in transit. IBM will pay these charges for return shipment to the customer's location. IBM tries to repair a system unit in one or two days. If the repair is performed at the National Support Center, shipping time should be added to the repair time. If the malfunctioning unit is the monochrome display, the matrix printer or keyboard, IBM tries to have a replacement unit available at a service location within twenty four hours of notification to IBM. If the customer ships the malfunctioning unit to the National Support Center, IBM attempts to ship a replacement unit within twenty four hours of receipt.

If a customer requests warranty service on a unit IBM would ordinarily elect to replace rather than repair, the customer may choose, for an additional charge, to have the unit repaired at the National Support Center instead of exchanged. IBM tries to repair the malfunctioning unit in one or two days plus shipping time.

Maintenance service is offered by IBM and is available under the terms and conditions of the IBM Personal Computer Service Agreement, Warranty Extension Option and Annual Option. The Warranty Extension Option is available only if selected prior to or during the warranty period. The agreement commencement date is concurrent with the start of warranty and continues for twelve months. After twelve months, the service agreement will be renewed automatically under the Annual Option, discussed later in this section. Written notice of any applicable price changes are provided prior to renewal. Customers not wishing to renew must withdraw their machines from the agreement.

The Warranty Extension Option provides for IBM-arranged pickup of a malfunctioning unit, and replacement with a similarly configured unit in good working order at a location designated by the customer. Pickup and delivery is available if the unit is located within a designated service area, normally a 3-mile radius of a service location. Service continues to be available by delivering to a service location or mailing to the National Support Center. IBM attempts to have a replacement unit available at a service location for pickup or delivery to the customer if within the designated service area less than twenty four hours from notification to IBM. If the customer ships the malfunctioning unit to the National Support Center, IBM tries to ship a replacement unit within twenty four hours of receiving the unit.

The Annual Option may be selected during the warranty period, and if accepted by IBM, the commencement date will be the day after the end of warranty. If this agreement is selected after the end of the warranty period, IBM must inspect the machine at the National Support Center. There is a charge for this inspection. If repairs are required to qualify for this agreement, IBM will provide an estimate; after customer authorization, IBM will perform the repairs. The customer will be billed for time and material.

The service provided by the Annual Option is the same as that provided by the Warranty Extension Option. The term of this option is twelve months, automatically renewed annually. Written notice of any applicable price changes will be provided prior to renewal. Customers not wishing to renew must remove their machine from the agreement.

Under both options, the customer may choose to have a unit repaired rather than replaced at the National Support Center. In that case, IBM tries to repair the malfunctioning unit in one or two days plus shipping time.

The following customer responsibilities apply during warranty and under the Service Agreements:

- Identifying the malfunctioning unit through problem determination using the Diagnostic Aid program.

●Notifying IBM, through the National Support Center's toll-free number, of the malfunctioning unit and providing all required information, including results of the Diagnostic Aid program, machine serial number, and location.

●Preparing the malfunctioning unit for shipping in the original or equivalent container. IBM will provide shipping containers for purchase by the customer.

●Removing all non-IBM devices or features before delivery to IBM.

●Accepting, unpacking and testing replacement (or repaired) units.

The National Support Center is accessible at a toll-free number to receive notification of hardware problems and to assist the customer in isolating problems. The Center will obtain certain customer information, provide advice on equipment disposition as per the customer's agreement, assist in isolating the malfunctioning unit, and coordinate pickup and delivery.

Agreements are not transferable in the event of the loss or sale of a unit. Agreements are purchased for a period of twelve months, payable through a one-time nonrefundable annual charge at time of purchase.

Time and materials service is available only by mailing to the National Support Center in Greencastle, Indiana. Labor, service, parts, and all transportation costs are billable to the customer. The customer must perform problem determination using the Diagnostic Aid program; telephone the National Support Center; remove all non-IBM devices and features, insure or assume risk of loss or damage in transit; and accept, unpack and examine the repaired unit.

In addition to the CSD service offerings the customer may purchase Advanced Service Aids, which permit the customer to isolate a problem to an under-the-cover field replaceable unit (FRU). Personnel using this diagnostic package must have completed the service training requirements for the IBM Personal computer. If the customer has the technical ability to follow written services procedures, the customer will be able to perform many of the necessary repairs.

Qualifying educational institutions will be eligible to receive the standard educational allowance, which will be available only for orders of VPA quantity. The standard educational allowance will be applied if it is greater than the volume purchase price reduction percentage. The educational allowance will not be applied to the pilot system quantity included in the VPA quantity.

The IBM Personal computer requires setup by the purchaser. The allowance for setup is one day. Detailed setup instructions are included with each machine. The customer is responsible for unpacking the system components, attaching them correctly, and running the diagnostic program. Customers using DOS disk and software requiring disks are responsible for copying the original disks (when copying is permitted) and following the terms and conditions of the IBM Program License Agreement.

TECHNICAL ASSISTANCE

A newly formed Personal Computer Assistance Center provides telephone assistance to customers who install IBM software for the IBM Personal computer, for three months after a system has been installed. Moreover, customers who have signed a VPA may designate a coordinator at one location who may call the center. Assistance for this coordinator will be available during the VPA period and for three months after installation of the last system shipped under the VPA. If software code appears defective, the center will document the problem and submit it to the Information Systems Division (ISD).

I received my computer shortly after the IBM PC was first introduced. Since I was writing a book about this machine, I needed much more detailed information than the average user would require. I found the IBM technical assistance team extremely helpful. Many of the IBM technicians have purchased their own IBM Personal computers and were enthusiastic about verifying my ideas. I felt that IBM personnel were quite excited about the machine. One of IBM's strong points lies in supporting their products with documentation, assistance, and immediate service. It can be safely said that even IBM does not yet realize the full operational potential of this computer. As more and more people use this device, new applications and procedures are being discovered.

SOFTWARE

The IBM Personal computer is still a new machine, thus software, especially from a hobbyist's standpoint, is not as available as for other personal computers. However, there are many ready-to-run programs available from IBM, and other companies offer compatible software. This book helps to fill the software gap. In text mode, you will find that many programs designed to be input by keyboard to other types of microcomputers will run on the IBM Personal computer with few modifications. Graphics programs, however, may require reworking in order for them to run properly. Chapter 2 overviews IBM Personal computer BASIC, noting some of the differences between it and other dialects of this language.

The experienced microcomputer hobbyist should have no lasting difficulties, even when converting programs for graphics operation, but a thorough reading of IBM's BASIC manual will be required along with much trial and error (input and debugging) at the beginning. I found graphics programming to be somewhat difficult at first, mianly because I was accustomed to other machines and their own dialects of BASIC. Graphics programming quickly seemed to make good sense, and is a much quicker method than other languages with which I have worked.

Because of the limited graphics capability of the IBM monochrome display, I found graphics programming for this monitor to be very challenging. When switching to the color/graphics monitor adapter and full graphics programming, one could easily become firmly entrenched in IBM graphics alone. The Advanced BASIC language (BASICA) offers many shortcuts to graphics programming; for this reason I highly recommend the purchase of the IBM disk operating system (DOS) program, which contains Advanced BASIC.

DOS is a valuable debugging aid and offers easy editing procedures. For example you can input a program for another machine into IBM BASIC, then switch to DOS and make near-instantaneous changes throughout the program in order to make it compatible with IBM BASIC. Consider the Set statement, which is common to many dialects of BASIC. IBM has no such statement and substitutes Pset or Preset. If a program is input using the Set statement, it will not run on the IBM machine. However, once the program is input via the keyboard, you can switch to DOS and issue a single command to change all Set statements to Pset or Preset. This will be accomplished electronically within the blink of an eye, possibly saving hours of rewrite time. This is but one of the many features of this very powerful operating system. The Debug feature (which is separate from the Edlin feature) allows for debugging at the machine level. DOS also offers batch processing and many other capabilities not common in other microcomputers.

Through its release of the IBM Personal computer, IBM Corporation has given the microcomputer field a truly revolutionary machine that will do many things not normally associated with microcomputers. The IBM Personal computer seems to offer more of everything and is a "fast" machine because of the 16-bit internal architecture of the Intel 8088 microprocessor. If you have not already done so, I feel you will quickly discover the ease of operation this machine has to offer, along with its highly sophisticated processing capabilities. The programs presented later have been written to take advantage of as many of these features as possible and, to some persons, will serve as a useful education in programming the IBM Personal computer.

HARDWARE OVERVIEW

For those who have not yet purchased an IBM Personal computer and for those who do not yet own every available option, this section provides descriptions of each of the block components of the entire IBM PC system.

System Unit/Keyboard

The system unit, shown in Fig. 1-3, is the heart of the IBM Personal computer. The system unit with its companion keyboard is rugged, easy to use,

Fig. 1-3. The system unit is the heart of the IBM Personal computer system.

and controls a variety of input/output devices. Each system unit comes with at least 16K (16,384 bytes) of memory for user programs. Based on the high-performance Intel 8088 microprocessor, each system unit includes in the 40K ROM an enhanced version of the popular Microsoft BASIC-80 Interpreter, and a jack for attachment of a user-supplied cassette recorder for loading or saving programs and data. A programmable speaker which can produce tones is also standard. The system unit can be expanded further through options that are customer-installed in five system expansion slots (one of which is used for a display or monitor adapter).

Memory may be incremented from 16K to 64K on the system board of the system unit, and then up to a system unit total of 256K. While each system unit has a jack for the attachment of a cassette recorder, one or two disk drives may be easily added for rapid access to programs and data.

Highlights of the system unit include:

- Intel 8088 Microprocessor
- 4.77 MHz clock speed
- Up to 256K random access memory
- 250ns memory access time
- 410ns cycle time
- Parity checking
- 63.5 watt power supply; cooling fan
- Approximate dimensions: 16-inch depth, 20-inch length, 6-inch height.
- Approximate weight: 21 lbs (without disk drive)

An enhanced version of the Microsoft BASIC-80 Interpreter (cassette level) is standard in the ROM of each system unit. Highlights of the BASIC-80 Interpreter include:

- Select 40 or 80 character display lines
- Full screen editor for easy program creation and modification
- Up to 16 foreground and 8 background colors (with appropriate monitor adapter)
- Automatic line numbering
- 40-character variable names (all characters significant)
- Multiple statements per program line

- 250 characters per program line
- Comments on program lines
- Up to 17-digit numeric precision
- Supports sequential cassette files
- Error trapping
- Addressable workspace up to 60K
- Integer/real/string variables
- Single- and double-precision floating-point numbers

The keyboard, shown in Fig. 1-4, is attached to the system unit with a 6-foot coiled cable, permitting adaptation to a variety of work environments. The 83-key keyboard, with an adjustable typing angle, offers commonly used data and work processing functions in a design that combines the familiar typewriter and calculator pad layouts. All noncontrol keys are typamatic (repeating). Ten program-supported function keys (total of 40 possible functions using keyboard shift keys) are standard. Special symbols, such as those used to draw lines, may be accessed with a combination of keys. Depending on the application program, from ten to forty special function keys may be supported. Other keys (like those used to print the current screen contents, correct a typing error, or "scroll" a long document) are clearly labeled. Access to all 256 characters (ASCII and special) is provided by the use of the ALT key.

The approximate dimensions of the keyboard are: 8-inch depth, 20-inch length, and 2.5-inch height. The approximate weight is six pounds. The IBM 80 CPS matrix printer may be attached for hard copy printout.

For video output, the user has a choice of connecting, with proper adapters, a high-quality IBM monochrome display, a color or black-and-white monitor, or, through a customer-supplied RF modulator attachment, a color or black-and-white TV set. Computer-generated video output may vary from a simple 40-by-25-character alphabetic display, to 80-character-per-line "text" application, to high-resolution graphics.

Fig. 1-4. The IBM keyboard contains 83 keys and attaches to the system unit via a 6-foot cable.

The keyboard and customer-supplied cassette recorder are plugged directly into the system unit. The display and printer are connected via an optional adapter installed inside the system unit.

When turned on, the system unit automatically runs a power-on self test to verify system readiness. If the validation is successfully completed, the BASIC ROM Interpreter (cassette level) is made ready and identified on the display screen. The user may not enter a program from the keyboard or load it from a cassette recorder. If a failure is found, an identifying number will appear on the screen.

If a disk drive is installed, the system unit automatically loads from the disk in drive A. This is typically the Disk Operating System (DOS) or application program. The DOS may in turn invoke the Disk or Advanced levels of BASIC, following by the manual or automatic execution of one or more BASIC programs.

The IBM Personal computer requires a video display device for display output. A cassette recorder or a disk drive is required for program or data storage. The IBM Personal computer is powered by a standard 110-volt, 60-Hz power source.

IBM Monochrome Display

The IBM monochrome display, shown in Fig. 1-5, is a high-resolution device with an 11½-inch diagonal, green phosphor screen. The screen area provides for 25 rows of 80 characters. Characters are 7 by 9 dots in a 9 by 14 box. Both upper- and lowercase letters can be displayed. The character attributes provide underline, blinking, high intensity, reverse image, and nondisplay. In addition to the normal alphameric characters, a large number of special characters are provided. A set of line graphic characters is supported for simple display drawings.

Fig. 1-5. The IBM monochrome display comes equipped with signal and power cables.

The IBM monochrome display is supplied with signal and power cables. The signal cable is plugged into the IBM monochrome display and printer adapter, which is inserted into the second system expansion slot on the left, as viewed from the front of the system unit. The power cable is plugged into the system unit.

The approximate display dimensions are 14-inch depth, 15-inch length, and 11-inch height. The weight is approximately 17 pounds.

IBM 80 CPS Matrix Printer

The IBM printer, shown in Fig. 1-6, is an 80 character-per-second bidirectional matrix printer. It uses pin-feed, continuous form (4-inch to 10-inch width), multipart paper. Under program control, the pitch can be selected for 40-, 66-, 80-, or 132-character lines. Both horizontal and vertical tabs are supported. Twelve character styles are available.

Several features of the printer make it especially easy to use. When first turned on, it runs a self test (Fig. 1-7). A bell sounds when it is out of paper, which is simple to load and adjust. The ribbon cartridge can be quickly changed, and the print head is a low-cost item that can be replaced by the user. The printer responds to a variety of commands from the system unit to control page spacing, select the desired character style, or skip to a specified row or column.

The printer requires a signal cable (Fig. 1-8) for connection to either the IBM monochrome display and printer adapter or the IBM printer adapter. A 6-foot signal cable may be purchased from IBM. The printer comes with a 6-foot power cable and requires a 12-volt, 60-Hz source. The approximate printer dimensions are 16-inch length, 15-inch deep, and 4.5-inch height. It weighs approximately 13 pounds.

IBM Monochrome Display and Printer Adapter

The IBM monochrome display and printer adapter is a plug-in card that provides for attachment of both the IBM monochrome display and the IBM 80 CPS matrix printer. The adapter provides cable connectors for attachment of the printer and the display at the rear of the system unit. The card (Fig. 1-9) should be plugged into the second system expansion slot on the left as viewed from the front of the system unit.

Color/Graphics Monitor Adapter

The color/graphics monitor adapter (Fig. 1-10) provides for the attachment of a television frequency display to the IBM Personal computer. Either a "direct-drive RGB" signal or a "composite" video signal can be selected. The display can be a monitor, or, through a customer-supplied RF modulator, a standard TV set. Either a color or black-and-white monitor or TV can be attached. Sixteen foreground and eight background colors are supported in text (character) mode. This attach-

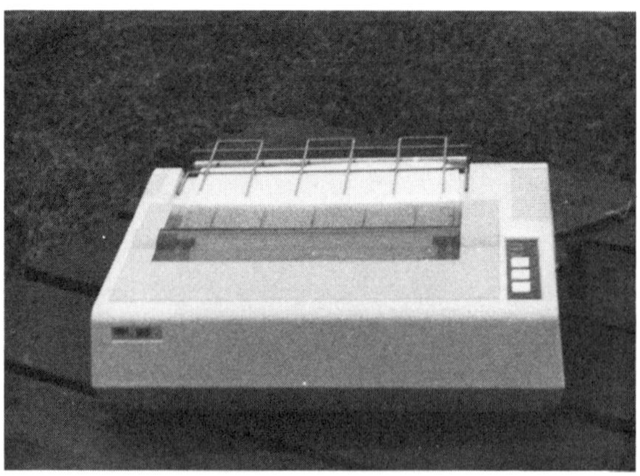

Fig. 1-6. The IBM 80 CPS matrix printer.

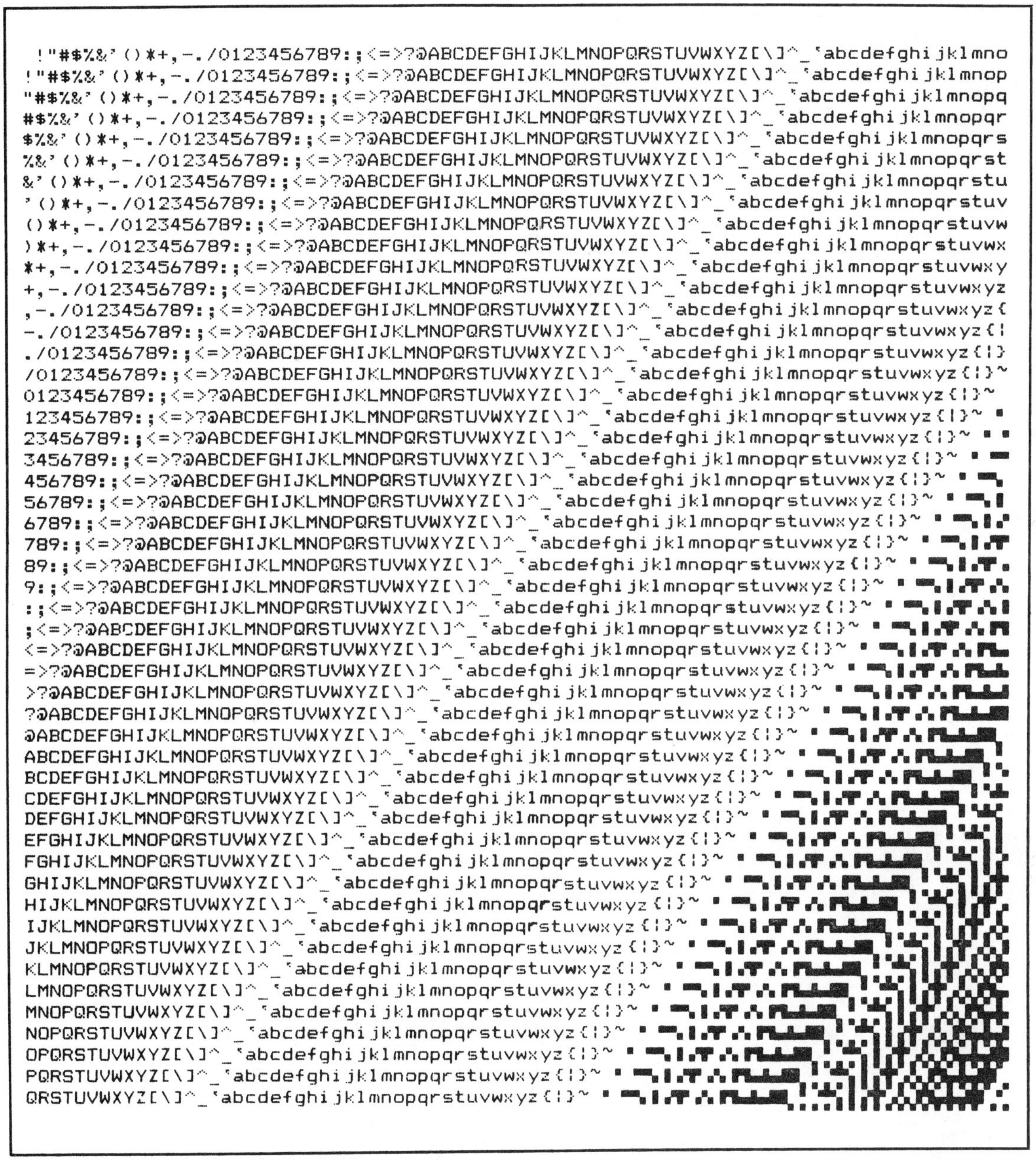

Fig. 1-7. When the printer is turned on, it runs a self test.

ment also provides support for four-color medium-resolution graphics (320 dots horizontal, 200 dots vertical). Two hundred fifty six characters are available in text mode, 128 in medium or high-resolution graphics. The adapter provides 16K of built-in memory to store multiple display screen contents and supports a customer-supplied light pen. The adapter should be plugged into the second system expansion slot on the left, as viewed from the front of the system unit.

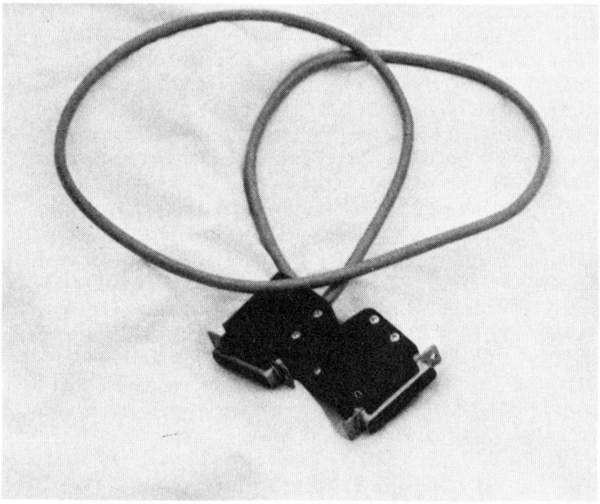

Fig. 1-8. A signal cable is used to connect the printer to adapters.

Printer Adapter

The printer adapter (Fig. 1-11) provides for attachment of the IBM 80 CPS matrix printer. This option is used when the color/graphics monitor adapter is selected instead of the IBM monochrome display and printer adapter.

16K Memory Expansion Kit

The 16K memory expansion kit allows up to 64K of memory to be plugged into the system board. This memory is available in 16K increments and must be used to provide the first 64K of memory.

32K Memory Expansion Option

The 32K memory expansion option is used to increase the memory beyond the 64K on the system board by installing one or more of these options. Each option provides an additional 32K of memory. The system board must first contain 64K of memory before this option can be used. Each option requires a system expansion slot.

64K Memory Expansion Option

The 64K memory expansion option (Fig. 1-12) is used to increase the memory beyond the 64K on the system board by installing one or more of these options. Each option provides an additional 64K of memory. The system board must first contain 64K of memory before this option can be used. Each option requires a system expansion slot.

5¼-Inch Disk Drive Adapter and Disk Drive

The 5¼-inch disk drive adapter (Fig. 1-13) allows up to two 5¼-inch 160K disk drives (Fig. 1-14) to be installed inside the system unit. This user-installable drive allows the IBM Personal computer to read, write, and store data on 5¼-inch disk. Storage capacity is approximately 160K per

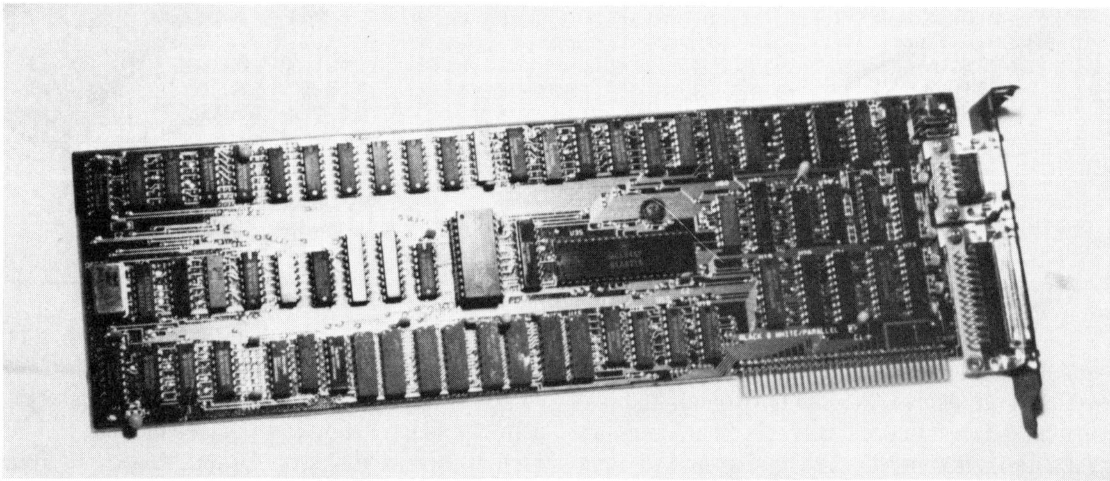

Fig. 1-9. The IBM monochrome display and printer adapter.

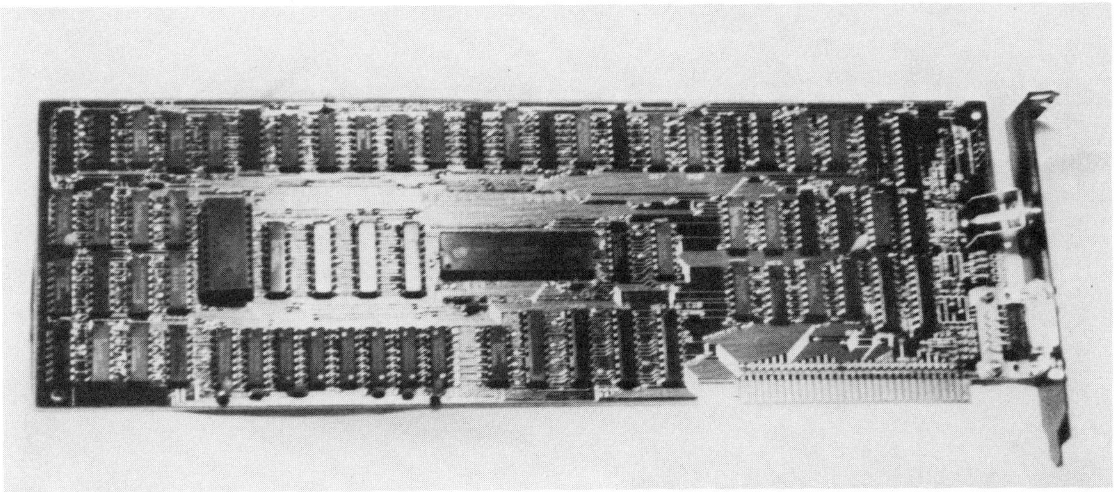

Fig. 1-10. The color/graphics monitor adapter.

disk. The disk drive has the following characteristics: 48 tracks per inch, 40 tracks per disk, 300 revolutions per minute, 8 ms track-to-track access time, and 20,480 bytes per second transfer rate. One or two drives may be installed in a system unit.

Asynchronous Communications Adapter

The asynchronous communications adapter (Fig. 1-15) provides you with a channel to data processing or input/output devices outside of the immediate system. These can be connected by telephone using a plug-in modem, or directly by cable when the device is nearby. The communication "target" may be a large host computer, a Series/1, another IBM Personal computer, a paper tape reader, a communicating typewriter, a laboratory instrument, or other machine(s) providing the RS-232-C asynchronous interface.

Fig. 1-11. The IBM printer adapter.

The asynchronous communications adapter is flexible enough to match most of the computers and related products available in the microcomputer market. Once communication has been established, the user's program performs reads and writes. Interrupts permit the program to perform data processing such as calculating; disk reading, writing and printing; and then to pause to resume communications when a signal appears on the line.

The asynchronous communications adapter has been verified to communicate with an IBM Series/1 with feature #1610, 2091/2092 attachment card using a sample program provided on the IBM Personal computer DOS disk, and an application program running on Realtime Programming System 5 and Event Driven Executive Version.

The asynchronous communications adapter provides an EIA RS-232-C interface. One 25-pin "D" shell, male-type connector is provided to attach various peripheral devices. In addition, a current-loop interface is located in the same connector. A jumper block is provided to select manually either the voltage or the current loop interface.

BASIC language application programs supporting communications will require a disk-based,

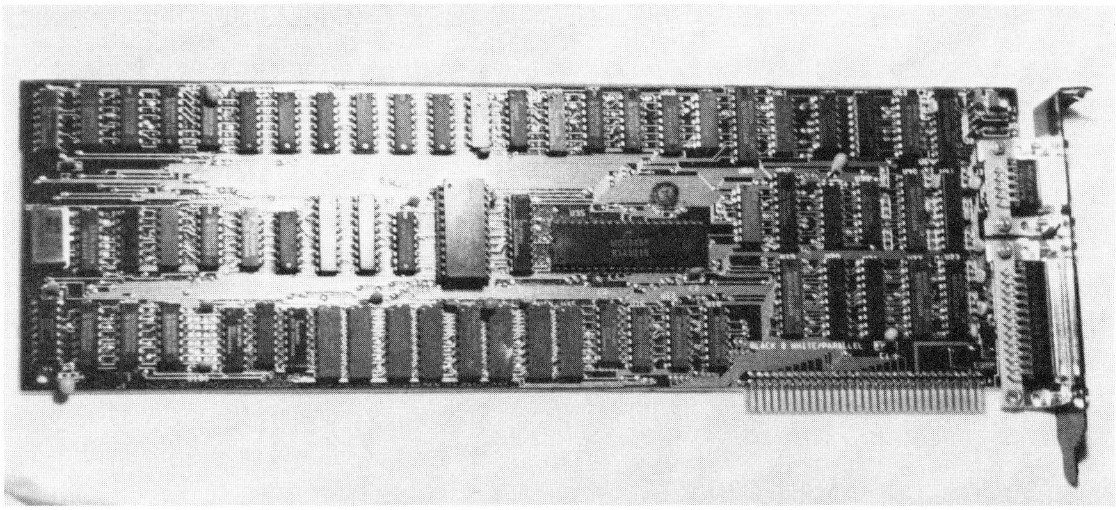

Fig. 1-12. The 64K memory expansion option.

minimum 32K system containing DOS and the BASIC language extensions which include communications support.

Printer Cable

The printer cable is a signal cable used to connect the IBM 80 CPS matrix printer to either the IBM monochrome display and printer adapter or the printer adapter. A printer stand is also available, which supports the IBM 80 CPS matrix printer and holds fanfold paper.

Game Control Adapter

The Game Control Adapter supports two

Fig. 1-13. The 5¼-inch disk drive adapter.

Fig. 1-14. A typical 5¼-inch disk used with the IBM Personal computer.

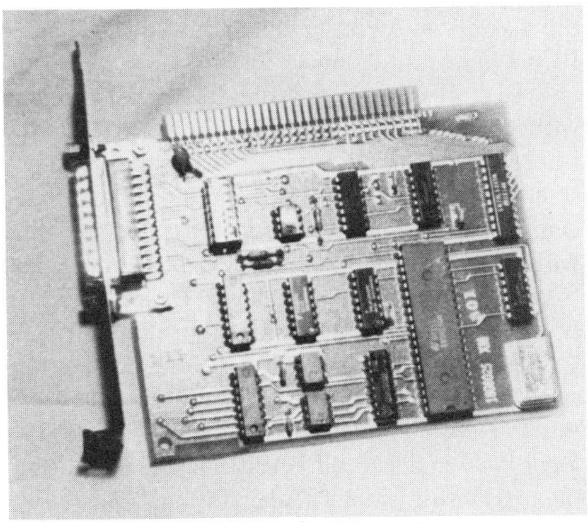

Fig. 1-15. The asynchronous communications adapter.

customer-supplied joysticks for video game interaction, allowing the user to move an object on the screen in any direction, or supports up to four customer-supplied game paddles for simple horizontal or vertical movement.

Hardware Requirements for This Book

Many of the programs in this book run in text mode and require only a minimum IBM system, namely the system unit, keyboard, IBM monochrome display, adapter board and 16K memory. Some programs run in the graphics mode, which requires the color/graphics monitor and adapter, along with IBM DOS. Any programs in text mode may also be run in graphics mode using a separate monitor, but not vice versa.

Chapter 2

IBM Personal computer BASIC is a powerful and versatile language. It is not too different from other BASIC dialects, but many programs written in BASIC for other machines will not run directly on the IBM PC. This is not unusual, as dialect modifications are often required for different machines. Fortunately, BASIC is easy to master and dialect modifications are learned just as easily.

The IBM Personal computer offers three versions of the BASIC: Cassette BASIC, Disk BASIC, and Advanced BASIC (BASICA). The three versions are upward compatible. Cassette BASIC is the nucleus of IBM BASIC; Disk BASIC does everything Cassette BASIC does and a little more; and Advanced BASIC does everything Disk BASIC does but also offers additional features.

Cassette BASIC is built into the IBM Personal computer in 32K of ROM. You can use Cassette BASIC on an IBM Personal computer with any amount of RAM. The only storage device you can use is a cassette tape recorder.

Disk BASIC and Advanced BASIC are both part of the IBM Disk Operating System (DOS). IBM DOS is a group of programs available on a 5¼-inch disk for about $20. It is loaded into memory using the disk drive. All programs in this book run using IBM DOS.

Disk BASIC requires a disk-based machine with at least 32K bytes of RAM. You load it into the machine using a disk drive. An internal clock keeps track of the data and time, and an asynchronous communications (RS-232) support, in combination with the IBM communications adapter, allows you to talk with other IBM computers. Disk BASIC also offers support for two additional printers.

Advanced BASIC (BASICA), the most extensive form of IBM BASIC, requires a disk-based machine with at least 48K RAM. Special features found only in advanced BASIC include event trapping, advanced graphics, and advanced music support. The additional graphics statements—Circle, Draw, Get, Paint, and Put—make it easier to create highly complex graphics with the computer and an optional color/graphics monitor adapter. The Play music statement in advanced BASIC allows easy use of the built-in speaker to create musical tones.

All forms of IBM BASIC contain an extended character set of 256 different characters. If you have the color/graphics monitor adapter, you can draw points, lines, and even entire pictures. The screen is all points addressable in either medium or high resolution.

BASIC STATEMENTS

ABS This function returns the absolute value of an expression, which is always positive or zero. This BAS (8*(-7)) will return 35.

ASC This function returns to the screen the ASCII code for the first character on the screen which follows. If A$ = "RADAR", then command PRINT ASC (A$) will then return the number 82, which is the ASCII value of the letter R.

ATN This mathematical function returns the arc tangent of a value. For example, ATN (3) will return the arc tangent of 3, which is 1.249046.

Auto AUTO, a highly useful command, speeds program writing; as it allows you to write programs without having to type in a number for each program line. It is not part of an actual program but is input prior to programming in order to generate the automatic numbering sequence. After you input Auto command and press the Enter button, a 10 will automatically be printed. After you type in the program line and hit Enter again, a 20 appears in the next line position, and so forth.

You can also use the Auto command in the body of a program. For example, if you input program lines numbered from 10 through 110, you can input AUTO 120, 10, and line numbers will be automatically generated thereafter beginning with line number 120 and will advance in increments of 10. You can also number program lines in steps of 5, 10, 15, 20, or whatever increments you choose using the Auto command. Inputting AUTO 5, 5 causes the first line number to be 5 and all succeeding lines to be numbered in increments of 5. Without these additional numbers, the default is automatically the number 10 and advances in increments of 10. When the additional numbers are inserted, the one immediately following the command will be the next printed line number. The one following the comma will set the incremental steps.

Beep The Beep statement causes the computer to output an 800-Hertz tone to the internal speaker. The tone lasts for approximately one-quarter second and is used as an audible prompt.

Bload The Bload command causes a memory image to be loaded into memory . When a Bload command is executed, the file is loaded into memory starting at a specified location. This command is immediately followed by the string expression for the file and then by an offset number which specifies the address at which loading is to start. The Bload statement is usually preceded by a DEF SEG statement, which defines the current segment of storage.

Bsave This command saves portions of the computer's memory on a specified device. If the device name is omitted, the machine defaults to the first drive (cassette or disk). When using a dual-disk system, this statement is quite useful for choosing which drive is to receive the input information.

Call The Call statement is a method of interfacing machine-language programs with BASIC. It calls a machine-language subroutine. This statement is followed by the name of a numeric variable whose value indicates the starting memory address.

CDBL CDBL is a function which converts the numeric expression following it to a double-precision number. The value of the number is accurate to the second decimal place after rounding.

Chain The Chain statement transfers control of the machine to another program, and passes along the variables from the current program to the one which is to be in control. This allows the operator to easily inset previously input variables from one program into a new one, and greatly decreases overall run time.

**CHR$** This function is the opposite of the ASC function. It is used to convert an ASCII code into its character equivalent. For example, CHR$ (82) will return the letter R. The CHR$ function is used for many purposes, including the writing of some limited graphics using the IBM monochrome monitor and adapter board. For example, CHR(219) causes a solid square to be printed on the screen. This is not available by depressing a single keyboard key.

CINT The CINT function is used to convert a numeric expression to an integer. For example, CINT(37.92) would result in 38. The numeric expression is converted to an integer by rounding its fractional portion.

Clear The Clear command frees all memory used for data without erasing the program which is currently in memory. It sets all numeric values to zero and all string variables to null.

Close The close statement is used to end all input/output to a device or file. This statement may be followed by designators that determine which files or devices are to be closed, but when used alone CLOSE causes all open devices and files to be closed.

CLS The CLS statement clears the screen. If the screen is in graphics mode, the entire screen buffer is cleared to the background color. The CLS statement is used with a program to erase all printed information input to the screen to this point.

COM The COM statement is used in conjunction with a communications adapter and enables or disables trapping of communications activity. The statement COM(n) ON enables the communications adapter. The same statement followed by OFF disables it. No trapping takes place and no communications activity is remembered. The COM statement followed by Stop disables the adapter. However, any communications activity that does take place is remembered. The variable which immediately follows COM is the number of the communications adapter; there may be a maximum of two.

Common The Common statement passes variables to a chained program. This statement is used in conjunction with the Chain statement.

CONT This command stands for continue and is used to resume the running of a program after a break. This avoids the necessity of rerunning an entire program when it has become necessary to stop it during execution.

COS The COS function causes the computer to return the trigonometric cosine function. For example, COS(3.14) will return a −1, which is the cosine of pi radians.

CSNG This function is similar to CDBL, but converts a numeric expression to a single-precision number.

CSRLIN CSRLIN is a variable which causes the screen to print the vertical coordinate of the screen cursor. This allows the operator to obtain the coordinates of the exact position of a point on the screen. This information may be used later within a program to print a keyboard input at the same location.

CVD, CVI, CVS These functions convert string variable types of numeric variable types. These functions are available only in Disk and Advanced BASIC. CVI converts a 2-byte string, while CVS and CVD convert 4- and 8-byte strings, respectively. Using these functions the actual bytes of data are not changed, but the way BASIC interprets these bytes is changed.

DATA The Data statement stores numeric and string constants within a program. These constants are accessed by a Read statement within the same program.

**Date$** DATE$ is a variable and a statement and is used to set or retrieve the date. The year must be in the range 1980 to 2099. As an example, if DATE$ = "8/29/83" the printout will be 08-29-1983.

DEF FN This statement defines and names a function written into a program. The statement is followed immediately by the written name of the function, and then by an argument or formula for determining when the function is to be named during the execution.

DEF SEG This statement defines the current segment of storage and is followed by an address which is a numeric expression in the range 0 to 65,535.

Delete The Delete command erases program lines. For example, DELETE 30 would erase program line 30. Using this command you can erase whole sections of programs. DELETE 30-200 would erase all program lines between and including 30 and 200.

DIM This statement specifies the maximum values for array variable subscripts and allocates appropriate storage. This is a command which is common to all dialects of BASIC.

Edit The Edit command is used to display a particular program line for editing purposes. The cursor is then moved to the faulty part of the line, where new information may be input. EDIT 40 recalls line 40 for editing purposes. The same line could also be recalled and edited by inputing LIST 40. (See List)

ELSE See *"If"* below

End The End statement is used within a computer program to stop program execution. It closes all files and returns the machine to the command level.

Erase The Erase statement is followed by the name of a specific array and erases it from storage.

Files The Files command causes the name of all files residing on a disk to be displayed on a screen. This command is available only in IBM DOS.

For, Next This statement does not differ from other dialects of BASIC and is used to perform a series of instructions within a loop a number of times. The For statement is followed by a variable and then by two numeric expressions, one being the initial value and the other the final value. For example, the program line FOR X=1 TO 10 would set the starting value of X at 1 and the final value at 10. A Next statement must follow in order to allow the loop to be repeated the set number of times.

GOSUB, Return: These are common statements within any dialect of BASIC. This allows for branching to a subroutine and returning from it. GOSUB 130 causes a branch to line 130 during program execution. At some point past 130 a Return statement is required. The latter statement causes BASIC to branch back to the program line immediately following the one containing the GOSUB statement.

GOTO GOTO is similar to GOSUB, but the branch is unconditional. Using the previous example, a line which reads GOTO 130 will create a branch to line 130, where execution will continue to the end of the program. There is no Return statement.

**HEX$** This function returns a string representing the hexadecimal value of a numeric expression input in decimal form. This expression must range in value from −32,768 to 65,535. For example, HEX$(32) will return the number 20, which is the hexadecimal equivalent of 32 decimal.

If As is the case in other dialects, the If statement decides the route of programming flow based upon the results of an expression. This statement is often preceded by an Input statement. The If statement may be followed by a Then and an Else statement, or by GOTO and Else. For example take the line IF A$ = "YES" THEN 250 ELSE 300. This means that if A$, which has been input earlier, is equal to the expression "YES", then the program flow is routed to line 250. If A$ does not equal "YES", program flow is routed to line 300. The Then statement could be replaced in this example by a Goto. The Else statement may or may not be used. It must always be followed by a Then or Goto statement.

**Inkey$** This is a variable which is common to most BASIC dialects and is used to read a character from the keyboard. For example, the line X$ = INKEY$:IF A$ = "" THEN 40 causes the program to stop at this line and then branch to line 40 when any key on the keyboard is depressed.

Input The Input statement is used within a program and stops execution until information is received from the keyboard. INPUT is often followed by a phrase in quotes. This phrase serves as a screen prompt. For example, INPUT "YES OR NO",B$ asks the operator to input a yes or no answer. This line will most likely be followed by one containing an If-Then statement which would act upon the input from the keyboard. INPUT may be used without an If-Then statement, such as INPUT "PRESS ENTER TO CONTINUE",B$.The program stops at this line, but continues when the Enter key is depressed. B$ is used here only as an example and any unused string variable will suffice.

Input# This statement reads data items

from a file or sequential device and assigns them to program variables. The expression is followed by the number used when the file was initially opened for input and by a variable that has an item in the file assigned to it.

Input$ This is a function which returns a string of a specified number of characters read from the keyboard or from a file number.

Key The Key statement controls the ten soft keys which are located on the left-hand side of the IBM Personal computer keyboard. It also turns the screen printout of the keyboard designations on and off. KEY ON causes a printout at the bottom of the screen listing keys F1 through F10, along with their string expressions. The latter is an abbreviated listing of what each key does. KEY OFF removes this display. KEY LIST causes a separate printout of key functions to be displayed. KEYn,X$ is used to change key functions. For example, KEY 1, LIST would cause KEY 1 to print the word LIST on the screen. When this latter expression is followed by appropriate ASCII coding, the soft keys take on command functions and will automatically input and run a short command.

Kill This command deletes a file from disk. If a file is named PGM, the command KILL "PGM.BAS" will erase the file from disk. The .BAS is the name of the file (along with PGM) as stored in DOS.

**Left$** This function causes the screen to return (print) the leftmost characters of a string expression. Let's assume that A$ = "MY NAME IS RON". If the next line reads B$ = LEFT$, (A$,2):PRINT B$, then the screen display will print out MY. This is the leftmost portion of A$, composed of the first two characters. If we inserted the line B$ = LEFT$(A$,5), then the first five characters would be output to the screen.

LEN The LEN function returns the number of characters in a string. As an example, A$ = "FRONT ROYAL, VA":PRINT LEN(A$) would cause a printout on the screen of fifteen, the total number of characters within the string. Notice that the spaces have also been counted, as they are part of the string expression.

Let The Let statement, as in most dialects of BASIC, assigns the value of an expression to a variable. For example, LET A=10 means that the variable A will always be equal to the number 10. However, in IBM BASIC the Let statement is optional. The previous example could be replaced simply by A=10. Since the expression is optional, there is no real reason to use it as this will slow programming slightly.

Line Input The Line Input statement reads an entire line, up to 256 characters, from the keyboard and places it into a string variable, ignoring all delimiters. This expression is sometimes followed by a prompt, which is the string constant displayed on the screen before input is accepted. The prompt is then followed by a string variable which is the array element to which the line will be assigned. In Disk BASIC, LINE INPUT may be immediately followed by a semicolon to allow the cursor to remain on the same line as the response.

List The List command, when used by itself, will display all lines of program currently in memory. You may also follow the expression with a line number such as LIST 200. Line 200 will then be displayed on the screen. If you input LIST 100-200, lines 100 through 200 will be displayed. You may edit lines using the List command, just as you would do with the Edit command.

Llist This command is identical to the previous one, except all lines specified are output to the printer.

Load The Load command retrieves a program from a specified memory device and reads it into current memory. This command is followed by a quotation mark and the name of the file. For example, LOAD"PGM loads the file named PGM into current memory.

Locate The Locate statement positions the cursor on the screen at the point specified. This statement is followed by the screen position. For example, LOCATE 10,30 positions the cursor at row 10 and column 30. This statement may then be followed by a Print statement to allow information to be printed starting at the 10,30 position on the screen. The Locate and Print statements must be separated by a colon if included in the same program line. When used jointly, the Locate and Print statements take the place of Print@statements, which are common to other dialects of BASIC. There is no Print@statement in IBM BASIC.

LOG The LOG function returns the natural logarithm of a numeric expression to the screen. For example, PRINT LOG(56) would cause the screen to print out the natural logarithm of 56. You may also use variables with the Log function and perform arithmetic operations with the parens. PRINT LOG(36/6) would return the natural logarithm of 36 divided by 6, or 6.

Lprint Lprint is identical to the Print statement, but outputs to the line printer. (See Print)

Lprint Using LPRINT USING is similar to LPRINT, but causes the printer to display a string constant. (See Print Using)

Merge The Merge command merges the line from an ASCII program file into the program which is currently in memory. This allows one program to be stored on disk or cassette, while another portion of the program is being worked out in RAM. When this latter portion is completed, the two may be merged.

**MID$** The MID$ function returns the requested part of the given string to the display to print that portion of A$ starting with the 4th character and ending seven characters past this point.

Motor The Motor statement is used to turn the cassette recorder on and off. MOTOR 1 turns the machine on, while MOTOR 0 turns it off. If the Motor statement is used by itself, whenever it is encountered in a program the state of the motor (on or off) will automatically be reversed. If the motor is on, it will be turned off when a Motor statement is encountered, and vice versa.

Name The Name command is used to change the name of a disk file. Assume that a program has been stored on disk under the name "RED". The command NAME "RED.BAS" AS "BROWN.BAS" renames the file "BROWN". In each case the .BAS designation is necessary, as all programs stored on disk from BASIC are automatically given this designation within the filename.

New The New command is often used prior to beginning a program. This command deletes the program currently in memory and clears all variables. If this command is not used before beginning a new program and another program already in current memory, the lines of the program you are working on will automatically take the place of the lines bearing the same numbers in the older program.

Next See "For" above.

**OCT$** This function returns a string to the screen that is equal to the octal value of a decimal numeric expression. For example, PRINT OCT$(24) will result in the screen displaying the number 30, the octal equivalent of decimal 24.

On The On statement is used in conjunction with a Gosub and Return or Goto to branch to one or more line numbers, depending on the value of the expression. The On statement may also be used in conjunction with the Key statement to branch to another line number when the soft keys are used.

Play The Play statement is used in Advanced BASIC only, and when coupled with a string expression outputs tones to the internal speaker. The Play statement is used to program computer music and is followed by string expressions composed of the letters A through G, which specify musical notes. Other string expression elements set the octave, note length, pauses, and music style.

Print The Print statement is used to display data on the screen. It may be followed by a phrase in quotation marks, in which case it will reprint all characters within the quotes. This statement may also be followed by a numeric or screen variable. For example, consider the program line A=1000:PRINT A. The number 1000 will then be printed on the screen. As another example, the line A$="ONE THOUSAND":PRINT A$ will cause the expression ONE THOUSAND to be printed.

Print Using The Print Using statement is used to display strings or numbers using a specific format.

Pset The Pset, along with Preset, statement is used to draw a point at a specified position on the display screen. This is used in graphics mode only and requires the IBM color/graphics monitor adapter. PRESET is almost identical to PSET, but if no color parameter is specified the background color (0) is automatically selected. If a color designator is used, the two statements are identical. PSET is followed by the X,Y screen coordinate. X specifies the row and Y indicates the column. Using PSET or PRESET, these coordinates will be followed by the desired color number, which must be in the range 0 to 3. These expressions replace the Set statements common to other dialects of BASIC. IBM BASIC contains no Set statement.

Randomize The Randomize statement causes the program to stop in order to allow an integer expression to be input via the keyboard. This reseeds the random number generator, allowing numbers which are to be randomized (See RND) to be altered each time. The integer expression must be between −32,768 and +32,767. Each time the program is run, the program will stop and a prompt will be displayed on the screen, telling you to input a random number seed. You may also input a fixed number with the Randomize statement. This number will be automatically input to the random number generator each time the program is run, and there will be no pause.

Read The Read statement is common to most dialects of BASIC and reads the value from a Data statement, assigning it to a variable.

REM The REM statement is a portion of a program which is not executed but is included to explain the functioning of that portion of the program. Remarks that follow the REM statement are not displayed or acted upon during the program run, but are there to indicate a program function and are seen during the line listing.

RENUM The RENUM command is used to renumber all program lines. When used by itself, it automatically numbers the lines in a sequence of 10. For example, if your program were

```
10 A = 5
15 B = 10
18 PRINT A + B
```

and you entered the RENUM command, your program would automatically change to

```
10 A = 5
20 B = 10
30 PRINT A + B
```

Proper programming must be treated with adequate number spacing to allow for the insertion of new program lines. However, sometimes reworking a program causes all line spaces to be filled. When this occurs, enter the RENUM command and list the new numbered program lines. You now have renumbering in increments of 10, and thus more spaces between lines to add new program lines. The RENUM command also changes all line number references following GOTO, GOSUB, Then and Else statements, so it is not necessary to make these corrections within the program lines to obtain the desired branching. An executable program will be just as executable after the RENUM command has been input.

The RENUM command may also be followed by numeric expressions which set the value of the first line number, the line in the current program where renumbering is to begin, and the increment to be used in the new program line sequence. For producing easy to understand programs, this command is extremely valuable.

Reset In IBM BASIC, the Reset command closes all files contained in disk storage and clears the system buffer. If all files are already contained on disk, the Reset command is the same as CLOSE.

Return See GOSUB above.

**Right$** The Right$ function returns the rightmost characters of a string expression. This is the reciprocal of the Left$ function. (See LEFT$)

RND The RND function returns a random number between 0 and 1. The same sequence of random numbers is generated each time the program is run unless the random number generator is reseeded. (See RANDOMIZE)

Run The Run command begins program execution. It may also be followed by a line number to begin execution at some point within the program. This command is available by depressing KEY F2 on the IBM Personal computer keyboard.

Save The Save command is used to save a

program in a file on cassette or disk. The command SAVE"PGM" will cause the program to be filed and listed under the name PGM. If using Cassette BASIC, the program is automatically filed on the default disk drive (drive A). When used as shown, PGM will be saved in a compressed binary format rather than in ASCII. This conserves storage space. You may also save the program in ASCII by using SAVE"PGM",A.

SIN The SIN function calculates the trigonometric sine of a number. For example, PRINT SIN(20) returns the sine of 20 in a single precision number.

Sound The Sound statement causes a tone to be generated through the internal speaker. The Sound statement is followed by a numeric expression in the range 37 to 32,767, which corresponds to the frequency of the tone. This may be followed by another numeric expression which determines the duration of the tone.

SQR The SQR function returns the square root of a numeric expression. For example, PRINT SQR(9) will return the number 3.

Stop The Stop statement ends program execution and returns the machine to the command level.

Swap The Swap statement exchanges the values of two variables or array elements. For example:

```
10  A$ = "TWO":B$ = "FOR"
20  PRINT A$,B$
```

The screen printout from this program will be TWO FOR. Using the Swap statement brings about a different printout:

```
10  A$ = "TWO":B$ = "FOR"
20  SWAP A$,B$
```

The screen printout will now be FOR TWO. The two expressions have been exchanged.

System The System command exits BASIC and returns to DOS.

Tab The Tab function advances the cursor to the column designated. For example, PRINT" HELLO" TAB (30) "THERE" will cause the screen to display HELLO at the left-hand side of the screen and THERE at column 30 on the same line.

Then See "If" above.

**Time$** The Time$ statement (or variable) sets or retrieves the current time. This is very similar to the Date$ statement.

Wait The Wait statement suspends the execution of a program while monitoring the status of a machine input port. The program execution is halted until the specified port develops a prearranged bit pattern.

Wend See "While" below.

While The While statement is used in conjunction with a Wend statement to execute statements within a loop as long as a certain condition is true. If a statement is true, the loop is executed until the Wend statement is encountered. This returns execution to the original While statement, and if the expression is still true the process is repeated. While and Wend statements are similar to GOSUB and Return, as long as a certain condition is true.

Width The Width statement is used to set the width of any line, expressed in number of characters. If no Width statement is used, the default is automatically 80 characters. This is the high resolution mode. WIDTH 40 sets the display to output lines with a maximum of 40 characters, the medium resolution mode.

Write The Write statement is very similar to the Print statement, and both are used to output data onto the screen. However, the Write statement inserts commas between the items.

Chapter 3

Many computers are equipped with small internal speakers for producing audible prompts in the form of a beep at about 1000 Hertz. The beep is often used when large amounts of data must be processed, taking much time before the information is ready to be output to the screen or printer. The beep signal alerts the operator that processing is complete and that it is time to input more information. This audible prompt allows the operator to leave the machine and wait until the sound is heard, rather than constantly monitor the screen looking for a visual prompt.

Three statements for producing an arranged sequence of audio tones are available with the IBM Personal computer. Two of them—beep and sound—are part of Cassette BASIC and Disk BASIC. The third—Play—is available only in Advanced BASIC, which is part of the IBM Disk Operating System (DOS).

BEEP

The Beep statement has a single purpose. It causes the internal speaker to output a quarter-second, 800-cycle tone. There is no frequency control, so the tone will always be 800 Hertz and one-quarter of a second in duration. This statement is quite useful and often follows If-Then statements to prompt the operator of an existing condition. For example, in the following program, assume that the variable *X* can be no greater than 20 and no less than 1.

```
10  INPUT X
20  IF X < 1 OR X > 20 THEN BEEP
30  IF X < 20 AND X > 1 THEN 40
40  GOTO 2000
```

After a value for *X* is input, the If-Then statements will compare the value of this variable to see if it is more than 1 and less than 20. If it is, the program branches and continues. The If-Then statement in line 20, however, also makes a comparison, to see if the value of *X* is less than 1 or more than 20. If either of these conditions occur, a beep is sounded from the speaker, indicating that the value of X is out of range. In this program, then, the beep is used to indicate an input error. Several Beep statements may be used together to indicate the nature of the malfunction. For instance

```
10  INPUT X
20  IF X < 1 THEN BEEP
30  IF X > 20 THEN BEEP:BEEP
```

produces different audio prompts for different conditions. If the output is a single beep, then the value of X is too low. If two beeps occur, then the value of X is too high. This routine is not very practical, because the beeps in line 20 will be so closely spaced that you may not be able to recognize them as two distinct beeps.

This can be easily overcome by building in an automatic delay within the same line as follows:

```
10  INPUT X
20  IF X < 1 THEN BEEP
30  IF X > 20 THEN BEEP:FOR T=1 TO
200:NEXT:BEEP
```

Line 30 now contains a For-Next statement to create a time lag within execution of the program. The machine must count from 1 to 200 before it can execute the next statement, the second Beep. If the lag created by the For-Next statement is too short, you can change its duration from 200 to 500 or 1000. If it's too long, then lower the value to 50 or 100. The time lag causes a clear definition (silence) between machine-produced beeps.

Some programmers automatically insert a Beep statement each time information is to be input. For example,

```
10  PRINT "INSERT THE PROPER VALUE";A
20  BEEP
30  INPUT A
```

combines a visual prompt with an audible one. The visual prompt is set up in line 10, wherein the screen will display "INSERT THE PROPER VALUE" for the value A. After the line is executed, the beep is heard (line 20), and execution stops until A has been properly input as specified in line 30.

This is useful in programs that use the For-Next delay tactic to display information, pause, and then automatically move on to the next program lines. Often, the operator will automatically depress Enter during the delay, thinking that such an input is necessary to continue execution. If the next line requires a keyboard input, the program will assume that a value of zero has been input, since Enter was previously depressed. By using audible Beep statements, the operator is alerted ahead of time (in program explanation lines) that an entry is necessary only when a beep occurs. This makes operating the computer during the program run much simpler.

SOUND

The only way we can code prompts is by building in automatic machine delays that cause a specific number of beeps to occur and represent a problem or occurrence within the program run.

If it were possible to control the duration and/or the frequency of the audio output from the speaker, even better coding would result. This can easily be brought about using the Sound statement, which is applicable to Cassette, Disk, and Advanced BASIC dialects.

The Sound statement also causes the computer to generate sound through its internal speaker. However after SOUND you must specify the desired frequency of the sound (in Hertz) and also the duration the sound is to be maintained.

Frequency is specified immediately after the Sound statement by another numeric expression, which must range from 37 to 32767. This specifies the frequency in Hertz. If the Sound statement is followed by the numeric expression 1000,18, then the sound will be at 1000 Hertz (1 kHz) and will last for approximately one second. The numeric expression for frequency will theoretically create an output up to slightly more than 32 kHz. This lies just outside of the normal human hearing range, however.

Duration is given in numeric expressions ranging from 0 to 65535. This expression specifies the number of clock ticks over which the sound is to be maintained. In the IBM Personal computer, eighteen clock ticks are equal to approximately one second. Using the Sound statement and the maximum duration numeric expression of 65535, the sound will be maintained for 3600 seconds, or one hour. Naturally, practical usage will shorten this time to a few seconds in most instances.

When the Sound statement is used, the program continues to execute until another Sound statement is reached. If the duration of this next Sound statement is zero, the current Sound statement is turned off. This assumes, of course, that the duration specified in the first statement is longer than the time required to complete the program, at least to the point of another Sound statement.

When using Advanced BASIC, you can use the Sound statement in such a manner that the output tone created is buffered. This means that execution will not stop when a new Sound statement is encountered. However, this feature is more applicable to the Play statement, which also requires that Advanced BASIC be used and will be discussed later. The program line:

```
10  SOUND 800,5
```

is approximately equal to the Beep statement. The sound is to be at a frequency of 800 Hertz to last for a duration of 5 clock ticks or cycles, which is about one-quarter second. However, if you change the 5 to an 18, the 800-Hertz tone will be produced for a full second. Changing it to 182 would cause the tone to be sustained for a full ten seconds. (The exact duration of a one-second tone in clock cycles is 18.2.)

The Sound statement can be used for audio prompt purposes in many different ways. Using similar programs contained under the discussion of the Beep statement, we might end up with:

```
10  INPUT X
20  IF X < 1 THEN SOUND 1000,18
30  IF X > 20 THEN SOUND 1000,18:SOUND
2500,18
```

Here, if *X* is a value less than 1, a single 1000-Hertz tone will be heard for approximately one second; but if the value of *X* is more than 20, you will hear the same tone for one second, followed by a much higher tone for another second. This out-of-range problem could also be signified by a 1000-Hertz tone for less than a value of 1 and a single 2500-Hertz tone for a value of more than 20. Further definition could be provided by using the same tone for both occurrences and extending the duration of one to three seconds or more. The Sound statement is quite useful, in that it offers definitions in forms of frequency changes, duration changes, or changes in both duration and frequency.

The Sound statement can be used to make music. Programming music with SOUND is much more difficult than with PLAY (available only in Advanced BASIC), but the end result can be identical to that obtained with PLAY. It is first necessary to determine what frequency must be generated to output a particular note, the note middle C for instance. With a musical note frequency chart, you would then use Sound statements to generate the various notes of the scale by inputting the correct frequencies for each one. Duration would depend upon the tempo of any piece being performed. A very slow tempo (called *Andante* in music terms) might mean that each quarter note would last for one second, a half note two seconds, and a whole note for four seconds; as in the following program:

```
10  SOUND X,18
20  SOUND Y,18
30  SOUND Z,36
```

Let's assume that *X* represents middle C, *Y* is middle D, and *Z* is middle E. This simple composition would then consist of the three notes C, D, and E. The first two would be quarter notes lasting one second each, and the last would be a half note lasting two seconds. The duration expressions following *X* and *Y* both stipulate 18 clock cycles (one second), while the 36 following the Z in line 30 represents 36 clock cycles equalling two seconds. Thus we have a full measure in four/four time consisting of two quarter notes and a half note. A duration expression of 9 would indicate an eighth note; an expression of 72 would give a whole note.

However, while the frequency expressions remain the same for C, D, and E in all tunes, the duration expressions would have to change to reflect varying tempos. If we were using a quick tempo (*allegro*), the duration expression 9 (one-half second) might represent a half note. Remember also that as octaves are changed, frequencies must be changed to arrive at the same note in another octave. Twice the frequency of middle C will not necessarily give you the same note an octave higher. Octaves are expressions of harmonic relationships, so direct multiplication will not necessarily apply.

Because of these complications, the Sound statement is not well suited for music programming. If one cannot run Advanced BASIC, the extra programming steps necessary to make Sound work are mandatory. The complexities involved will likely be overwhelming, so that purchasing IBM DOS will be desirable in the long run.

The Sound statement can be used to augment the comprehensibility and pleasantness of running many different types of computer programs. Sound effects can easily be produced by combining many Sound statements to create warbling or deep-space audio impressions. RND statements will help, but should be applied only to the frequency expression. The program that follows shows a simple method by which random sounds can be generated:

```
10  SOUND RND*1500 + 37,4
20  GOTO 10
```

This program creates a continuous loop, causing the Sound statement to generate a random sampling of tones, each for a duration of approximately one-fifth of a second. Be sure to append the "+37" as shown in line 10, to prevent a program halt caused by an "Illegal Function Call." Without the +37, should a random number of 10, 20, 30, or less than 37 appear, the expression is out of range, since it must fall between 37 and 32767. The +37 next to the expression 1500 assures that the minimum random value will be at least 37, even if the random number generated is 0. The Sound statement causes the first random sound to be generated. This process repeats, producing a myriad of unusual tone sequences.

One can tinker with this program by increasing or decreasing the frequency expression (always appending +37). The same can be done with the duration expression; however, I have found shorter durations much more pleasing for unusual sound effects.

If you have Advanced BASIC, you may use the Sound statement, followed by MB and then the frequency duration expression, to send this portion of the program to a buffer. Doing so allows the program to continue to run after the Sound statement is encountered. Sounds generated by the speaker will continue for the specified duration. Without the MB designator, the program will halt until the Sound statement is executed. Using MB with the Sound statement requires Advanced BASIC programming.

PLAY

The serious computer music enthusiast will use the Play statement almost exclusively. Using PLAY, you do not have to directly input the frequency or duration of each note in terms of Hertz. This is established by a single expression and applies to all notes within a musical piece or within a certain part of a musical piece. The Play statement may be used to generate a single note, but this is more appropriate to the Sound or Beep statement. The Play statement is followed by a string expression consisting of as many as ten music commands and various notes.

The Play statement is used with a definition language, which forms the character string. Part of this language involves the music notes A through G. In IBM Advanced BASIC, if you input the letter A into the string following the Play statement, the A note will be output from the speaker. It will be necessary to set the tempo in this statement as well, but the duration of the note is determined by a single numeric expression. For example, the number 1 specifies a whole note, 2 a half note, 4 a quarter note, etc. The numeric range may be from 1 to 64, so even 1/64 notes can be included in your compositions. However, you must remember the previous discussion regarding the Sound statement and especially the line which indicated that a whole note at one tempo may be a half note or quarter note in another tempo when speaking of duration alone.

The Play statement also contains a tempo designator, a numeric expression ranging from 32 (the slowest tempo) to 255 (the fastest tempo). The length of each note (1, 2, 3, 4, etc.) is based upon a fraction of the tempo. For example, a quarter note played at a tempo designated by 50 would last for a duration of 50/4. The tempo expression has to do with clock cycles, but is different from the duration expression used with the Sound statement.

In the character string, the notes are specified by the letter symbols A through G. If you want the machine to output a D note, include D in the string expression. The number symbol (#) or the positive symbol (+) immediately following the letter expression indicates a sharp; a minus symbol (–) following a letter expression indicates a flat. For example,

AA#B-BBDEF

will bring about the notes A, A sharp, B flat, B, B, D, E, and F. The plus symbol could also have been used in place of the number symbol to indicate a sharp, but being a frustrated musician, I always used the number symbol, which is quite similar to the sharp symbol used in musical compositions.

The next portion of the string expression is the letter L, following by a numerical expression of from 1 to 64. This establishes the tempo of the note that follows it. For example,

L1A

indicates that the A note is a whole note due to the numerical expression 1. If we used L4 instead, then the A would be represented as a quarter note. Again, the numerical expression cannot be less than one, nor more than 64. You may be able to understand this a little better by remembering that, in effect, a 1 is always placed over the number that follows the L. For instance, 1/1 is a whole note, 1/2 is a half note, 1/4 is a quarter note, and so on. When using these designations, however, the overhead one is assumed, and the number that follows the L becomes a fractional divisor.

Another designation within the string is MF, which stands for music foreground. Music which is created by the Sound or Play statement will run in foreground automatically if this designation is not used. However, MF may be used to switch from MB (music background), mentioned earlier. Using the MF designation, each note or sound will play for its specified duration; the next note or sound will not begin until the previous one has concluded. The remainder of the program (music or otherwise) will not continue until the note or notes which make up this string have played.

The music background (MB) expression is used to play a tune, while at the same time the rest of the program continues to execute. Let's assume you wanted the speaker to output, "Mary Had a Little Lamb," while a graphic representation of a lamb was being drawn on the screen. Using the previous MF expression, the entire song would have to play before the program lines (that draw the lamb) would be executed. However, using the MB expression, the song data would be held in a buffer and would be run separately but concurrently from the graphics portion of the program. Using this method of programming, you would hear "Mary Had a Little Lamb" while the lamb was being drawn on the screen. The MB expression is often used to generate random sounds (Sound or Play statement) when computer games and graphics are executing. You can imagine a colorful ball bouncing about the screen while random electronic noises are generated at the same rate as the on-screen motion. This can significantly enhance the effect of any program.

It is necessary to understand more about how humans make music. Assume a piece of music in 4/4 time requires a duration of four seconds for one bar. This would mean that a whole note would last for four seconds, a half note for two, and a quarter note for one second. But is this really true? From a practical standpoint, the answer is no. Each note will be held for a period of time that is slightly less than the time allotted to it. Each note (in many instances) is separated by a fractional pause from the following note. This time is required to readjust the instrumentation and to reposition the shape of the mouth for wind or brass instruments. Special music expressions indicate how long to hold these pauses in some instances. When notes are to be played staccato, a quarter note may only be held for the length normally required to execute an eighth note. This is one half of the normal time required for a quarter note, but the musician will automatically pause for the space of time which would be required to play another eighth note, so the effect is one-eighth on/one-eighth off. The players usually hold a note for about seven-eighths of the time that note is supposed to last.

Notes are held for their full duration in legato music. We've all heard a slide trombone linearly gliss or slide from one note to another; a similar effect can be obtained by varying an audio frequency generator. Different notes seem to run together, and there are no defined breaks between them. This discussion was necessary in order to explain the next three string expression terms used with the IBM Play statement. The IBM Personal computer can produce normal, staccato and legato music.

MN stands for "music normal" and will play each note for seven-eighths of the time specified by L (length). You probably won't be able to detect the silent spaces with your conscious mind (depending upon the tempo), but they will be there, since each note has a definite beginning and definite ending.

ML stands for "music legato." Each note will play for the full period of time set by L. The notes will be run together; slurs will occur from the end of one note to the beginning of the next. There will be no sharp beginnings or endings from note to note, and the entire song will seem very smooth to the human ear.

Music staccato is specified by MS. Each note will play for three-fourths of the time specified by L. Using this mode, each note will have a sharp or harsh beginning and will be clearly separated by a recognizable pause from the next note. If MS were not available, it would be necessary to use MN and shorten the length of each quarter note (for instance) to an eighth note, and follow each with a pause expression (P) to create the required periods of silence. This would make for difficult programming. (The pause expression will be discussed later in this chapter.)

The IBM Personal computer has a 7-octave range. Within each octave, there are twelve possible notes: A, B-flat, B, C, C-sharp, D, E-flat, E, F, F-sharp, G, and G-sharp. Thus there are 84 different notes. The Play statement may be used with alphabetical designations of notes in conjunction with an octave expression (which will be discussed next) to play any of these 84 notes. However, you may also use the N expression followed by a number from 0 to 84 to specify any of the 84 possible notes in the seven octaves. N1 would specify A in the lowest octave; N84 would indicate an A-flat (or G-sharp) in the highest octave. N followed by a zero indicates a rest or pause. N makes programming easier since alphabetical designators, sharp or flat symbols and the octave expression are unnecessary.

The octave expression (0) sets the current octave for the notes that follow. A numerical expression from 0 to 6 follows the 0. Middle C is in octave 3; each octave goes from C to B. When an octave expression is inserted in the string, all notes which follow will be within that octave.

The letter P is used to designate a pause which, in music terminology, is called a rest. As with most of the other alphabetical expressions, P will be followed by a numerical expression between 1 and 64. For example, P1 indicates that a pause is to occur for a duration equal to that of a whole note. P64 will create a rest for a duration equal to a sixty-fourth note. In music programming, the P expression is used almost as frequently as those expressions that cause musical notes to be generated. All musicians know that a rest has the same importance as a note.

The last expression, which will be part of the string following the Play statement, is denoted by T for tempo. Tempo sets the number of quarter notes that may occur within one second. The default is 120 (120 notes per second), a nice, moderate tempo. When T is omitted, a song will automatically be played at this tempo. The number following T must be from 32 to 255.

A PRACTICAL EXAMPLE

When writing music programs using the Play statement, I prefer to use an X variable to follow the Play statement and execute a specified string. This is used in conjunction with the first character command discussed, which involves simply writing in the notes from A to G following the Play statement. By using the X variable, Read/Data statements may be used to specify the notes.

The program that follows uses the Play statement to generate ten different musical numbers in a somewhat abbreviated state. The game is called Name That Tune and is similar to the popular television game of the same name. Contestants on these shows were played a few notes from a song and asked to guess the song title. If the guesses were wrong, another note was added to the first series, and then another, until the song was correctly identified.

This program's makeup is quite complex, so a discussion of it will help you understand the programs that follow in a later chapter.

This program incorporates ten well-known, easily recognizable songs. It is fairly complex because of the number of branch statements necessary to access information from Data statements, and to exhaust or restore them as the situation warrants.

When the program runs, it asks the player whether he needs instructions; if so, there is a branch to line 930, which includes the complete instruction set. The instructions are quite detailed and fill up more than a single screen "sheet." Therefore line 1030 is used midway in the instructions to stop the scrolling, in order to give the player time to read this portion of the information. When the timing loop concludes, the rest of the information is printed while most of the top portion scrolls off the screen.

Once the instructions are finished, there is a screen prompt asking the player to input the number of notes he wishes to hear. Most persons will begin with three notes, although youngsters may require more. The player simply inputs the number of notes desired and presses Enter. The number of notes will then be output to the speaker of the IBM Personal computer. Sometimes fewer than the desired number of notes will occur, because of musical pauses written into the Data statements that contain the song information. Most pauses, however, occur after a song has progressed to a point where it can be reasonably identified.

After the selected notes are heard, the screen prompt asks the player to name the tune and prints the number of notes presented. If the player wants to make a guess, he simply types the name of the song and presses Enter. If the guess is incorrect, the word "WRONG!" appears at the center of the screen; a few seconds later, another prompt appears asking for the number of notes desired for the next guess. Assuming the first series contained three notes and the second series is to contain five, on the next play, the first three notes will be heard again, followed by two more. The prompt sequence repeats itself, asking again for the name of the tune. The player's first guess is also displayed as a reference. This entire sequence repeats itself again and again until the name of the song has been guessed. When that occurs, the screen displays the name of the song, followed by "THAT'S RIGHT!", and the entire song plays from beginning to end. The next song is then automatically ready, and the prompt sequence begins again. This sequence can continue for ten tunes.

The songs I selected for this game are:

- Mary Had a Little Lamb
- Yankee Doodle
- Blue Skies
- Jingle Bells
- Go Tell Aunt Rhodie
- London Bridge
- The Marine Hymn
- The Army Song (also known as When the Caissons Go Rolling Along)
- Old MacDonald Had a Farm
- Twinkle, Twinkle Little Star

When the tenth song has been guessed, the program automatically branches to line 830, which prints "THANK YOU FOR PLAYING NAME THAT TUNE" at the center of the screen. This prompt is surrounded by musical note symbols, which are generated by ASCII character 14.

All of these songs should be familiar to you. However, if the player mentally identifies the song but can't think of the name, the player simply inputs 200 the next time the screen prompt asks for the number of notes. The song name will be printed on the screen and played through. This is necessary: if you can't guess the name of the song, there is no way to advance to succeeding songs.

In IBM Advanced BASIC (BASICA), the Play statement is followed by a character command selected from a set of twelve. The basic format for playing music with this program is illustrated by the following program segment:

```
10   READ A$
20   PLAY "XA$;"
30   DATA   G,F,E—,F,G,G,P4,F,F,F,P4,G,
B—,B—,B—,P4,G,F,E—,F,G,G,G,G,F,F,G,F,E—
AA
40   GOTO 10
```

This program will play "Mary Had a Little Lamb" when run in IBM Advanced BASIC. Line 10 reads the first item from the Data statement in line 30, which is the letter G. This corresponds to middle G on the musical scale. Line 20 contains the Play statement, followed by the X variable and the A$. This means Play A$, or (for the first go-round) play middle G. The GOTO statement in line 40 branches back to line 10. The next Data item is read, which is middle F, and is then played. This process continues to the end of the Data line. The last piece of information (AA) is used in the Name That Tune program as the variable indicating that the current song is complete, and a branch should be made to the next one. This can be understood by adding the following line between lines 30 and 40 of the previous program:

```
35   IF A$ = AA THEN 5000
```

This line causes the program to branch to line 5000 when AA is encountered at the end of this Data statement.

Name That Tune contains ten Data statements (line 470 through 560) to play ten different songs.

Name That Tune Program Listing

```
10 REM NAME THAT TUNE
20 REM COPYRIGHT ROBERT J. TRAISTER $ AS
SOCIATES 9/30/82
30 REM PROGRAM MUST BE RUN IN ADVANCED B
ASIC (BASICA)
40 CLS
50 KEY OFF
60 SCREEN 0,1
70 LOCATE 14,20
80 PRINT"WELCOME TO THE MUSICAL GAME OF
NAME THAT TUNE
90 FOR TL=1 TO 1500
100 NEXT TL
110 LOCATE 20,1
120 INPUT"NEED INSTRUCTIONS (Y/N)? ";Q$
130 IF Q$="Y" THEN 930
140 IF Q$="N" THEN 160
150 IF Q$<>"Y" AND Q$<>"N" THEN 120
160 CLS
170 RESTORE 470
```

Name That Tune Program Listing (continued from page 31)

```
180 TT$="MARY HAD A LITTLE LAMB"
190 GOTO 290
200 RESTORE 480:GOTO 290
210 RESTORE 490:GOTO 290
220 RESTORE 500:GOTO 290
230 RESTORE 510:GOTO 290
240 RESTORE 520:GOTO 290
250 RESTORE 530:GOTO 290
260 RESTORE 540:GOTO 290
270 RESTORE 550:GOTO 290
280 RESTORE 560:GOTO 290
290 LOCATE 1,1
300 PRINT"HOW MANY NOTES DO YOU WANT TO
HEAR? ";NN
310 INPUT NN
320 IF NN=200 THEN CLS:LOCATE 14,34:PRIN
T TT$
330 Y=NN
340 FOR X=1 TO Y
350 READ A$
360 IF A$="AA" THEN RQ=2:TT$="YANKEE DOO
DLE":GOTO 630
370 IF A$="BB" THEN RQ=3:TT$="BLUE SKIES
":GOTO 630
380 IF A$="CC" THEN RQ=4:TT$="JINGLE BEL
LS":GOTO 630
390 IF A$="DD" THEN RQ=5:TT$="GO TELL AU
NT RHODIE":GOTO 630
400 IF A$="EE" THEN RQ=6:TT$="LONDON BRI
DGE":GOTO 630
410 IF A$="FF" THEN RQ=7:TT$="THE MARINE
 HYMN":GOTO 630
420 IF A$="GG" THEN RQ=8:TT$="THE ARMY S
ONG":GOTO 630
430 IF A$="HH" THEN RQ=9:TT$="OLD MACDON
ALD HAD A FARM":GOTO 630
440 IF A$="II" THEN RQ=10:TT$="TWINKLE T
WINKLE LITTLE STAR":GOTO 630
450 IF A$="JJ" THEN 830
460 PLAY"XA$;"
470 DATA G,F,E-,F,G,G,G,P4,F,F,F,P4,G,B-
,B-,P4,G,F,E-,F,G,G,G,G,F,F,G,F,E-,AA
480 DATA C,C,D,E,C,E,D,P4,C,C,D,E,C,P4,O
3,B,O4,P4,C,C,D,E,F,E,D,C,O3,B,G,A,B,O4,
```

```
C,P4,C,BB
490 DATA C,G2,F8,E-16,F16,P8,G2,F8,E-16,
F16,P8,G3,C4,P6,C8,E-16,P8,C4,CC
500 DATA E,E,E,P8,E,E,E,P8,E,G,C,D,E2,F,
F,F3,F8,F,E,E,E8,E8,G,G,F,D,C2,DD
510 DATA A2,A4,G4,F2,F2,G2,G4,B-4,A2,F2,
A2,A4,G4,F2,F2,G4,F4,G4,A4,F3,EE
520 DATA G,A,G,F,E,F,G2,D,E,F2,E,F,G2,G,
A,G,F,E,F,G2,D2,G2,E,C3,FF
530 DATA C,E,G2,G2,G2,G2,G2,P4,O5,C,O4,G
2,E,F,G2,G2,F2,D2,C1,GG
540 DATA G8,E8,G,G8,E8,G,G8,E8,G8,A8,G8,
E8,G,E8,F8,G8,F,D8,G8,F,D8,C1,HH
550 DATA F,F,F,C,D,D,C2,A,A,G,G,F2,P4,C,
F,F,F,C,D,D,C2,A,A,G,G,F1,II
560 DATA C,C,G,G,A,A,G2,F,F,E,E,D,D,C2,P
4,G,G,F,F,E,E,D2,G,G,F,F,E,E,D2,C,C,G,G,
A,A,G2,F,F,E,E,D,D,C1,JJ
570 NEXT X
580 CLS
590 LOCATE 14,20
600 PRINT"CAN YOU NAME THAT TUNE IN "Y"
NOTES?",T$:INPUT T$
610 IF T$=TT$ THEN CLS:LOCATE 10,30:PRIN
T T$:LOCATE 14,35:PRINT"THAT'S RIGHT!":Y
=100:GOTO 730
620 IF T$<>TT$ THEN CLS:LOCATE 14,35:PRI
NT"WRONG!":FOR TL=1 TO 3000:NEXT TL:CLS
630 IF RQ=2 THEN 200
640 IF RQ=3 THEN 210
650 IF RQ=4 THEN 220
660 IF RQ=5 THEN 230
670 IF RQ=6 THEN 240
680 IF RQ=7 THEN 250
690 IF RQ=8 THEN 260
700 IF RQ=9 THEN 270
710 IF RQ=10 THEN 280
720 GOTO 170
730 Y=100:IF RQ=2 THEN RESTORE 480:GOTO
340
740 IF RQ=3 THEN RESTORE 490:GOTO 340
750 IF RQ=4 THEN RESTORE 500:GOTO 340
760 IF RQ=5 THEN RESTORE 510:GOTO 340
770 IF RQ=6 THEN RESTORE 520:GOTO 340
780 IF RQ=7 THEN RESTORE 530:GOTO 340
790 IF RQ=8 THEN RESTORE 540:GOTO 340
```

```
800 IF RQ=9 THEN RESTORE 550:GOTO 340
810 IF RQ=10 THEN RESTORE 560:GOTO 340
820 RESTORE 470:GOTO 340
830 CLS
840 LOCATE 14,20
850 PRINT"THANK YOU FOR PLAYING NAME THA
T TUNE"
860 FOR CV=10 TO 70 STEP 2
870 LOCATE 8,CV
880 PRINT CHR$(14)
890 LOCATE 22,CV
900 PRINT CHR$(14)
910 NEXT CV
920 END
930 CLS
940 PRINT"THIS IS THE MUSICAL GAME CALLE
D NAME THAT TUNE. THE IBM PERSONAL"
950 PRINT
960 PRINT"COMPUTER WILL PLAY TEN DIFFERE
NT, POPULAR SONGS. THE OBJECT OF"
970 PRINT
980 PRINT"THIS GAME IS TO GUESS THE NAME
 OF EACH SONG IN AS FEW NOTES AS"
990 PRINT
1000 PRINT"POSSIBLE. WHEN YOU START THE
GAME, THE COMPUTER WILL ASK YOU HOW"
1010 PRINT
1020 PRINT"NOTES YOU WISH TO HEAR. TYPE
IN THIS NUMBER, THEN PRESS <ENTER>>"
1030 FOR TL=1 TO 10000:NEXT TL
1040 PRINT
1050 PRINT"YOU WILL THEN HEAR THIS NUMBE
R OF NOTES FROM THE COMPUTER. WHEN"
1060 PRINT
1070 PRINT"PROMPTED TO DO SO, TYPE IN YO
UR GUESS FOR THE SONG NAME OR"
1080 PRINT
1090 PRINT"SIMPLY PRESS <ENTER> IF YOU D
ON'T HAVE ANY IDEA. IF YOUR GUESS"
1100 PRINT
1110 PRINT"IS CORRECT, THE COMPUTER WILL
 TELL YOU SO AN THEN PLAY THE WHOLE"
1120 PRINT
1130 PRINT"SONG. IF YOU GUESS IS WRONG,
```

```
YOU MAY REQUEST MORE NOTES. IF YOU"
1140 PRINT
1150 PRINT"ARE STUMPED COMPLETELY AFTER
HEARING ALL OF THE NOTES, TYPE IN"
1160 PRINT
1170 PRINT"THE NUMBER, 200, WHEN ASKED F
OR THE NUMBER OF NOTES. THE COMPUTER"
1180 PRINT
1190 PRINT"WILL THEN TELL YOU THE TITLE
AND PLY THE ENTIRE SONG."
1200 PRINT
1210 PRINT
1220 INPUT"PRESS <ENTER> TO BEGIN";A$
1230 GOTO 160
```

Program Summary

Lines 10 through 150 set up the screen and provide the opportunity for the player to receive instructions. The program enters its main section at line 160, which clears the screen. The Restore statement names line 470, which contains the data for the song "Mary Had a Little Lamb." Line 470 contains the Data statement for this song. Line 180 specifies the value of the string variable (TT$) as "Mary Had a Little Lamb." Line 190 branches to line 290, which prints the first screen prompt, asking for the number of notes the player desires to hear. The keyboard input is assigned to the variable "NN". Line 320 is the escape line specifying that if NN equals 200, the screen is to be cleared and TT$ is to be printed on the screen.

Assume the player wants to hear five notes. The value of NN will be five. Line 330 assigns this value to Y, and line 340 starts a For-next loop. The number of cycles in the loop is equal to the number of notes the player wants to hear. Line 350 begins a portion of the program quite similar to the one previously shown. Information is read from the first Data statement (line 470). Lines 360 through 450 do nothing at this point. They exist to identify the conclusion of each song and to cause the appropriate branches. For the first five notes of the first song we can skip to line 460, which causes the computer to play the first note in the Data statement, a G. Line 570 causes the loop to recycle and the next note to be played. This process continues until the first five Data statements have been read and the notes they represent are output from the speaker.

At this point line 580 clears the screen, and lines 590 and 600 create the screen prompt, requesting the player to "Name That Tune." Notice in line 600 that Y has been inserted in front of the word "Notes." This allows the player to be aware of the number of notes he has heard for scorekeeping purposes. When the player types his guess of the song's title, his guess is assigned to the string variable T$. Line 610 compares T$ (the player's guess) with TT$ (the actual name of the song). If the two are equal, the screen is cleared and the computer prints "THAT'S RIGHT!" centered. The same line also contains a GOTO statement which branches to line 730. This will be discussed later.

If the player's guess is incorrect, line 620 will detect the error, clear the screen, and print "WRONG!!" centered. This line also contains a timing loop, after which lines 360 through 710 take effect. For the first song the variable RQ has not been assigned any value, so line 720 causes a branch to line 170. Line 170 contains the Restore statement for Data line 470, which has the information for "Mary Had a Little Lamb". The result is a restoration of all data in line 470, so the next Read statement will access the first Data item instead of the sixth (assuming the player originally requested five notes for his first guess). The screen prompt appears again, asking for the number of notes; suppose the player requests seven this time. The For-next loop starting at line 340 then cycles seven times and plays the previous five notes plus two additional ones. It is absolutely essential to restore the Data statement in order to hear the first five notes again.

Now assume the player makes the correct guess, which is detected by line 610 causing a branch to line 730. Here, Y is assigned a new value of 100. (Its previous value was seven because the hypothetical player wanted to hear seven notes.) The new value was chosen because it is adequate to access all items in the Data statement. If the Data statements contained more than 100 notes, a higher figure would have been necessary. The next portion of line 730 tests for the value of RQ. At this point, the variable RQ has not been assigned any value, so line 820 takes over and again restores the data in line 470. Seven items have already been accessed, so restoration is mandatory in order to hear the entire song. Line 820 also contains a branch to line 340, which substitutes 100 for Y. The loop will theoretically cycle 100 times. This causes all items in the Data statement to be read and played as notes from the IBM Personal computer speaker.

While the For-next loop is set to cycle 100 times, the Read statement encounters AA at the end of line 470 before the hundredth cycle. This is immediately detected in line 360, which then assigns two to variable RQ, assigns a new value (Yankee Doodle) to TT$, and branches to line 630. This line tests for the value of RQ; since it is two, there is another branch to line 200, containing the Restore statement for Data line 480, which has the information for the song Yankee Doodle. The data in line 470 has been exhausted and must not be restored or the song will be repeated. Line 200 also contains a branch to line 290, which begins the entire sequence again.

Remember that in this phase of the program RQ has been assigned the value two, TT$ equals Yankee Doodle, and the song information contained in Data line 470 has been exhausted. As the player inputs the number of notes he wants to hear for the next song, Data line 480 is accessed. Lines 610 and 620 again verify the accuracy of the next guess. If it is incorrect, line 630 branches back to line 200, which restores the Yankee Doodle line and continues to do so until the correct guess has been entered. When that happens line 610 branches to line 730, which sets the value of Y at 100, restores line 480 and branches to line 340, which plays the entire song after printing "THAT'S RIGHT!" on the screen. This complex sequence continues through the remaining eight Data lines containing the song information.

Inevitably, it will be desirable to change the tunes in the program. To do so, change Data lines 470 through 560 to reflect the new information. One must also change the value of TT$ in lines 360 through 440 and in line 180, so TT$ contains the new song names.

If you are musically inclined and can read music, the process I have used for generating music should be easily mastered. By examining the Data lines, one will see that in some instances the items contain only a letter to identify the note. Some contain minus signs indicating a flat. Plus signs designate sharps. Still other items are followed by numerical designators, used to indicate the duration each note is to be held. If there is no numerical designator, each note may be thought of as a quarter note. The designator 1 indicates a whole note, 2 a half note, 4 a quarter note and 8 an eighth note. The letter P designates a pause or rest; if followed by a numerical designator, P indicates the length of that rest. The last Data item in each line is used to branch to other program lines; thus AA-JJ are not notes.

I composed the Data lines mostly from my son's beginning music book written for the trumpet. This publication contains very simple songs that were easily input. Complex songs should not be much more difficult to input, although the input time will be longer. Playing music on any instrument involves some knowledge of mathematics, as the musical manuscripts contain representations of audio tones and the lengths they are to be held. The computer can think faster than you can think mathematically and will play exactly what it is told. Therefore, to input musical information to the IBM Personal computer is quite similar to the input of a mathematical formula. The statements contained in Advanced BASIC make this a very simple task, with the information corresponding directly to the information contained in any musical manuscript.

You may wish to include more tunes than I have. This is more difficult than changing the ten tunes, as it is necessary to add several more If-then and branch statements for each additional song input. You can do this by following the same programming techniques used to develop this program.

THE CONCEPT

The writing and performance of a musical composition is heavily based upon mathematics. Each note symbol, whether it be an eighth note, sixteenth note, half note or whole note, may be thought of as a partially assigned variable. The symbol for a quarter note by itself, for example, tells the musician very little. When it is inserted into a musical manuscript measure along with the staff time designator, it then becomes fully assigned to a specific value. The assignment will depend on the line or space where the note is inserted and also on tempo markings and staff indications of sharps and flats. The first portion of a musical manuscript indicates the key in which the piece is to be played, the time given to each measure, and the tempo at which this time is to be measured. At this stage, the note symbol is fully assigned.

This discussion closely resembles the assignment of a specific value to a variable in computer programming. I have stated that the note by itself is partially assigned, since one can tell (approximately) whether it will eventually be given a high or low value. The oval symbol portion of the note will receive a lower assignment if it is filled than if it is left open. Without the staff lines one has no idea at what frequency this note is to be played, so the partial assignment indicates relative length rather than frequency.

When music is performed, the musician reads the score and physically executes the tone for the duration specified. In 4/4 time, a quarter note will be sustained for one-quarter of the total time devoted to any single measure. In 3/4 time, the same note symbol will be sustained for one-third the total allotted to a single measure. We know that the note symbol by itself is a quarter note if it consists of a filled oval attached to a single stem. If the stem contains a flag at its end, this means an eighth note. Two flags indicate a sixteenth note, and so forth. The partially assigned variable (without the staff designator) indicates only the name of the note in regard to allotted time within a measure, but we need the additional information to put it to use.

To make a comparison in computer terms, let's take the letter X. We know that this is a variable, but that's all we know. If the X is followed by a $, as in X$, we know that this is a string variable, but we cannot put it to use until an assignment is made. The program line:

```
10  X = 100
```

assigns that variable, and this line corresponds to the musical staff and the information the staff line contains.

Because of this close similarity, the programming of music for the IBM Personal computer (or any computer, for that matter) can be made quite simple by looking at all musical manuscripts as one would a mathematical formula. Using the Play statement in IBM Advanced BASIC, we can make the transference from musical manuscript to computer program almost directly. The T command following the Play statement is used to set tempo. If you wish to play middle G as an eighth note, simply follow the Play statement with "G8". If you want to change to a sixteenth note, convert to "G16". Even here we are dealing with a partially assigned variable. The G is a definite assignment for frequency, but the 16 only indicates that that note will be sustained for one-sixteenth of the full measure. When a tempo designation is assigned, our variable is fully assigned, and the exact length and frequency can be determined.

If you can read music, you can rapidly commit it to the program using IBM Advanced BASIC. If the tempo command is omitted, the computer automatically defaults to 120, a moderate rate. The tempo command may be as low as 32, which is extremely slow and would be musically defined as

Fig. 3-1. A section of musical manuscript showing different types of notes.

Larghissimo. Increasing the tempo results in *Largo, Lento,* and *Adagio* at a tempo setting of 65 to 75. The default temp of 120 is musically classified as *Allegretto* or *Allegro,* medium fast.

Figure 3-1 shows a section of musical manuscript specifying several different types of notes. The program designation following the Play statement would read as follows:

G4,G4,G4,G4,F4,F4,F4,F4,E2,E2,A1

The first measure consists of four Gs, each a quarter-note. The next measure consists of four quarter-note Fs. The third contains two E half notes, and the final measure contains a whole note A. We can see that the program portion which will cause the computer to output these tones is identical to that of the notes mentioned. The numerals following the notes correspond to their relative sustain time. No tempo statement would be necessary here if the default of 120 is satisfactory. If a faster tempo is desired, a "T200" might suffice. All of these data items can be committed to a Data statement. They would then be assigned to a string variable at the Read statement, and the Play statement would execute these notes.

Musical rests are programmed similarly by using the P command following the Play statement. The command P4 indicates that a rest is to be held for the equivalent of a quarter-note, P8 an eighth note, and so forth. The octave command is used to select one of seven octaves numbered from 0 to 6. The sample musical manuscript discussed here was composed solely of notes in the middle range, which is the computer default (octave 4). Assume the second note is to be played one octave higher than the first note. The data information would then read:

G4,05,G4,04 . . . . . .

The first G will be played in the default octave 4, the next command goes to octave 5 and again plays G, and the succeeding command is necessary to return to the default octave. If this were not done, the remaining notes would be played in octave 5.

I was very surprised at how easy it was to convert the musical manuscript information to computer program form. Although my major in college was music, I do not consider that an advantage compared to those who have not had this background but who can read music. Transferring a musical manuscript to a computer program is not like composing, but is more like copying. Those with no performing experience who can identify notes and read music purely from a scholastic standpoint can program as effectively as an artist.

One can use the computer as a compositional aid in the absence of a piano or other instrument. Harmony cannot be played because of the necessity of producing one note at a time. However, one can write a melody line and then a harmony line and play each separately. The IBM Personal computer cannot take the place of a music synthesizer, which is a true musical instrument, whereas the computer is not. Most music will be generated for entertainment purposes or to add interest to another type of program. Music is often output from the computer to accentuate movement on the screen. A child's learning program can be accentuated by playing a simple song to indicate a correct answer or other accomplishment. Music is another addition to microcomputers which has enhanced the overall use of these devices.

Speech...

Chapter 4

For the last three decades, science fiction movies have often presented futuristic scenes of robots with internal computers that could interface directly with humans. Commands were given verbally by humans to robots and by robots to humans. In the early seventies, the movie *2001–A Space Odyssey* was extremely popular. One of the most interesting aspects of this film was "Hal," the computer that talked to its human pilots in a soft human-like tenor voice. Of course, Hal later went on a rampage until one of the crew members finally succeeded in "pulling the plug." This computer had been programmed with so much information that it had attained awareness of its own existence. The most appealing thing about the computer was its ability to talk to human beings and, to a lesser extent, understand what was said.

The idea of constructing a mechanical or electronic device able to communicate with mankind in human language has appealed to many for a long time. In the past, tape recorded words have been accessed to allow this to take place in a limited form. A human being simply spoke a word into a microphone, committing it to one section of magnetic tape; other words were committed to other sections. Then, based on a preset cueing and switching technique, these words were combined to form crude speech. Such systems were often massive, complex and not very effective. Speech entails much more than pronouncing words in only one way. Humans use inflections to a very high degree; such patterns are even more complex than vowel and consonant sounds.

Consider the letter E, for example. When used alone, it is rarely pronounced with a true E sound. It may become "eh," or when used with other letters, be completely silent. The letter C, in combination with certain vowels, may be pronounced as "see." More often, it takes on the "cah" sound. The letter S often goes hand in hand with the same sound of the letter C. Consider the word receive, for instance. This could be phonetically spelled "resieve"; most persons would pronounce it that way. When dealing with consonants and vowel combinations, the English language allows "psy" to sound like "sī" or "sy".

The point is that the pronunciation of any letter within a word often depends on its relationship to other letters in the same word. If we always pronounced C as "Cee," I as "eye," and B as "bee," instead of "buh," then committing human speech patterns to a computer and obtaining a highly accurate playback would be much simpler.

Now consider the problem of inflection. For example, when used within a sentence the word "and" is always pronounced in the same basic manner; but according to its importance in a sentence. It may be "and??" or "and!!" For a computer to duplicate exactly the human speech pattern and all inflections we use, many other parameters, in addition to the vowel and consonant makeup of each work, must be considered.

The way humans speak words and utter sounds differs according to the message. When I was in the commercial radio business, a popular test given to announcers applying for jobs involved the sentence "You did not say I could go." The individual was asked to speak this sentence seven times, putting the emphasis on the first word the first time, then the second word, and so on. Try reciting the following lines, emphasizing the italicized word:

You did not say I could go.
You *did* not say I could go.
You did *not* say I could go.
You did not *say* I could go.
You did not say *I* could go.
You did not say I *could* go.
You did not say I could *go*.

You probably will find that the emphasis given each successive word will be different depending upon the word. When proper emphasis is given, the entire meaning of the sentence is changed. Unknowingly, you will also change the emphasis given every other word in the sentence. Emphasis has to do with the duration of the word, its timing relationship with other words in the sentence, the loudness with which the word is spoken (in relationship to other words), the pitch or frequency of each vowel and consonant sound, and many other voice pattern modifications. The way these sentences are pronounced involves much more than the words placed before the reader. Human beings will automatically recall past experiences or will manufacture a fictitious situation in which sentences would be said to another human being, thus allowing for the correct inflection. So far computers cannot do this. Electronic machines now are only able to act upon information that has been input, a very small fraction of the knowledge required to duplicate human concepts that sentences would bring to mind.

Fortunately, humans can understand ideas communicated in other than perfect fashion. Consider the slang phrase "How's it going?" We know this means "What is your current physical, mental, and emotional state based upon recent occurrences?" A computer, however, would have to define what was meant by "it," which in this context can be thought of as a variable. When asked this question, the human being defines "it" (in most cases) as the single most important past occurrence, which is creating happiness or sadness, or any of a number of other states of mind. This is weighed against past states of mind and is automatically rated on some mental scale. If the individual is feeling very good, the response may be "fine" or "excellent." If things are not so good, an "okay" may suffice. On the other hand, "Things are rotten" may be more appropriate. Even this last statement involves the variable "things." The questioner assigns a constant to this variable based upon his past experiences. It's not so difficult when two humans are communicating, but when a human must communicate with a nonhuman, difficulties arise.

This situation becomes far more complex when a living creature tries to communicate with a nonliving entity (such as a computer), or vice versa. First, let us examine communication between a human and a family dog, Fido. While certainly not human, Fido is still a living creature and experiences many of the same feelings and emotions that we do. During many thousands of years humans and dogs have learned to communicate. When a dog wags its tail, we know the dog probably is happy. When that tail is tucked between its legs, a dog is frightened or unhappy. Many movies have portrayed dogs in life-saving roles in which they summon human help by running up to them, barking, and then running off a short distance again and again. This may indicate the dog wants to follow. Even as recently as the late sixties, many humans thought we were the only race with the ability to think. Animals were said to do everything instinctively, without using the mental processes we refer to as thinking. I believe this concept has basically been refuted, possibly because humans are becoming more secure in their existence and don't feel superior based on quirks of nature. Many animals do think. I will argue this with my dying breath, regardless of what a few self-ordained religious fanatics claim through no more than their own arrogance.

Computers, on the other hand, do not think. They do mimic the human thinking process to a minimal degree. However, a thinking process and true thinking are altogether different. As we progress in computer science, we will undoubtedly learn much about the mechanics of the human thinking process. At present, the term "thinking" is a variable in itself and has been defined in large part through opinion rather than fact.

Speech patterns need not be perfectly human in order to be understandable. For many decades, amateur radio operators have been communicating by means of Morse Code, which in no way sounds human. This is a simple binary code in which there are only two possible states: on or off, long or short, dot or dash. It is not possible to communicate much inflection or emphasis using this code, although the code symbol for the question mark, exclamation point and comma, may be used to indicate a question, special emphasis, or a pause in speech. While Morse Code is basically used to spell out words, most amateur operators use an abbreviation system which is understood by practitioners of the hobby. These abbreviations are human-designed and human-oriented. For example, the code phrase "•••——•——" represents a V and a Y. The code word "vy", then, stands for "very". "Gud" is "good," and "vy gud" means "very good." Obviously, Morse Code and the many abbreviations used to speed transmission in no way aurally resemble human speech. We are able to decipher what is meant by each transmission.

When communicating with the digital computer, a computer language is used which might be better described as a human language. This language is actually an interface between the thinking process of the human and the logic processes of the computer. In BASIC, the statement Print indicates to the machine that the following phrase or assigned variable is to be displayed. Print, however, is a word which is understood by human beings. A microprocessor acts only on a binary code that in no way resembles the word print. This command is converted within the computer to binary code, which the computer can understand. The output from the microprocessor is then converted to signals which cause a printout on the screen in a form humans can understand. This process is similar to speaking with an individual who understands a different language from your own, through an interpreter who understands both languages.

It would be nice to have a computer system that could output speech information exactly as a human does, but this is not now possible. The main point to remember is that all we really need is an oral line of communication between the machine and the human operator. Most machines already offer visual communication by means of a cathode-ray-tube display, or hard copy form using a printer. Often the screen prompts are abbreviated; for example, "input data," which means "insert the information you want the computer to act upon." It's not necessary or even desirable to print in most instances in minute detail exactly what you're expected to do; the simple "input data" command is sufficient.

People who become frustrated with computer systems that do communicate orally probably are frustrated because they expect the machine to be just like a human being. It's important to distinguish between communicating and conversing. Taken at face value, both words mean about the same thing. But when applied to devices rather than human beings, they take on different meanings. Efficient communications involve sending and receiving instructions within the shortest time possible, using the minimum data required. Conversing is more of an exchange of ideas, emotions, and complex concepts, and thus is not nearly as restricted as an efficient communication. There are those who would argue with my terminology, but I think the differences between these two words with respect to computers makes my point.

Whenever we communicate with a computer, an action is required. This is not necessarily so with human beings, or the person to whom the communication is directed. For example you could ask a friend, "What are your opinions on the energy crisis?" The friend may choose not to respond and simply walk away. On the other hand, all input to the computer demands a response. The response may be in the form of printed matter or the IBM Personal computer might display "Syntax Error," which means you did not ask the question or insert the command in a manner that it could understand. In either case, the computer always responds to your input. Communications, then, require an exchange of "hard" information. A conversation will involve this as well as opinions and emotional feelings.

THE BASIC SPEECH PROCESS

Speech is a product of respiration. Normally, air contained in the lungs is passed over the vocal cords, causing them to vibrate at the desired frequencies. When babies learn to talk, this requires a combination of mental and physical functions. The brain retains the concept of the word (how it sounds), but physical training is required to get the brain to trigger the correct flow of air from the lungs, along with mouth and tongue movements to add accent to the sounds which are generated. Most persons don't even think of respiration as being part of the speech process. Try clamping your mouth shut, holding your nose, and humming. You can produce a sound for only one second until pressure builds up within the throat, mouth, and nasal passages, stopping all flow of air from the lungs. The air is still there, but it is no longer moving across the vocal cords. You can make another sound by inhaling (still with your mouth and nose held shut). The lungs are pulling the pressurized air from the head back across the vocal cords. In either case, a movement of air within the human system is required to produce sounds from the vocal cords.

Readers who have had the opportunity to speak into a microphone while observing the signals of the speech pattern on an oscilloscope realize that the human voice does not consist of a single varying tone. Rather, it is a complex combination of many different tones and harmonics of these same tones which produces not only recognizable speech, but also other identifiable speech characteristics such as timbre and frequency. Audible signals generated by the human vocal cords are unique from person to person. No two waveforms would be identical, even if both persons were pronouncing the same word. The word by itself is only a small portion of human speech. The way a word is pronounced conveys information as well. Take the word "now," for example. If used in an angry statement, such as "I want this done *now*!" it would sound different (and look different on the oscilloscope) from the sound if this same word were used meekly in the sentence, "Do you want me to do this *now*? While the word "now" means the same thing in both sentences, it has different purposes when used as above.

We pronounce words and emphasize them through sound groupings called phonemes (pronounced fo-neems). Phonemes are the basic speech sounds; when properly combined, they can be used to pronounce any word. We change the frequency at which phonemes are uttered to give emphasis or further meaning to a word. For example, "Now!" is usually said quickly and with few major frequency shifts on any phoneme. On the other hand "Now?" starts with the first phoneme at a lower pitch than the last one, with a steady rise in frequency. This is the way we pronounce most words used to ask a question. Analyzed into phonemes, the word "now" would be something like "nah-owl-uh." By placing a "k" in front of this word, it could easily take on a phonetic sound of "kuh-nah-owl-uh". This is the way a simple speech synthesizer acting on a string of phonemes might pronounce the second word. However, in the English language we know that the "k" is silent, so why is it there? Its purpose (in our language) is to indicate that the "ow" is to take on the "o" sound; thus the correct phonetics would be "nuh-owe." The same phonetics would apply to the word "no," since both are pronounced identically.

THE SPEECH SYNTHESIZER

Many types of speech synthesizers contain the phonetics of human speech in on-board memories. When triggered by the computer, they act upon the original input information, which is in printed form, and assign a different phonetic to each letter or letter combination. Good synthesizers consider the entire word, and thus can provide different phonetics for our sample words "now" and "know." The phonetics are tied together through highly complex circuitry contained on a single chip, whose purpose is ultimately to output a string of phonetics in audible form. The identification and assignment process is only one part of this process. Output from the chip is fed through audio stages which consist of electronic filters and buffers, so as to arrive at an output to the speaker that is within the human voice range. The exact science of how this is done fills many books.

When speech synthesizers were first made available to the public, they were mostly experimental in nature. Through hours of arduous machine-level programming, you could get them to say a completely recognizable word providing you knew what the machine was trying to say in the first place. These devices were certainly interesting but were not practical from a user's standpoint, since the vocabulary was quite limited and each word was arrived at through difficult programming.

Later, costly synthesizers were made available that contained limited preprogrammed vocabularies. These were triggered by output information from the computer. Of course, one had to stay within the restricted vocabulary, because if the word wasn't already on board the synthesizer, it could not be made up.

The speech synthesizer stores sounds rather than words. The computer provides a code for a phoneme and the synthesizer pronounces it. By stringing several phonemes together, along with the appropriate pitch and intonation information, the synthesizer says a word. If the synthesizer contains the capability to pronounce enough phonemes, it can say any word in any language. None currently have this capability, but enough phonemes are contained to pronounce most words well enough for them to be understood. What has been discussed is often called *unlimited speech:* a word is input from the keyboard and is then spoken by the synthesizer.

Votrax Type-'N-Talk Synthesizer

Votrax is a division of Federal Screw Works and is located in Troy, Michigan. This company has long been well known for its voice synthesizers. A few years ago a book involving speech synthesizers for the computer hobbyist would have been impractical, since most commercial units cost far more than even the most powerful microcomputer. This has recently changed; now anyone can buy an unlimited speech synthesizer for a moderate price. I contacted Votrax to see whether they had a synthesizer that would interface with the IBM Personal computer, and found one available for less than $400.

When the unit arrived my worst fears were realized. Here was a tiny unit, weighing less than two pounds, that looked more like a miniature preamplifier than a voice synthesizer, which obviously must require vast amounts of circuit space and be fitted with a minimum of 273 controls. The Votrax unit (Fig. 4-1) has only two controls on the front panel, one of which is for volume. The frequency control was even more of a surprise, as I had expected to be constantly adjusting it in order to get any intelligible speech patterns.

Dejectedly taking my synthesizer in hand, I stopped at a local electronics hobby store to pick up a plug with which to connect the owner-supplied speaker to the Votrax unit. Despite being disappointed with what I had so far, I did learn that connecting the unit to the IBM machine was simply a matter of attaching one end of the interface cable to the synthesizer and the other end to the asynchronous communications adapter output plug at the rear of the IBM Personal computer. Votrax provides a separate power supply which attaches to the rear of the unit by means of an octal plug.

With the device connected to the computer and

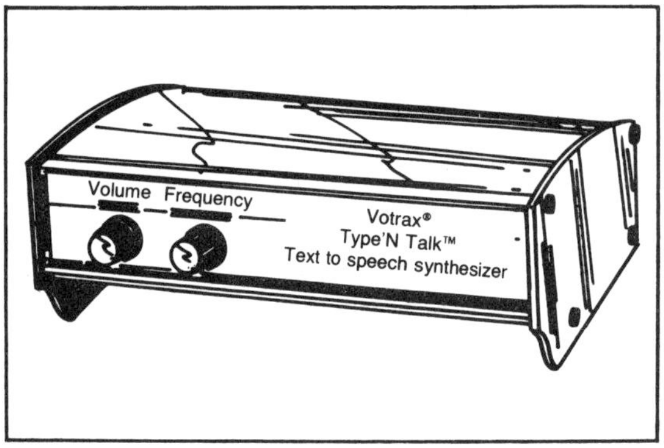

Fig. 4-1. The Votrax Type-'N-Talk speech synthesizer. (Courtesy Votrax Division, Federal Screw Works.)

the speaker attached, I pushed the "on" switch on the system unit and the pushbutton switch on the synthesizer. I immediately heard "system ready" from my speaker. This indicated that the synthesizer was functioning properly and was indeed receiving signals from the computer.

It was at this point that I finally opened the Votrax owner's manual. Was I surprised! I couldn't believe what I was reading. I had in my possession a synthesizer, miniature in size and costing less than $400, with an unlimited vocabulary. A Votrax data sheet supplied the four-line program to be run on the IBM machine to activate the communications adapter, but all indications were that from this point, the synthesizer would speak whatever words were typed in. I admit I had strong doubts at this point, but quickly inserted the program and typed in the phrase "The quick brown fox jumped over the lazy dogs back 1 2 3 4 5 6 7 8 9 10." When I pressed Enter, the synthesizer immediately said what I had typed; it was surprisingly accurate and easy to understand. It did pronounce the final ten as "one zero," but this was my fault and had nothing to do with the Votrax unit. To say that I was immediately hooked would be an understatement. I then sat before the keyboard for six hours, inputing various words, word groupings, and letter groups. This is truly an amazing unit and is priced well within the reach of most computer hobbyists.

The following information has been reprinted from some of the excellent documentation Votrax supplies with its speech synthesizer. This device may also be used with many other types of personal computers. My experience with it has included only the IBM Personal computer at a transmission rate of 9600 baud.

Type-'N-Talk is a serial communicating peripheral device which appears to a computer very much like a serial printer. It receives information transmitted to it on Pin 3 (RD) of its DB 25 connector (an RS-232 standard). Once this information is received, Type-'N-Talk normally retransmits the information on Pin 2 (TD) of its RS-232 connector. As each character is received, it is checked and then normally placed in the input buffer. If the character has special meaning, Type-'N-Talk takes immediate action. In the case of a carriage return character, the device immediately becomes busy, indicates this condition with line 5 (RTS goes low) on its RS-232 connector, and accepts no additional characters. Type-'N-Talk remains busy until all of the information in its input buffer has been passed to its output queue (128 phoneme capacity). Normally, this step uses the text-to-phoneme algorithm and the output queue is used to store phonemes on the way to the synthesizer. If the computer used does not have hardware handshaking connected (RTS/CTS Pins 4 and 5), information sent to the device during the busy period will be lost.

Type-'N-Talk requires a high signal on both pins 4 (CTS) and 8 (DCD) of its RS-232 connector in order to accept information sent to it. If appropriate signals are not available from the computer, these lines may be connected to line 20 (DTR) at the Type-'N-Talk end (just jumper all three wires together). In addition, the baud rates must be set at the same value on both the computer and the Type-'N-Talk. The audio connection to the device is made through a "mini-plug" connector (3.5 mm, ⅛ inch), not an RCA-type connector.

To restate:

- Serial information must be received by Type-'N-Talk on Pin 3.
- Serial information is transmitted from Type-'N-Talk on Pin 2.
- Pin 1 is chassis ground and Pin 7 is signal ground; at least Pin 7 must be connected.
- Pin 4 is the clear to send (CTS input; must be

held high for the device to receive; can be attached to Pin 20 if no request-to-send (RTS) signal is available from the computer.

●Pin 5 is the request-to-send (RTS) output and should be attached to the clear-to-send (CTS) into the computer or any line that can serve as a "busy" indicator.

●Pin 8 is the data carrier detect (DCD) input and must be held high for operation; it can be attached to Pin 20 if no signal from the computer is available.

●Pin 20 is the DTR and is high as long as the device is powered up.

●A mini-plug (3.5 mm, ⅛ inch) must connect the audio output to the speaker or amplifier used.

●Baud rates of the computer and the device must be set for the same value.

Figure 4-2 provides a table of specifications for the Votrax Type-'N-Talk unit, which uses a microprocessor-based text-to-speech algorithm. It contains a 1-watt audio amplifier and is built around the SC-01 speech synthesizer chip offering a data rate of 70-100 bits per second. It contains a 750-character buffer and has data switching capabilities.

Type-'N-Talk is a completely self-contained text-to-speech synthesizer. The unit is as easy to program as typing data or programs into a computer. It may be easily interfaced to a computer, modem or any RS-232-C compatible serial device.

Physical		
Width	7.7 inches (19.3 mm)	
Depth	5.2 inches (12.3 mm)	
Height	3.1 inches (6.5 mm)	
Weight	2 lbs. (0.896 Kg.)	
Environment		
Temperature	Operating:	40 to 100 degrees F (4 to 38 degrees C)
	Storage:	−35 to 150 degrees F (−37 to 65 degrees C)
Humidity	Operating:	20% to 90% (no condensation)
	Storage:	5% to 95% (no condensation)
Electrical		
Power	Input to transformer*	120 Vac, 60 Hz, 20 W
	Input to TNT*	—pins 1-3, 26 Vac, 180 mA
(see note below)		—pin 2, 20 Vdc, 50 mA
		—pin 4 is 0 volt reference
Interface	RS-232C compatible, 75-9600 baud Frame bits = 1 start, 8 data, 1 stop	
Audio	1 watt into 8 ohm speaker, ac coupled	

Fig. 4-2. Specifications for the Votrax Type-'N-Talk unit. (Courtesy Votrax Division, Federal Screw Works.)

It contains a low data rate Votrax SC-01 phoneme-based speech synthesizer CMOS chip with unlimited vocabulary. The Type-'N-Talk text-to-speech translations are performed completely independently of the host computer. Thus the user's computer is free to perform other tasks while speech is in process, with no effect on the throughput of the user's computer. The vocabulary spoken by this unit is unlimited and user-defined. The text-to-speech synthesizer creates speech from electronic phonemes using a set of rules that describes English pronunciations.

The unlimited vocabulary repertoire is inserted directly into the user's software programs in the same manner as statements are printed on the CRT or printer. This eliminates the need for extra memory in the IBM Personal computer, which would usually be required for prestored vocabulary techniques.

Type-'N-Talk Description and Interconnections

Two voice control knobs, volume and frequency, are located on the front panel. The back panel contains the on/off pushbutton switch, power jack with 5-pronged DIN connector, RS-232-C serial port, baud select switch, and the speaker jack Type-'N-Talk is supplied with a 110-volt power supply. Any 110-volt ac outlet is appropriate for the power supply. The low-voltage side of the power supply is plugged into the power jack.

Any 8-ohm speaker can be attached to Type-'N-Talk via the speaker jack.

The unit is provided with an RS-232-C serial interface. A 25-pin DIP connector is provided.

Eight signal lines are used:

- Ground (2 pins) (GND)
- Transmit data (TD)
- Receive data (RD)
- Clear to send (CTS)
- Request to send (RTS)
- Data carrier detect (DCD)
- Data terminal ready (DTR)

Different cable configurations are required, depending on whether the unit is to be used in the Send-Receive or Receive-only modes, or with a modem only.

Connector cables for Type-'N-Talk may be separately ordered. Cables are in stock for the TRS-80 Color (RS-232-C), the Apple II with serial card (RS-232-C) and the ATARI 800 with serial interface (RS-232-C). Cables may be specially ordered for other computers.

Inputing Data

Data in the form of ASCII codes can be sent to Type-'N-Talk when the handshake line (RTS line) is not busy (at logic 0). There are three classes of data: speech data, mode controls/commands, and null data.

Text is defined as any printable ASCII character not preceded by an Escape code or a phoneme delimiter. All text received is stored in the input buffer until spoken. A subset of the printable characters produce durations of silence or have no effect.

Phonetic data is defined as any printable character enclosed by phoneme delimiters. Phonetic data is stored in the input buffer and can be mixed with text if desired. When data in the input buffer is being spoken, phonetic data is routed directly to the output queue, bypassing the text-to-speed algorithm.

Certain ASCII characters will have no effect on the operation of Type-'N-Talk, and if desired by the user, can be echoed.

Unit Assignment/Selection

Up to eight Type-'N-Talk units may be daisy-chained with a terminal or printer from a single serial interface. Unit select codes allow independent or shared use of the data stream.

When a Type-'N-Talk receives an assignment code, it will store the corresponding unit number as its own. It then adds one to the assignment code and transmits this downline. This feature enables multiple Type-'N-Talk units in a daisy chain to all be assigned with only one assignment code from the user's computer.

Several optional modes of operation are available and can be selected by using control codes.

These modes can be dynamically set in accordance with the user's application.

In the *PSEND* mode, all phoneme codes resulting from a translation of the input buffer are directed to the Transmit Data output of the Type-'N-Talk unit's RS-232-C interface. This feature allows the user's computer to collect the phoneme codes corresponding to the text sent to the Type-'N-Talk and create a phonetic library or change the phonemes for different pronunciations.

The *PSEND OFF* mode is the standard mode of operation. All phonemes generated from the input buffer are placed into the output queue, where they can be removed by the speech synthesizer upon demand.

The *ECHO* feature is used selectively (On/Off) to relay data received by a Type-'N-Talk unit to the next unit or peripheral in a daisy chain.

In the *caps on* mode, capitalized letters are treated in two different ways. If only the first letter of a word is capitalized, such as proper nouns, the word is translated by the text-to-speech algorithm. When two or more letters are capitalized at the beginning of a word, the entire word is spelled out, letter-by-letter. This automatically separates acronyms, which are capitalized, from an English-text string. For example, the words "TIN" and "BOB" are pronounced "tee--eye-en" and "bee-owe-bee". The words "Tin" and "Bob" are pronounced "tin" and "bob."

The *caps off* mode is useful for systems that can only use uppercase characters. All uppercase characters are folded into their lowercase equivalent so that all text is translated and not spelled out. Mixed upper- and lowercase text are treated as all lowercase.

Type-'N-Talk powers-up in the *timer on* mode. If more than four seconds elapse after a character in a text string is sent to Type-'N-Talk, the text in the input buffer at the moment is translated and spoken.

The input timer is useful when ON-LINE applications send a prompting message without being followed by a carriage return. If for any reason this timer feature is not desired, it can be disabled with the Timer Off command.

The *reset* command resets all Type-'N-Talk modes to their power-up settings. The Type-'N-Talk assignment number returns to 0.

The Type-'N-Talk accepts several commands as follows:

●BACKSPACE (HEX 8) deletes the last character in the input buffer.

●TALK-CLR (HEX D) (carriage return - CR) causes the data in the input buffer to be spoken, then cleared. There are two alternate ways that TALK-CLR can be executed without sending a CR. The first is the result of an input buffer full condition. The second is the result of the input timer expiring (see Timer Off). When text is being translated, data input will be momentarily halted by the RTS signal going True.

●STOP-TALK (BREAK = RD) spacing for more than one data frame) causes all pending speech output to be cancelled.

Vocabulary Programming

Vocabulary may be entered into the user's computer in the same way as other data or programs are entered. Messages may be typed as literal statements using standard English text.

Vocabulary programming is as simple as typing a sentence. Once users have predefined the vocabulary in their software. Vocabulary can be sent to one or more output systems by defining it within that same software.

If the computer is functioning as a Computer Aided Instruction (CAI) system, the software may be adjusted so that messages intended for display on a CRT will be spoken by a Type-'N-Talk instead. Type-'N-Talk speaks and functions independently of other output devices. Its synthetic speech can draw attention to information that otherwise might be overlooked in a visual presentation.

Software

Computer-aided instruction programs and games are currently being written by nationally recognized suppliers that use the speech synthesis capabilities of Type-'N-Talk. As the library of available programs grows, Type-'N-Talk owners will be advised.

USING THE TYPE-'N-TALK

The real reason you might purchase the Type-'N-Talk device is its operation with the IBM Personal computer. Interconnections are quite simple and take only a few minutes: attach one end of the interface cable to the rear of the Type-'N-Talk unit; the other end plugs directly into the asynchronous communications adapter at the rear of the IBM machine; the octal plug from the Type-'N-Talk power supply is inserted into the rear of the synthesizer; the power cord goes to any 115 Vac wall outlet. Now activate the computer in the usual manner and then depress the on/off switch on the back panel of the Type-'N-Talk. This discussion assumes that you have already wired an 8-ohm speaker to an appropriate mini-plug which inserts in the jack on the Type-'N-Talk back panel.

When the switch is depressed, the synthesizer should immediately announce "system ready." This means the synthesizer is properly interfaced with the computer. If this does not occur, it may be necessary to adjust the volume control on the synthesizer to a higher setting. It may also be necessary to adjust the frequency control on the front panel to the midway point. This latter control adjusts the speed at which the Type-'N-Talk outputs its words. It has the same effect as speeding up and slowing down a tape recorder. As speech rate increases, so does the speech frequency. The midrange setting will produce a pleasing baritone voice. Lowering the setting will make the unit sound like a tape recorder whose audio has been input at 7½ inches per second and then played back at 3¾ ips speed.

A simple four line program input in IBM BASIC permits testing the synthesizer for as long as desired:

```
10  OPEN "COM 1:9600, N, 8, 1" AS #1
20  LINE INPUT "ENTER PHRASE:";A$
30  PRINT #1, A$
40  GOTO 20
```

Line 10 sets the asynchronous communications adapter at 9600 baud. Line 20 prints a screen prompt, "Enter Phrase:" Line 30 causes the asynchronous communications adapter to send the phrase which was input to the Type-'N-Talk in ASCII code form. Line 40 forms a loop which allows another phrase to be input.

When this program is run, "Enter Phrase:" will appear on the screen. At this point, type the word or phrase you want the Type-'N-Talk to say and press Enter. The Type-'N-Talk synthesizer then says the desired phrase.

To automatically access the asynchronous communications adapter in order to execute a spoken phrase within a program, use the same program discussed earlier with a few modifications. Line 40 would be deleted and line 20 would be changed to:

```
20  A$ = "I AM A COMPUTER"
```

At this point in the program, "I AM A COMPUTER" would be output from the Type-'N-Talk synthesizer. Any statement previously printed on the display would be spoken instead. It can easily be seen that programming in voice prompts rather than screen prompts requires no special techniques. One can even commit the asynchronous communications adapter setup information (in quotes in line 10) to a string variable (B$, for instance) to shorten programming time. This would allow specifying OPEN B$ AS #1 to access the RS-232 interface.

In most instances any word or phrase can be typed just as you normally would; it would be understandable when spoken by the synthesizer. In my terminology, however, understandable does not mean perfect speech. For example, if you input the word "computer," Type-'N-Talk will say "compooter." Almost anyone would know that this means "compewter". However, I was not satisfied and tried several different combinations to get the machine to pronounce the word the way we do. Instead of "computer," input "compeuter"; the synthesizer will pronounce it perfectly. You could also input "computer" for a perfect pronounciation.

It is surprising how quickly one becomes accustomed to the little idiosyncrasies of the speech synthesizer. With a few minutes of experimentation I discovered that almost any phoneme is possible, although one has to resort to phonetic spellings in some instances to get the most pleasing pronunciation. As a further test, I input the phrase "How now brown cow." The synthesizer was perfect with the first three words, but not with the last word. The spoken phrase come out "How now brown *coe*". I tried changing the spelling of this word to "cowl" and ended up with "coe well". I finally got the right combination with either "cal" or "kal." I found that in many instances, the machine took on a typical California accent when the letter "A" was substituted for the "owl" sound.

One can get into the synthesizer chip and make changes; however, I found that phonetically spelling words which did not sound right was the easiest method. For example, the word "clothes" came out "claw thes," but this was immediately corrected by using "cloze." This should also be used for the word close. The word "color" sounds best when spelled "cuhler." There are also some problems with words that begin with "e" as in "English." This word will be pronounced correctly when it is input as "inglish."

Getting the best pronunciation is simply a matter of playing with the synthesizer for a few hours, after which one begins to understand how it reacts to English spellings. You begin to compensate automatically during program writing. In most instances, you can input the normal spelling of a word and the synthesizer will say it perfectly, or closely enough for reasonably good comprehension. With a little extra effort, one can greatly improve those words which are not pronounced exactly as you would pronounce them.

Once I felt I had mastered inputing words and phrases in English, I tried German, French, and Russian to see how the synthesizer would react. Not being fluent with any of these languages, I experienced a few problems. Some French words are especially difficult, because phonemes are used for which there seem to be no English counterparts. I was finally able to obtain reasonably good pronunciations of the few words I did know in these foreign languages, as in "spray kan zee doitch," "parley voo fron say," and "o chee chorn ya." I am certain that a person more familiar with these languages and with English phonetic spellings of their vocabularies would be far more successful. Figure 4-3 shows a vocabulary programming pronunciation correction guide reprinted from the Votrax Type-'N-Talk. User's Manual. It is not necessary to memorize the phonetic spelling of every word, as this seems to come naturally after using the machine a short time. The manual is handy in case you get stuck and need guidance.

Generally speaking, correcting the pronunciation of the vowels involves more substitutions than those used for consonants. Votrax points out that this is because there are only five vowel letters to represent eighteen vowel sounds. Spelling rules accommodate by combining the vowel (and occasionally the consonant) letters in many different ways in order to achieve specific sounds which make up our language. There are three categories of vowel sounds defined with the American English spelling system: short vowel sounds, long vowel sounds, and diphthongs (2 vowel sounds in sequence spoken as a single unit). Some long vowels overlap with diphthongs, but the user need only be concerned about what letter sequences are required to say the sounds he desires.

When a vowel letter is doubled, it will usually produce a long vowel sound. The word "keep," for example, has a long "e" vowel sound. Therefore when the synthesizer pronounces the word "read" like "red," you may quickly replace the "ea" with "ee" ("reed") to achieve the appropriate pronunciation for the present tense form of this word. Examples of other letter sequences that produce long vowel and diphthong sounds may be found in Fig. 4-4.

To create a short vowel sound, you may have to manipulate the consonants that follow the vowel. For single syllable words with short vowel sounds, the synthesizer has a high degree of pronunciation accuracy. The words "bat," "spot," and "net" are produced correctly. To maintain the short vowel sounds when adding more syllables to these words,

Word List	Correction	Word List	Correction
advertisement	advertise ment	everyone	every one
baseball	base ball	extensive	extensiv
beautiful	butiful	generator	generayter
break	brake	goto	go to
breakfast	brekfest	item	ightem
bringing	bring ing	machine	mosheen
calculation	cal culation	machinery	mosheenery
capacity	cuppacity	output	out put
cassette	case et	paste	payst
certain	certin	phoneme	phone eem
character	kerekter	procedures	prowceejers
children	chilldren	program	prowgram
circuit	cirkit	promise	promiss
clients	clyents	pronunciation	pronunsiation
clothes	cloze	radio	radeo
close	near by	replace	reeplace
color	cuhler	requirement	require ment
comfortable	comfterble	rodeo	rowdeo
customer	custummer	scissors	scizors
data	dayta	shoes	shooz
definition	deffinition	singer	sing er
delete	deleet	software	softwayr
easiest	easy est	specify	specifuy
english	inglish	today	tuday
equivalent	eequivalent	typewriter	type writer
error	airor	vocabulary	vowcabulary
error	mistake	ware	wair

Fig. 4-3. A vocabulary programming pronunciation guide. (Courtesy Votrax Division, Federal Screw Works.)

you double the consonant before adding "...er," "...ing," or "...end"; thus we have "batter," "spotted," and "netting." Without the double consonant, the vowel sound is automatically assumed to be long. To misspell the word "definition" to get a short vowel pronunciation of "e," double the "f" to get "deffinition."

Through further experimentation, I found that individual letters of the alphabet may be input and are pronounced exactly as we would pronounce them, as in "a," "bee," "cee," "dee" and so forth. The numbers 1 through 9, when input as numbers and not spelled out, are pronounced in strict accordance with standard human pronunciation. This can help to abbreviate words during the input process.

For example, consider the word "today." When input using this spelling, the synthesizer says "tah day." This can be corrected by inputing "tuday." However, another way would be to input "2 day." This easily generalizes two phrases. For example, "Are you going to buy one for me?" becomes "R U going 2 by 1 4 me?" One can see that this substantially lessens the number of keys which must be struck to enter a phrase, thus speeding programming. "You are okay" becomes "U R O K". It is absolutely essential to put a space between each letter when using this form of input. If letters run together, the computer will try to say them. I ran my fingers across the keyboard at random, inputing a series of letters (without spaces in between). The synthesizer output "skupzug", "mizgub" and even "arfloteeba". Whatever you input, the synthesizer is going to treat in a logical manner and pronounce the jumbled letter string based upon its internal programming.

At the back of the Votrax User's Manual is a statement regarding Federal Communications Commission regulations governing the use of this device, especially in regard to radio and television interference. It reads: "This unit generates radio frequency energy and if not installed and used

LETTER SEQUENCES PRODUCING LONG VOWEL SOUNDS			DIPHTHONG LETTER SEQUENCE	
Long Vowel Sound	**Letter Sequence**	**Example Word**	**Diphthong Sequence**	**Example Word**
a	ai	maid	ow	power
a	ay	day	ou	house
a	a-e	save	oi	noise
e	ee	keep	oy	boy
e	cei	receive	you	you
e	ie	retrieve	u	music
e	y	every	ew	few
i	ey	eye		
i	ye	type		
i	i-e	line		
i	y	my		
o	o-e	home		
o	oa	goat		
o	ow	grow		
o	a	war		
u	oo	soon		
u	ou	group		
u	u-e	tune		

Fig. 4-4. This table shows examples of letter sequences that produce long vowel and diphthong sounds.(Courtesy Votrax Division, Federal Screw Works.)

properly—that is, in strict accordance with the manufacturer's instructions—it may cause interference to radio and television reception. It has been tested and found to comply with the limits for a Class B computing device in accordance with the specifications in Subpart J of Part 15 of FCC Rules, which are designed to provide reasonable protection against such interference in a residential installation. However, there is no guarantee that interference will not occur in a particular installation.

If the unit causes interference to radio or television reception, which can be determined by turning the unit off and on, you should try to correct the interference by following one or more of the following measures:

- Reorient the receiving antenna
- Relocate the unit with respect to the receiver
- Move the unit away from the receiver
- Plug the unit into a different outlet so that the unit and receiver are on different branch circuits.

If necessary, consult the dealer or an experienced radio/television technician for additional suggestions. You may find the booklet "How to Identify and Resolve Radio-TV Interference Problems" prepared by the Federal Communications Commission helpful. It is available from the U.S. Government Printing Office, Washington, D.C. 20402, Stock #004-000-00345-4.

This disclosure is typical in the microcomputer industry because of the clock frequencies at which most processors operate. My IBM Personal computer sits on an RCA color television receiver and uses it as a monitor in the color/graphics mode. My Type-'N-Talk unit also sits on the same television. There are many cables which input the modulator, the antenna terminals and so forth. For entertainment purposes the receiver gets its signal from the local cable system. I tried many different combinations to produce television interference and got nothing. As a long-time amateur radio operator, I'm quite familiar with radio and television interference. I know how to correct the situation and what causes interference. The IBM Personal computer and the Votrax synthesizer seem to be completely "clean" of rf interference, so I would not anticipate any reader having such problems. It has been my experience that most forms of radio and television interference stem from faults or poor design characteristics within the television or radio itself, and are rarely created by properly designed processing systems. In fringe areas where extremely weak television and radio broadcast signals are the rule rather than the exception, it is conceivable that some interference problems could result from using such equipment. Even so, bypassing or repositioning the computer and synthesizer should completely correct the problem.

My next uses of the Votrax Type-'N-Talk speech synthesizer involved going through programs I already had, which had been designed to output prompts to the display screen. A few additional program lines were inserted to automatically trigger the asynchronous communications adapter. By this short process I was able to convert all screen prompts to synthesized voice prompts, or both. Because of required phonetic spellings in some instances for proper output from the synthesizer, it was sometimes necessary to spell the voice prompt phrase differently from that of the screen prompt. This entailed only a few extra minutes of programming time.

The speech synthesizer was obtained more for experimentation and "play" purposes than as a highly useful accessory to the IBM Personal computer. However the synthesizer quickly became an integral part of my system, and I depend upon it in nearly every stage of programming. The synthesizer adds a new dimension to running a computer program, especially where non-computerists are involved. My thirteen-year-old son was not extremely excited about computer programming; he was more interested in simply running the programs I had already written. When the Votrax speech synthesizer was added, he immediately wanted free access to the keyboard, at first to play, but then to begin programming. He now is most interested in programming, which I attribute to the synthesizer.

When personal computers were first offered to the American public, there was a very significant element of science fiction involved in their use. For many years we have seen movies and read stories of the future, where everyone had a personal computer and depended on it much as we rely on the automobile today. Americans quickly become accustomed to the exotic innovations that the electronic age continues to produce. Personal computers have now become commonplace in our society. The speech synthesizer has sparked the science fiction element, and new interest has arisen in microcomputers that talk back.

Sound Effects

Chapter 5

There is nothing especially difficult about writing programs for the IBM Personal computer to output musical numbers or even human speech when using a speech synthesizer. However, the simplest audio outputs involve sound effects, and the programs used to produce these are exceedingly simple. It may not be apparent at first that a tone generator such as the one contained in the IBM Personal computer can be used to create a whole range of audio effects that don't seem to bear any resemblance to true audio tones. Clicks, pops, and many other effects are quite easily programmed, and the Sound statement is best used for such purposes.

While programming music and speech takes a bit of forethought and planning, some of the best sound effects are often arrived at through random experimentation. The IBM Personal computer has a very efficient audio generator that is capable of outputing frequencies from 37 to 32, 767 Hertz. The upper range of these frequencies lies above the human hearing limit, but dogs, cats, and other pets will certainly pay attention to these ultrasonic sounds.

Sound effects are used exactly in the same manner as graphics or on-screen text displays. All of these capabilities of the IBM Personal computer are incorporated to enhance the program run. Many people tend to separate the audio outputs of personal computers from the pure processing features. This attitude can greatly increase programming efforts. Just as a good on-screen graphic display can enhance most programs, a good audio presentation can do as much or more.

For example, I recently wrote an alphabetizing program in which up to 1000 words could be randomly input and alphabetically displayed on the screen or on printer. The IBM Personal computer did the alphabetizing internally and then displayed the alphabetized list. If the word list is quite long, much machine time is consumed by the internal sorting of the values of each letter. With the original program, the computer would seem to sit and do nothing while the list was being processed. It was as if the machine had shut down. Twenty minutes or more may be required to sort a long list. It was necessary for me to constantly check the screen, waiting for the visual prompt to inform me to press the Enter key in order to start the on-screen or hard copy print. Although it was possible to do other things while the machine was processing, the constant visual checking was a nuisance. I solved the problem by utilizing the audio output available with this computer. All that was necessary was to incorporate a Beep statement within a For-Next loop. When the machine was finished processing a string of beeps was output, alerting me that the information was ready for presentation. With this addition the words could be input and the processing begun when the list was complete. I could then leave the computer without wondering whether it was time to activate the display. When processing had been completed, a series of short beeps was output from the internal speaker which could be heard from quite a distance. In this case the audio prompt was far more valuable than the original visual one which simply printed "PROCESSING COMPLETE" on the screen.

At the present time microcomputers depend on visual displays and prompts for 99 percent or more of their output. When audio and video outputs are incorporated in the same program, the computer becomes more user-friendly, and information is transferred from computer to human much more efficiently. As we move further into the microcomputer age it is not inconceivable that devices to permit us to receive information by touch and perhaps by smell will be available. These two senses are also quite instrumental to human perception. Imagine a computer which displays a graphic orange on the screen and then by means of some unique peripheral, wafts a tangy aroma of this fruit your way. Many will say this is impossible, but so were computers in the recent past.

An audio prompt such as the Beep statement is not what I call an enhancement sound effect. By itself, the beep means nothing. To the programmer, however, the beep from the alphabetizing program is a variable which has been mentally assigned. Through this assignment process, the string of beeps tells us that processing is complete, just as effectively as the printed phrase on the screen. The beep would mean nothing to someone who is unaware of how the program is written and who had not made a mental assignment of the audio variable.

Fortunately the IBM Personal computer and its audio capability are quite versatile; many different sound effects can be programmed, for which automatic mental assignments have been made from childhood. Most of the things we sense are really variables that have eventually become assigned through experience. This is not completely true of all the things we sense, since some of these cause instinctive reactive reactions. For example, placing your hand on a hot surface does not require any mental assignment. There is a built-in automatic response to jerk your hand away . . . but you do assign the feeling to the presence of heat, although you realize this consciously only after your hand has been jerked away. If you had to go through the mental process of saying "This is a hot surface; I'd better take my hand away so I won't be burned," the time lag might result in crisp flesh. Nature realizes the brain's conscious processing is too slow to prevent injury from input received by sensory organs. The instinctive reaction comes first; the brain analyzes sensory phenomena after the event is already over.

At present instinctive reactions are not as important to the computer/human interfacing of information as is the conscious output of information. Sound effects can be quite important and helpful and are rarely used to maximum advantage.

Sound effects can be used in computer programs any way you want them to be used. Video game programs often incorporate sound effects, but these are often limited to weird ululations which simulate what humans think a flying saucer might sound like. Since none of us have ever heard an actual flying saucer (although many claim they have), this sound is an assigned variable; the assignments having been made from a long series of science fiction movies. It makes no difference that a flying saucer may not sound like this, only that we identify this sound with the flying saucer. The video game will also display a flying saucer traveling across the screen, which strengthens our original impression. The visual effect is more important to the actual playing of the game, since part of the game will probably involve shooting down the saucer or maneuvering it in some fashion. The game could be played just as efficiently without the audio effect, so why is it present? Simply because audio effects add to the enjoyment or the realism of the event being portrayed.

Of course in some cases the audio effect may be all-important. To use a similar example, the ATARI game Space Invaders involves constant on-screen action. Occasionally, a flying saucer will travel across the top of the screen. At the same time the player's attention may be riveted near the bottom. Without the audio sound effect, the player might not even be aware that the flying saucer is on the screen. In this case the sound effect, coupled with the video image, forms a special combination. Removing either the audio effect or the visual image would decrease the player's efficiency in shooting down the object. This type of situation can also be applied to pure microcomputer applications.

To add audio effects to a computer program, one must know something about human nature. The age of the person or persons who will be receiving the information is especially pertinent. Microcomputers are now used in grade schools to teach small children math and other subjects in an enjoyable manner. The flash card routine is one of the best-known computer learning sequences. One version of this program will draw two or more large numbers on the screen with a mathematical sign specifying the operation to be performed. For example, "4 + 4 =   " may be displayed. The child is then supposed to input the proper answer. If the correct answer is input, the word "RIGHT" will be displayed. The word "WRONG" is the result of an incorrect answer. At the same time, an audio prompt or output is heard. This is where human nature becomes important. For some reason, Americans tend to associate a rather high-pitched single note with "good", whereas a raspy low-pitched note indicates "bad." This is evident in many TV game shows where pleasant bell-like chimes are heard for a correct answer, while a raspy buzz is heard for a wrong answer.

The natural selection of these tones has something to do with the human psyche, it is known that certain tones bring about calmness or a sense of satisfaction among humans, while others grate on our nerves. There are exceptions; most of us can relax to the relatively low-pitched sounds of the surf beating against the shore, yet we recoil and wince at the sound of chalk squeaking across a blackboard or a metal pot being scraped with a spoon. These high-pitched sounds do nothing to keep us calm. Both the surf and the scraping are not pure audio waveforms, but are a complex combination of many different frequencies. From the computer standpoint we can safely use a low-pitched tone to indicate a wrong answer or a malfunction of some sort, and tones of a medium to high pitch to indicate a pleasing event.

The duration a tone is held is also very important. A short 800-Hertz beep is rather pleasing to most people, but hold this tone for ten or more seconds and it begins to grate on our nerves. Also, whereas one beep may indicate a pleasing occurrence, a string of beeps may trigger some sort of primordial alarm within our psychological makeup.

Let's get away from the idea of sound effects and discuss audio prompts. These can be used to especially good advantage when someone with no previous computer experience is operating a machine. Assume the screen will display all information that is to be output, and that it is necessary to press the Enter key several times during the program to complete the run. A standard program might simply print "PRESS ENTER TO CONTINUE", but since there is other information on the screen, this prompt may go unnoticed and may even add to the confusion. Instead of using the visual prompt, consider using the Beep statement to inform the operator that whenever the beep is heard, he is to press Enter and then examine the screen. This removes pressure from the operator who is struggling with a new situation. As soon as the program is initiated, all that is necessary is to examine the screen to extract the desired information. Whenever a beep is heard, one presses the Enter key. This allows the total workload of the operator to be split between two senses, sight and hearing. The operator will make a distinction between the on-screen information and the audio prompt and assign responsibilities to both outputs.

True audio sound effects can be used to make a game or learning program far more pleasurable. I advocate using graphics and sound to augment programs traditionally presented solely in text form. The audio portion of these enhancements may take the form of music, random sounds, or electronic simulations of natural sounds. The latter are true sound effects. Several programs are presented in the next chapter which will electronically simulate some real-life sounds. These are designed to be incorporated into already existing programs and used as enhancement subroutines. Sound effects programming is not a completely separate part of computer programming, but a natural extension. It is not essential that the sound effects be identical to the natural sounds.

Screen displays in both text and graphics form can set the stage for sound effects, or vice versa. For example, if you draw a graphic bird on the screen and run a sound effect of a bird singing, everyone will immediately see the connection. If you ran the bird call alone, the effect might be as easily understood. I previously referred to a high-pitched ululation which was supposed to represent the sound of a flying saucer. The sound effect mimics the flying saucer only because the saucer also appeared on the screen. Without the graphic representation, the sound effect might be that of a space gun or even a common earth-side siren. The point is that sound is only one means of representing an event. While some events can be identified immediately from audio information, others require the use of additional senses. Microcomputers are presently restricted to sight and sound, so we must use these so an operator can perceive a concept while relying only on these senses. It is often necessary to exaggerate audio and video effects to make up for the absence of smell and touch.

Graphic animation is a very important part of the IBM Personal computer, and sound can be used to accentuate on-screen motion. If an object is moving erratically across the screen, an erratic combination of sounds will augment this. The IBM graphics language is quite powerful and includes the capability of matching on-screen movement with similarly moving sounds. Visualize graphically an animated ball bouncing from the bottom of the screen to the top, and then down again in a diagonal path from left to right across the screen. It is quite easy to program a computer to output a low staccato note when the ball is at the bottom of the screen and a high note when it's at the top. The sound, then, matches the position of the ball on the screen, changing as the position changes. The feeling of motion is much stronger when the machine's sight and sound outputs are combined. For this particular example it would be necessary to add only two additional computer lines containing Sound statements. These would be keyed each time the graphic image is reset.

To begin your experimentation with IBM Personal computer sound effects, try this program:

```
10  FOR X = 37 TO 2000
20  SOUND X,1
30  NEXT X
```

When the Sound statement is committed to a For-Next loop such as shown here, a series of different notes are strung together in what sounds like a continuous, ever-changing output. The tone will go from low to quite high, but will do so smoothly, much like the first part of a fire siren. This particular program will take about one minute to run completely, but can be speeded up by decreasing the time command, which is a part of the Sound statement. By changing the 1 to a 0.1, the sequence will be shortened by a factor of one-tenth. Now if the time command goes below 0.1, the note will take on a raspy effect, and a harmonic is produced which is equivalent to the cycling speed of the For-Next loop. Extremely short duration values for any note will often create a raspy effect which can be used to good advantage.

Using this program, you can create many different sound effects simply by changing the value of X. The minimum value must be 37 or higher, since that is the frequency limit for the IBM Personal computer. As shown, the program will produce a continuous sound step sequence starting at 37 Hertz and increasing in steps of one to 2000 Hertz. The upper frequency limit is well above 30,000

Hertz, but the human hearing range is limited to a maximum of 15,000 to 20,000 Hertz. Very high frequency sounds will show as staccato clicks if the duration is held to a factor of one or less.

Sounds produced by the program will actually be a long series of different notes that step upward in frequency. These are individual notes, but the spacing between each is of such a short duration that the pauses cannot be detected. In some cases, however, you may want to produce a series of notes which are accented for individuality. All that is necessary is to slow the computer slightly with a time delay loop. By adding the following line to the previous program, each note will be followed by a short silence, and each note will definitely be separated from all others:

```
25   FOR Y = 1 TO 1000:NEXT Y
```

When this new program is run, the sound statement in line 20 will output a tone at 37 Hertz . The additional line causes the machine to count from 1 to 1000 which takes a short period of time. During this period, there will be no output from the speaker. When the Next statement is encountered in line 30, the loop recycles and a 38-Hertz note is output, followed by the same period of silence as before. The nested time delay loop separates each note by a silence that humans are able to detect.

The sample program begins at a very low frequency (37 Hertz) and increases to a high one (2000 Hertz). We can reverse this sequence by using:

```
10   FOR X = 2000 to 37 STEP -1
20   SOUND X,1
30   NEXT X
```

When this program is run, the starting tone will be 2000 Hertz and the output will oscillate down to 37 Hertz. By stringing this and the previous program together, we arrive at a simulation of a fire siren which will start low, go high, and then go low again. The speed at which one complete low-high-low sequence is output will be dependent upon the time value associated with the Sound statement. One can also speed the process considerably by using a higher step value. A value of 100 (plus or minus) will greatly shorten the sequence; most humans won't be able to tell the difference anyway. It is very difficult for our ears to detect slight changes in frequency, especially at the speed at which the computer is operating. Experiments will indicate a step value most applicable to producing the sound effect you desire.

Figure 5-1 shows another program which takes advantage of the computer's ability to generate and act upon random numbers. The For-Next statement has been deleted, and the GOTO statement in line 30 produces an endless loop. The Sound statement in line 20 acts on a random number. The frequency is determined by the value of 2000 multiplied by the random number produced by the machine. This number may be anywhere from 0 to a value of less than 1. The number 37 is added to the value in case the random number output is less than the minimum value required by the Sound statement of 37. Therefore, the lowest frequency that will be generated by this program is 37 Hertz, while the highest frequency will be 2036 Hertz. Each time the Sound statement is encountered, a different frequency value will be output by the random number generator. Each note is held for a very short duration; the result is a melange of random notes. This program produces a sound effect which has been used for years on television programs, in movies, and elsewhere to audibly invoke intricate electronic functionings. There is a definite feeling of intense movement which has long been associated with the processing functions of computers. This is a fairly accurate representation, because the sounds do occur at the approximate switching speeds of the computer on which they are run. This program could easily be limited to a lower frequency range by replacing the value of 2000 with a lower value. It can be increased in the same manner.

Undoubtedly, you have noticed that sound effects programs do not require much code. The pre-

```
10 REM RANDOM ELECTRONIC SOUNDS
20 SOUND (2000*RND)+37,.5
30 GOTO 20
```

Fig. 5-1. An example of a random-sounds generating program.

vious program contains only two active lines, and the second line is simply an endless loop return. One can lengthen the duration of each note produced by this program by inserting a higher figure for the time command portion of the Sound statement. One can even randomize this statement for a completely different effect.

When do you use sound effects? All I can say is that I use them whenever I have the opportunity. Anytime I write a program that shows an object on the screen or even alludes to an object in the text, I will often program an enhancing sound effect that will better convey the idea or setting for which I'm striving. Such enhancements can make the difference between a useful but rather drab program run, and one which is both useful and enjoyable. Pleasing programs are often determined by just a few lines.

I'm not speaking here of efficient processing as much as humanizing the program run. The most efficient programs from a pure processing standpoint are those which contain the minimum number of lines, prompts and output information. The computer attacks efficiency on a microsecond basis; humans are not so picky. If the addition of audio or graphic enhancements means that the computer must take 100 microseconds to output information rather than 10 microseconds, so what! Humans can't tell the difference anyway. Computer efficiency and the efficiency of the computer/human bond are often two different subjects. If a graphic or audio enhancement increases the attention span and thus the efficiency of the human to grasp output information, then such enhancements add greatly to the overall efficiency of information extraction. This is what all good programmers should try to achieve.

Music, voice, and audio effects have for too long been considered as little more than toys making up computer games. This is far from the truth, and as serious programmers continue to utilize the audio capabilities of the microcomputer, music, voice, and audio effects will become an integral part of more programs. If you refrain from approaching audio programming as a separate entity and look at it as a natural extension of graphics and text mode programming, your overall programming efforts will be far more rewarding, both for you and for those who use your program.

Sound Effects Programs

Chapter 6

Unlike many types of computer programs, those that are used to produce sound effects are not especially critical, and the same basic sounds may be produced using Sound statements whose frequency and time duration values may differ substantially. The programmer usually starts with a basic program and changes the values within the Sound statement by small degrees, in order to arrive eventually at a combination most to his liking.

The programs presented in this chapter were written specifically for and tested on the IBM Personal computer. You can run them exactly as shown to produce the effects described. They are also valuable examples of ideas that you can modify to produce completely different effects. If you don't see the sound effect you're looking for in these pages, try to input a program close to what is desired. You may then change the frequency and duration to produce the required sound. Most of the programs that follow will run in standard IBM BASIC, although some programs do require Advanced BASIC. The programs are extremely simple and can be input in a few minutes time. They are also designed to be strung together; examples will be presented in this chapter. In most instances you will want to include these programs in others already written. Normally these programs will be run as subroutines and accessed by appropriate GOTO and GOSUB statements. Many are so short that they can be committed to already existing For-Next loops without substantially slowing computer processing time. All are subject to much modification, which you are encouraged to do wherever appropriate.

FIRE SIREN

Figure 6-1 produces a fire siren sound. The program is an endless loop; the siren will continue until the program is manually halted. The computer will output a series of tones from 200 to 1000 Hertz and will then decrease in frequency until reaching the low value.

Line 30 begins the For-Next loop for the low-to-high portion of the output. The value of A is used as the frequency command within the Sound statement in line 40. A duration value of .1 machine cycle

```
10 REM SIREN
20 REM COPYRIGHT ROBERT J. TRAISTER AND ASSOCIATES 11/17/82
30 FOR A=200 TO 1000
40 SOUND A,.1
50 NEXT
60 SOUND A,15
70 FOR A=1000 TO 200 STEP -1
80 SOUND A,.1
90 NEXT
100 GOTO 30
```

Fig. 6-1. Fire siren.

was chosen after some experimentation. You may wish to use higher or lower values. The fire sirens in my area begin at a low value, then hold the high-frequency value for a short time before stepping down in frequency. When the For-Next loop has been completed, the output is 1000 Hertz. The Sound statement in line 60 causes this frequency to be sustained for a few additional seconds before the high-to-low loop is entered in line 70. This latter loop is simply the reverse of the former one and starts at 1000 Hertz, stepping down to 200 Hertz. As soon as the second loop times out, there is a branch to line 30 and the program repeats.

You may decide that a 200-Hertz value is too high or low to begin with, and you may wish to experiment with the values of A (in lines 30 and 70). My idea of how a fire siren should sound may be different from yours. This program is approximate and will allow you to regionalize the siren sound to match those in your area. I used it successfully in a game program involving a graphic fire scene. The program has many applications to game programs and can also be used to indicate an illegal function call, or to alert the operator to some malfunction requiring his attention during a program run. It's guaranteed to attract attention, especially when the sound goes off unexpectedly.

WHOOPER SIREN

This program (Fig. 6-2) simulates another type of siren, a whooper siren, often used by police cars, ambulances and other emergency vehicles. The sound is similar to the one in the fire siren, but the low-high-low sequence takes place during a much shorter period of time. Also, the high-to-low frequency differential is much lower.

Half of the fire siren program is used, since whooper sirens traditionally go from low to high and then repeat instead of stepping from high to low before resuming. The Sound statement in line 40 utilizes the frequency values set up in line 30. The time command was originally input as 0.0001, but the computer expresses this in a scientific math language represented by the number shown in line

```
10 REM WHOOPER SIREN
20 REM COPYRIGHT ROBERT J. TRAISTER AND ASSOCIATES 11/17/82
30 FOR A=900 TO 1000
40 SOUND A,8.999999E-02
50 NEXT
60 GOTO 30
```

Fig. 6-2. Whooper siren.

40. The Next statement in line 50 causes the loop to recycle, and when it has timed out, the Goto statement in line 60 returns the program to its beginning. This is another endless loop program, but when used with other programs, the loop would probably be removed and another For-Next loop added to cause a conclusion after a definite time duration.

You can experiment quite a bit with this program. If the step values of A are increased, many deep space sounds can be produced. You can also slow things up by lengthening the duration command. This is an exceedingly simple program, one you can have an awful lot of fun with, especially if the value of A is randomized. This program may be used for the same applications as the program described previously, and the fast-oscillating "whoop" can be even more startling than the relatively slow fire siren sound produced by the last program.

BIRDCALL

Figure 6-3 simulates a flock of chirping birds. Believe it or not, while I was trying to think of a program idea, a bird entered my attic and caused a tremendous ruckus while trying to get out. It was probably attracted by the sound my computer was producing. The bird was ejected and I returned to programming.

Birdcalls are easy to approximate but quite difficult to perfect. I am not completely satisfied with this program. Three different frequencies are used: 3000, 3500 and 4000 Hertz. The first two sounds are committed to the variables A and B in lines 30 and 40, whereas the 4000-Hertz tone is stated as a number in line 90. This was done for demonstration purposes and all Sound statements are processed by the computer in the same way, except that it is unnecessary to assign the variables in lines 50 and 70.

Three time delay loops in lines 60, 80, and 100 are used. These provide a fraction of a second of silence to separate each individual sound, although the time is so short that it is not very noticeable. The sequence is 3500-3000-4000. This combination gave me the most realistic sound, but if you are a bird watcher, you may be able to improve simulating the calls of specific types of fowl.

This program allows much room for experimentation. Notice that all of the For-Next time delay loops produce the same time delay. It may be more effective to make one or more loops longer than the other(s). The audio output from this program will sound very much like a flock of birds, although a radio amateur friend says that it sounds more like the audio transmission associated with slow-scan television. I take this as a compliment since off-the-air sounds are often referred to as birdcalls by other radio amateurs. The program must be fairly good or that bird would never have flown into my attic.

TELEPHONE RING

Simulating the ring of a telephone on the IBM

```
10 REM BIRDCALL
20 REM COPYRIGHT ROBERT J. TRAISTER AND ASSOCIATES 11/17/82
30 A=3500
40 B=3000
50 SOUND A,.9
60 FOR X=1 TO 50:NEXT X
70 SOUND B,.9
80 FOR X=1 TO 50:NEXT X
90 SOUND 4000,.9
100 FOR X=1 TO 50:NEXT X
110 GOTO 30
```

Fig. 6-3. Birdcall.

```
10 REM TELEPHONE RING
20 REM COPYRIGHT ROBERT J. TRAISTER AND ASSOCIATES 10/31/82
30 FOR X=1 TO 100
40 SOUND 500,.02
50 NEXT X
60 FOR X=1 TO 1500
70 NEXT X
80 GOTO 30
```

Fig. 6-4. Telephone ring.

Personal computer is very easy. Since different types of telephones ring differently, there is a broad range of tones to choose from. I chose to simulate the ring heard by the calling party through the telephone receiver after he has finished dialing a number. A later program will simulate the actual ringing sound when someone is calling you.

For the program in Fig. 6-4 I chose a frequency of 500 Hertz, which is inserted in the Sound statement found in line 40. I wanted a raspy sound, so a duration factor of 0.02 was incorporated. The For-Next loop beginning in line 30 does not control the audio frequency as it has done in other programs. This simply allows for a set number of tones to be output before ringing stops. At the end of the ring sequence the program enters a time delay loop, found in lines 60 and 70. Line 80 branches back to the beginning of the program and the ring sequence repeats. This time delay loop is necessary because telephones don't ring constantly. The ring occurs for a few seconds and is followed by silence for an equal duration before the ring begins again.

This program closely simulates what you will hear when a number has been dialed and you are waiting for your party to answer. I tried several frequency values for the Sound statement in line 40 and found 500 Hertz to be most pleasing. You may wish to raise or lower this figure, depending on your impression of how such a ringing should sound.

TELEPHONE DIAL SOUND

Undoubtedly, you have noticed the clicking sounds sometimes heard when you place a long distance call to an area not yet on the tone system. You may punch in a number and then hear a series of clicks, which are really the sounds of the line being switched on and off by means of an electronic dial. If you don't know what I'm talking about, as soon as you input and run the program, Fig. 6-5, you will know immediately.

To generate staccato clicks, a short-duration, high-frequency tone must be used. I chose 15,000 Hertz and a duration of 1 machine cycle. Line 40 contains a For-Next loop which places a space between each click. Since there are millions of numbers which can be dialed, I chose to randomize the number of cycles within the For-Next loop. The minimum number of clicks is 1; the maximum number is 10, representing dialing a 0. Lines 20 through 50 produce one number. Another time delay loop is then entered to provide spacing between each dialed number. Line 70 returns the program to the beginning, and another number is then clicked out. When you hear the sounds, I think you will agree that they are very realistic and sound exactly like what you've heard hundreds of times on your own telephone.

```
10 REM TELEPHONE DIAL
20 FOR X=1 TO 10*RND+1
30 SOUND 15000,1
40 FOR Y=1 TO 100:NEXT Y
50 NEXT X
60 FOR Z=1 TO 1000:NEXT Z
70 GOTO 20
```

Fig. 6-5. Telephone dial.

TELEPHONE RING/DIAL SEQUENCE

We can go one step further by combining the telephone ring and dial programs to produce an audio series. This series sounds like a number being dialed and the connection being made when the phone on the other end starts ringing. This program (Fig. 6-6) simulates the dialing of an 8-digit number, followed by the ringing of the phone on the other end.

This is a slightly modified combination of the previous two programs. The dialing sequence is found in lines 40 through 90; the ringing sequence is contained in lines 120 through 140. Each subroutine has been committed to a For-Next loop to control the number of dial clicks and telephone rings. Line 30 allows eight different random numbers to be dialed; the dial click sequence is nested within this loop. As soon as the eight numbers have been produced, there is a moderate time delay which is created in line 100. This simulates the silence heard after the last number is dialed and before the ring occurs.

The ring sequence is nested within a For-Next loop beginning at line 110. This causes the ring to occur five different times. The first ring occurs in lines 120 through 140 and consists of 99 different short outputs. The time delay is then entered in line 150, which establishes the silence between each ring. Line 160 returns the program run so that the next ring may be output. When five rings have occurred, the program has finished.

TUNED TELEPHONE RING

The program in Fig. 6-7 simulates the sounds heard when a telephone rings. Most telephones use a tuned ring system in which the second note creates a pleasant harmony with the first. The two notes are produced so rapidly that there is the effect of both being generated at approximately the same time. My telephone rings using the notes C and E. My sound effects program uses these same notes. The IBM Personal computer BASIC manual provides a chart in the Sound statement section which assigns a specific frequency to each musical note. Middle C is generated by the frequency 523.250 Hertz. Middle E is at 659.260 Hertz. This program incorporates these frequencies in Sound statements, lines 50 and 60, to create the desired harmony.

No time delay loop is found between these two

```
10 REM TELEPHONE RING/DIAL SEQUENCE
20 COPYRIGHT ROBERT J. TRAISTER AND ASSOCIATES 4/1/82
30 FOR A=0 TO 8
40 FOR X=1 TO 10*RND
50 SOUND 15000,1
60 FOR Y=1 TO 100:NEXT Y
70 NEXT X
80 FOR Z=1 TO 1000:NEXT Z
90 NEXT A
100 FOR TD=1 TO 1500:NEXT TD
110 FOR B=0 TO 5
120 FOR X=1 TO 100
130 SOUND 500,.04
140 NEXT X
150 FOR TD=1 TO 1500:NEXT TD
160 NEXT B
170 END
```

Fig. 6-6. Telephone ring /dial sequence.

```
10 REM TUNED TELEPHONE RING
20 REM LOW TONE=C  HIGH TONE=E
30 REM COPYRIGHT ROBERT J. TRAISTER AND ASSOCIATES 5/23/82
40 FOR X=1 TO 30
50 SOUND 523.250,.5
60 SOUND 659.26,.5
70 NEXT
80 FOR TD=1 TO 1500:NEXT TD
90 GOTO 40
```

Fig. 6-7. Tuned telephone ring.

statements; they are therefore produced almost simultaneously. There is a time delay loop in line 80 which provides the spacing between rings.

This program is an endless loop, so the ring sequence will last until the program run is manually halted. You can also create periods of silence by using another Sound statement, followed by the number 32767 and then a duration command.

The duration is given in clock ticks which occur 18.2 times per second. Therefore if you use a duration command of 18.2, the silence will last for one second. A duration of 180.2 will give silence for twenty seconds. I have been using For-Next time delay loops for so long that I have a general idea of what time delay will be produced by each value range, so I prefer to use these. You may choose to do otherwise.

CLOCK TICK

Taking a hint from the dial click program, I tried to simulate the tick of a clock on the IBM Personal computer. I originally intended this program to be used as part of a time bomb game program I was writing; it did work very well.

The program is quite simple and consists of only three lines:

```
10  SOUND 12500,.35
20  FOR X = 1 TO 600:NEXT X
30  GOTO 10
```

The click sound is produced by the reproduction of an extremely short 12,500-Hertz tone from the signal generator. The time delay loop in line 20 simply places a space between each tick. Subsequent ticks are generated by the branch to the program start set up in line 30. The program run will sound very much like a windup bedside alarm clock. Such a program is useful in computer games and in other situations where it is necessary to give the impression of time running out.

Going Further

It took me quite a while to deduce the method for producing a clock tick on the IBM Personal computer. I originally thought a low-frequency tone would work; when I was about to give up, I tried a high frequency, which resulted in the clock tick program above. Since I now had the sound effect of a bedside alarm clock, I decided to go a step further and write a complete alarm clock program that would actually tell time and could be used to wake up someone. Some people, accustomed to the constant tick of a windup clock, find they cannot sleep when they use one of the fancy electronic clocks that make no sound. The program in Fig. 6-8 provides all of the advantages of an electronic digital readout clock *and* it ticks like a bedside mechanical version.

IBM DOS 1.1 includes an automatic clock. When DOS is first keyed up, the date and current time are input. To display the time, use a Print Time$ statement, which is part of a continuous loop. Each time the seconds tick away, the display is written over the previous one, giving the impression of animation. This is exactly the way most

```
10 REM ALARM CLOCK
20 COPYRIGHT 9/22/82 ROBERT J. TRAISTER AND ASSOCIATES
30 CLS
40 KEY OFF
50 INPUT"TYPE IN THE ALARM TRIGGER TIME (EXAMPLE:01:30:00) ";A$
60 CLS
70 LOCATE 2,30
80 PRINT "ALARM TIME="A$
90 LOCATE 14,37
100 PRINT TIME$
110 IF TIME$=A$ THEN 150
120 FOR X=1 TO 600:NEXT
130 SOUND 12500,.35
140 GOTO 90
150 SOUND 2000,1
160 SOUND 800,1
170 KEY(1) ON
180 ON KEY(1) GOSUB 200
190 GOTO 150
200 CLS
210 GOTO 90
```

Fig. 6-8. Alarm clock.

electronic clocks display time. It was necessary to input the alarm time and to have the computer test for this condition during the program run.

When the program is first run, you must make certain that the correct time has been input while in DOS and before going to BASIC. The screen will prompt you to input the alarm trigger time. This value is committed to A$. Following this portion of the program, the screen will display the alarm time at the top, while lines 90 and 100 cause the actual time numerals to be displayed at the center of the screen. Line 110 checks the value of TIME$. If it is equal to the alarm trigger time (A$), there is a branch to the alarm portion of the program which will be discussed later. Line 120 is a For-Next time delay loop. This could have been placed after the Sound statement in line 130 which produces the ticking sound. Line 140 returns the program to line 90, where the TIME$ is again printed over the present screen display. In other words this program constantly refreshes the on-screen display to reflect the current time.

Let's go through a typical program run: The time numerals are printed at the center of the screen. There is a time delay, a tick, the time numerals are reprinted (in the same position), another time delay, another tick, and so forth. The value of X in line 120 can be altered to cause different tick speeds. This combination produces about one every second.

When the displayed time is equal to the alarm trigger time, this fact is detected in line 110 and there is a branch to line 150, creating a whooping alarm by constantly outputing a 2000 and an 800-Hertz tone. These are set up in lines 150 and 160. At the same time, Soft Key F1 is turned on. The alarm will continue until F1 is depressed. When this occurs, there is a branch to line 200 which clears the screen (thus stopping the alarm), and the time numerals are then printed again. The clock continues to keep time after the alarm is shut down.

To reset the alarm, you must manually stop the program, which is on a continuous loop, and immediately run it again. You will again be asked for the alarm time, and the time numerals will then reappear. The program is again armed to respond when the alarm trigger time is again reached.

Although not contained in this program, it would be a simple matter to create a built-in safety feature. Many electronic alarm clocks have this feature, which prevents you from going back to sleep (at least for any long period of time). An alarm sounds; you turn it off, but it sounds again five or ten minutes later. All that would be necessary to modify this program would be to assign a value to the new alarm trigger time (after the reset button is pressed) which would be equal to the present time plus five or ten minutes. The branch in line 210 would be the same, but the new value for A$ would be the present time plus five or ten minutes.

Although a sirenlike alarm was used here, you could just as easily incorporate any of the many music programs contained in the next chapter. When A$ is equal to TIME$, the music program would be keyed up; instead of a siren, you could be awakened to the pleasing strains of your favorite musical number.

This is a good example of a program that depends heavily on both sight and sound to offer a service to the human user. The clock program displays current time, which is highly useful in itself; but without the audio alarm feature, the system would be useless as a wakeup alert. If you do not need to be constantly informed of the time, you can forget the time display and simply leave the screen blank. The computer will still keep track of the time and sound the audible alarm at the appropriate moment.

From a practical standpoint there is a problem: your computer will probably consume far more power than a standard alarm clock. However, the alarm clock won't tick, and the computer will, so if you need the sounds of a clock tick to go to sleep and still want the advantages of an all-electronic timekeeper/alarm, the power tradeoff may be worthwhile.

CRICKETS

If you're accustomed to sleeping with the window open, sooner or later Old Man Winter is going to take his toll. Closed windows shut out fresh air and pleasing night sounds. In rural areas, the pleasing chirp of crickets often acts as a sedative and can have the same soothing effect as the clock tick mentioned previously. If you experience problems in this area, you might want to consider the program in Fig. 6-9, which simulates a cricket chirp. Unfortunately, there is no volume control on the audio output of the IBM Personal computer, so the sound may be a bit loud. You can always throw a towel or some piece of clothing over the openings to muffle the sound.

A cricket chirp is produced by a complex series of high-pitched musical notes. I chose frequencies of 1800 and 2000 Hertz for this program. The lower frequency is sustained for about twice the duration of the higher one, which is necessary to more closely imitate the insect. This program is a continuous loop and will chirp all night without the possibility of any six-legged "critters" crawling into bed with you. Notice that the ratio is nine low-frequency chirps to one chirp at 2000 Hertz. The For-Next loop in lines 20 through 40 outputs the low-frequency tone. When the loop has timed out, the high-frequency chirp occurs. There is a time delay loop in lines 60 and 70 to separate the complex sounds which generate a single chirp; the program then branches back to the beginning using the Goto command in line 80. You can experiment with this program quite a bit and probably produce a large number of different insect sounds.

PHASER

The television series Star Trek (and later the

```
10 REM CRICKETS
20 FOR X=1 TO 10
30 SOUND 1800,.05
40 NEXT
50 SOUND 2000,.02
60 FOR X=1 TO 1800
70 NEXT X
80 GOTO 20
```

Fig. 6-9. Crickets.

movie) has made the term "phaser" a household word. Carried by the crew of the Enterprise these weapons produced a very fast whooping or warbling effect when used to disintegrate Klingons and other deep-space phenomena. The program shown in Fig. 6-10 reproduces this sound and lends itself well to many different types of game programs.

The trick lies in scanning and producing a set range of frequencies within a short period of time. To accomplish this, I used a For-Next loop whose values control the frequency of the output tones. The loop is found in line 20 and increases by increments of 100 Hertz. There is a rapid increase from 300 to 1800 Hertz, especially when the very short duration command following the Sound statement in line 30 is considered. This program is a continuous loop; one can "phase away" into the wee hours of the morning. When used as part of a game program one would want to nest this program in a For-Next loop, which would cause the sounds to be output for a set duration.

FLYING SAUCER

The program shown in Fig. 6-11 is quite similar to the phaser sound in Fig. 6-10. A more limited range of frequencies is used, and a step factor of 200 is incorporated to speed up the oscillation. This program produces the usual flying saucer sound associated with many video game programs, usually a very fast-paced whoop starting at a moderate frequency and changing rapidly to a high one. Like many other programs in this chapter, this one is quite useless by itself; but it can be a substantial enhancement to an already existing space game program.

CONVEYOR

Most of the programs presented so far have used moderate- to high-frequency audio tones. Although this will be the case for many programs, it may be necessary to use low-frequency combinations, especially if you want to simulate sounds made by motorized mechanical contraptions. I call the program shown in Fig. 6-12 Motorized Conveyor, but the output has also been used to simulate the lumberings of Sherman tanks in a game program. The low-frequency drone gives the impression of something large and mechanical.

At line 20 you can see that I began at the low end of the IBM audio spectrum. X represents the audio tones that will be output; the minimum for this computer is 37 Hertz. The audio output changes in steps from one Hertz to 100 Hertz. There are no time delay loops. As soon as the audio output reaches 100 Hertz, the program repeats because of the Goto statement in line 50.

DOOR BUZZER

Another electromechanical device that produces an audio output is the old-fashioned door buzzer, the kind found in old black-and-white movies. Figure 6-13 simulates a door buzzer. It uses very high frequencies in the audio range with an extremely fast step factor (1500). A very short duration command following the Sound statement in line 40 produces a raspy harmonic, which gives us the sound we need. The Sound statement and the For-Next frequency loop are nested in another

```
10 REM STAR TREK PHASER SOUND
20 FOR X=300 TO 1800  STEP 100
30 SOUND X,.1
40 NEXT
50 GOTO 20
```

Fig. 6-10. Star Trek phaser sound.

```
10 REM FLYING SAUCER SOUND
20 FOR A=500 TO 1500 STEP 200
30 SOUND A,.5
40 NEXT
50 GOTO 20
```

Fig. 6-11. Flying saucer sound.

```
10 REM MOTORIZED CONVEYOR
20 FOR X=37 TO 100
30 SOUND X,.05
40 NEXT
50 GOTO 20
```

Fig. 6-12. Motorized conveyor.

```
10 REM DOOR BUZZER
20 FOR X=1 TO 20
30 FOR A=5700 TO 16000 STEP 1500
40 SOUND A,.01
50 NEXT
60 NEXT X
70 FOR TD=1 TO 1500:NEXT TD
80 GOTO 20
```

Fig. 6-13. Door buzzer.

For-Next loop which begins in line 20. This provides for the correct number of pulses to produce the door buzzer. Line 70 is a time delay loop which spaces the buzzes at an even rate. Line 80 makes this program a continuous loop, so the buzzer will continue to sound at regular intervals until the program is manually halted.

RANDOMIZED SOUNDS AND DURATIONS

An earlier program used a randomized frequency command in the Sound statement. This program is similar, but the duration of each random sound is randomized, and the end result is a program which will produce many different effects. These range from sirens to whoops to evenly-spaced musical scales. The audio frequency is randomized in line 20 of the program, shown in Fig. 6-14. This is done by adding the step command shown. Line 30 assigns a random value to X, which is used with the Sound statement in line 40 for the duration command.

This program really consists of two parts: Lines 20 through 50 randomly step the audio output from 37 to 1000 Hertz (minimum and maximum). Lines 60 through 80 do the same thing, but from high to low. One never knows what will be produced when this program is run. You can play with the frequency and duration commands to arrive at highly unusual sound effects; you may even discover a sequence which can form the basis for another program that will output only one type of sound.

CONVERTING EXISTING PROGRAMS

Now that a number of sound effects programs have been presented, let's explore the ways they may be used as parts of major programs. In many cases, the sound effects programs as shown will have to be modified slightly. This often means the use of existing For-Next loops in the master program, into which the sound effects portions are inserted.

Figure 6-15 shows a game program complete with sound effects. When originally written, no sound effects were used, these being inserted later. This program is called Anti-Aircraft and graphically portrays a moving airplane which you attempt to shoot down by pressing the F1 Soft Key. This causes the anti-aircraft gun at the bottom of the screen to fire a salvo at the approaching aircraft. If a hit is scored, the plane explodes in flames and falls to the ground. It is then replaced by a new plane, and the sequence is repeated.

This program requires the color/graphics adapter board and a suitable color monitor and must

```
10 REM RANDOMIZED SOUNDS AND DURATIONS
20 FOR Y=37  TO 1000 STEP 100*RND
30 X=RND*1
40 SOUND Y, X
50 NEXT
60 FOR Y=1000 TO 37 STEP -100*RND
70 SOUND Y,X
80 NEXT
90 GOTO 20
```

Fig. 6-14. Randomized sounds and durations.

```
10 REM ANTI-AIRCRAFT
20 REM COPYRIGHT ROBERT J. TRAISTER AND
ASSOCAITES 11/14/82
30 SCREEN 1
40 CLS
50 KEY OFF
60 INPUT"NEED INSTRUCTIONS(YES/NO)?";A$
70 IF A$="YES" THEN GOSUB 560
80 IF A$="NO" THEN 100
90 IF A$<>"YES" AND A$<>"NO" THEN 60
100 CLS
110 X=10
120 XX=15
130 DRAW"BM160,199 S=XX;R5U3L2U2L1U1L1D1
L1D2L2D3R2"
140 DRAW"BM160,100 S=X; C3 F1 L2 G1 L1 H
1 L2 H2 R2 F1 R5"
150 PAINT(156,102),2,3
160 DIM J(100)
170 DIM K(100)
180 DIM L(100)
190 GET (130,96)-(165,106),J
200 PUT(130,96),J
210 DRAW"BM160,100 S=X; A3 C3 F1 L2 G1 L
1 H1 L2 H2 R2 F1 R5"
220 GET(150,76)-(165,102),K
230 PUT(150,76),K
240 KEY(1) ON
250 ON KEY(1) GOSUB 500
260 FOR X=10 TO 280
270 PUT(X,5),J:SOUND X+27,.01:PUT(X,5),J

280 IF X=145 AND POINT(169,9)>0 THEN 290
 ELSE 310
290 LOCATE 1,19:PRINT CHR$(0)+CHR$(0)+CH
R$(0)
300 LOCATE 2,19:PRINT CHR$(0)+CHR$(0)+CH
R$(0)+CHR$(0)
310 NEXT
320 FOR X=1 TO 300:NEXT
330 GOTO 260
340 CIRCLE(X+15,5),20,2
350 PAINT(X+15,5),2,2
360 FOR EX=1 TO 5
```

Fig. 6-15. Anti-aircraft.

```
370 FOR E=300 TO 1800  STEP 150
380 SOUND E,.1
390 NEXT E
400 NEXT EX
410 GET(X-5,0)-(X+35,25),L
420 FOR T=1 TO 100:NEXT T
430 PUT(X-5,0),L
440 FOR Y=2 TO 170 STEP 4
450 PUT(X,Y),K:SOUND 1000,.01:PUT(X,Y),K
460 NEXT Y
470 SOUND 100,2
480 FOR G=1 TO 400:NEXT G
490 RETURN
500 FOR B=180 TO 0 STEP -20
510 SOUND 250,.35
520 CIRCLE(165,B),2,1:CIRCLE(165,B),2,0
530 IF X>137 AND X<147 THEN GOTO 340
540 NEXT
550 RETURN
560 CLS
570 PRINT"THIS IS A GAME OF SKILL WHERE"

580 PRINT"THE PLAYERS ATTEMPT TO SHOOT"
590 PRINT"DOWN AN AIRCRAFT. YOU MUST STR
IKE"
600 PRINT"THE AIRCRAFT AT A CERTAIN SPOT
"
610 PRINT"NEAR THE TAIL SECTION. WHEN"
620 PRINT"YOU SCORE A CORRECT HIT, THE"
630 PRINT"PLANE WILL EXPLODE AND FALL"
640 PRINT"TO EARTH. KEY F1 IS THE FIRING
"
650 PRINT"BUTTON. GOOD LUCK!!"
660 PRINT
670 PRINT
680 INPUT"PRESS <ENTER> TO BEGIN";B$
690 CLS
700 RETURN
```

be run in Advanced BASIC (BASICA). Even if you do not have these items on your IBM Personal computer, the program allows us to discuss the insertion of sound effects statements.

The first sound effect is the airplane itself as it flies across the screen. Put and Get statements are used to accomplish the on-screen animation; these are committed to a For-Next loop beginning at line 260. This assigns a value of X which varies from 10 to 280. This For-Next loop was originally used to specify the varying screen coordinates of the airplane, but we can also use it to specify the audio frequency used with the Sound statement found at the center of line 270. The Sound statement assumes a position within the current For-Next loop. The audio frequency is equal to X + 27. Therefore, the frequency will vary from 37 Hertz (10 + 27) to 307 Hertz (280 + 27). The duration command is quite small (time-wise) and creates a raspy sound. When the For-Next loop is entered, the graphic airplane is written on the screen by the first Put statement in line 270. Then the first audio output occurs with the Sound statement. The last Put statement in this line erases the plane from its present position and the run continues to line 310, where the process repeats as the loop recycles. The sound effect portion of this program, if written by itself, would be:

```
260  FOR X = 10 TO 280
270  SOUND X + 27,.01
280  NEXT X
```

If you inserted this program as is, however, the sound effect would not match the flight of the airplane. The For-Next loop shown in line 260 controls the positioning of the airplane. Therefore, sound is created each time the plane assumes a different position. In the original program, then, the For-Next loop controls screen position as well as sound effects and a number of other machine functions. Since the sound effects are to help accentuate the motion of the aircraft, it is necessary for the audio output to change correspondingly with the video output. You can see by this example that to insert the sound effects portion of the program, it was necessary to use only a single statement (Sound). The rest of the program remains unchanged. In this example, it was not even necessary to add another program line, although that could have been done immediately before or immediately after line 270.

The next sound effect in this program is controlled by lines 360 through 400. This portion of the program is activated when a hit is scored and is used to simulate an explosion. This effect is a whoop siren routine which sounds nothing like an explosion, but at least it simulates some kind of unusual on-screen happening. Unlike the previous insert, this one required extra program lines and may be thought of as a subroutine.

Line 360 establishes a For-Next loop which controls the duration of the sound. The nested loop in line 370 controls the frequency, which is stepped in values of 150 from 300 to 1800 Hertz. This portion originally occupied lines 361, 362, 363, and 364 of the original program, but the finished program was renumbered before printing. The explosion sound is a subroutine or mini-program added between the original lines of the same program.

After the airplane explodes, it makes a vertical dive to the ground, and sound effects are appropriate here as well. These are added by the Sound statement in line 450. Another For-Next loop in the original program has been borrowed, but the frequency (1000 Hertz) is specified with the statement. The For-Next loop in line 440 simply reproduces the 1000-Hertz sound many times as it cycles. The Sound statement in line 470 was also added to produce a low-frequency beep when the aircraft strikes the ground.

Lines 500 through 540 control the firing sequence of the gun and draw the projectiles on the screen. A Sound statement was inserted in line 510, which contains its own assigned commands for frequency and duration and is keyed each time the loop cycles. Whenever a projectile is fired, a short-duration beep accompanies it.

Thus complete sound effects have been added to this program to react to every on-screen movement, with the addition of a few lines. There are many other ways of placing the same basic effects in this program. The above seemed to be the easiest method; SOUND statements can be placed anywhere within presently existing For-Next loops.

Adding sound effects to an existing program, then, is simply a matter of deciding where or when you want them to occur, and then finding a method within the program for implementing the Sound statements. In animation programs it is advantageous to use existing loops, since adding new ones will slow the graphics considerably. For the explosion sound, all on-screen action freezes until the sirenlike ululation has completed. This is no great disadvantage, but it would be if an additional For-Next loop was used, for example, to control the sound effects of the crashing descent of the plane. By borrowing existing For-Next loops, program execution is not noticeably affected with regard to speed, so the Sound statements and their pleasing audio effects complement the existing program with no deleterious effects.

As an exercise, why not run some of your existing programs (ones you have written) and decide where you would like unusual sound effects. Then attempt the slight modifications, one at a time, while noting the results. If you do not feel ready, try using the Beep statement, which doesn't require external frequency and duration commands. Once you've gotten the program to beep at the right point, you can begin to expand your sound effects at the same point in the program. The following program is an example:

```
10  INPUT A
20  PRINT A/2
```

This simple program allows you to input a number; after pressing enter, the screen will display this number divided by two. The following program shows a sound effect version of this using the Beep statement:

```
10  INPUT A
15  BEEP
20  PRINT A/2
```

or

```
10  INPUT A
20  BEEP:PRINT A/2
```

Both programs are identical. In the second version an extra line is not required, since two statements have been committed to the same line.

When the latter type of program is run, the machine will do exactly the same thing (display half of A), but when you press Enter, a beep will occur. This is an extremely simple example; the Beep statement can be used to good advantage throughout the lengthy program, indicating to the user when an answer appears on the screen. The absence of a beep might mean it is necessary to input additional information; or you could reverse the process and let the beep signify a request for user input.

In place of the Beep statement (shown in line 15 of the first example), you could insert a multi-line sound effects subroutine or even music if desired. It may be easier for you to think of the special audio commands in IBM BASIC as Print statements which output sound instead of screen information. For example, if you want to print the word HELLO on the screen, you would input the line Print "HELLO". If you want to "print" a sound, you would simply type Beep or Sound 1000,1 (for example). What I'm pointing to is that there is nothing exotic about the specialized audio statements in IBM BASIC, and they should be treated in exactly the same manner as those statements with which you may be more familiar. It is just as easy to produce a single tone in a program run as it is to print a word on the screen, and just as easy to set up unusual sound effects as it is to print a column of numbers using a For-Next loop and the Print statement. The Print and Sound statements in IBM BASIC are identical, except one outputs video information to the screen and the other outputs audio information via the internal speaker.

PASSING TRAIN

Nearly everyone has had the experience of hearing a train approaching a station in the distance with its whistle blowing. You've probably noticed that the whistle seems to have a higher pitch, which becomes successively lower as the train approaches. The whistle is blaring at one pitch only, but because of the Doppler effect, the sound waves' are compressed by the speed of the train, which results in a higher-pitched sound.

The program, shown in Fig. 6-16, uses a Sound statement in line 40 to step from 1700 to 37 Hertz. Each sound burst is of extremely short duration. When low duration factors are used, the IBM Per-

```
10 REM TRAIN
20 FOR X=1700 TO 37 STEP -4
30 IF X=100 THEN SOUND 30000,.05:END
40 SOUND X,.01
50 NEXT
```

Fig. 6-16. Train.

sonal computer will lock onto the last frequency command and continue to output it. This is undesirable for such effects, so line 30 has been added to conclude the program when X equals 100. Therefore the lowest frequency this program will output is 100 Hertz, even though the minimum frequency in the For-Next loop established in line 20 is 37 Hertz. When X equals 100, the generator outputs a 30,000 Hertz tone which is inaudible, but which "unfreezes" the audio generator and removes any extra tones that might be output. The program may be used as is to produce an approaching train sound effect within a larger program. The whole sequence takes only a few seconds, so these program lines may be accessed in a larger program by means of a Goto or Gosub statement.

ELECTRICAL GENERATOR

Figure 6-17 shows a sound effects program that will simulate the startup of a large electrical generator. You can hear it slowly build up speed until its humming has reached a maximum. These effects are produced by two For-Next loops. The one contained in lines 20 through 60 combines three different tones. The second is twice the first, while the third is three times the first. This produces the complex warbling audio output that is required.

Once X has reached a maximum value of 1000 Hertz, the maximum speed sound is maintained by the loop found in lines 70 through 110. The same Sound statements are used in this last For-Next loop, but the frequency is no longer stepped. The frequencies of the last three Sound statements are 1000, 2000 and 3000 Hertz, respectively.

```
10 REM ELECTRICAL GENERATOR
20 FOR X=37 TO 1000
30 SOUND X,.1
40 SOUND 2*X,.1
50 SOUND 3*X,.1
60 NEXT
70 FOR Y=1 TO 20
80 SOUND X,.1
90 SOUND 2*X,.1
100 SOUND 3*X,.1
110 NEXT Y
```

Fig. 6-17. Electrical generator.

MUSICAL CROWD SIMULATION

Figure 6-18 shows a program which generates audio tones that give the impression of rapid crowd movement. It's what I call a "busy" sound effect, in that many tones are produced with short spaces of silence in between. Such effects are often used on television programs and in movies in conjunction with a picture of a scurrying crowd. The music seems to match the crowd's movements.

Three different Sound statements are used in this simple program; each time the loop cycles, the value of X in each statement is multiplied by a random number. This usually produces three separate tones, although occasionally the random numbers may produce the same frequency for each Sound statement. A value of 37 is added to each of the randomized numbers, as sometimes the random number which is multiplied by X will be so small that the product is less than 37 Hertz, the minimum that may be used with the Sound statement. By adding 37 to each of the randomized numbers, we make certain the minimum tone value will never be lower than 37.

```
10 REM MUSICAL CROWD SIMULATION
20 FOR X=370 TO 1000
30 SOUND RND*X+37,.1
40 SOUND RND*X+37,.1
50 SOUND RND*X+37,.1
60 NEXT
```

Fig. 6-18. Musical crowd simulation.

The output from each Sound statement is held for a duration which is long enough to establish the tone, but fast enough to produce the scurrying effect. If you want, you can add many randomized Sound statements to this program to expand the range of effects produced.

PHOTON TORPEDO FIRE

Returning to the Star Trek space adventure series, Fig. 6-19 shows a program which will simulate the effect heard on television each time Starship Enterprise fired a torpedo. Recall that this was a high-pitched sound which quickly stepped to a low frequency. The For-Next loop starting in line 20 steps from 4000 Hertz to a low frequency in increments of 150. This produces the fast frequency decay needed. Three Sound statements are used in lines 30 through 50. The value of X is inserted for the frequency command. In the last two Sound statements, the value of X is divided by two and three respectively. Since short duration commands have been used with each of the Sound statements, it is necessary to remove the unwanted output from the generator, which will continue to be heard after the program has ended. Line 60 unfreezes the generator when X falls below 200. This is the same method used in a previous program.

The photon torpedo sound may be effectively used in computer games which involve firing an object at a passing target. The sound effect routine is built into an existing For-Next loop or accessed as a subroutine in conjunction with a firing sequence.

MACHINERY

The program shown in Fig. 6-20 simulates many types of large mechanical devices such as motors, air conditioners, conveyor belts and so forth. Low-frequency commands are used in conjunction with the Sound statements in lines 30 through 50 to produce the sound of mechanical movement. This program is a continuous loop, so it is not necessary to use an "unfreezing" line, as was the case with the previous program. The program will run continuously until execution is manually halted.

BAT SCREECH

For the spelunkers (cave explorers) in the crowd, the program in Fig. 6-21 will recall the audible screeches made by some bats. These tiny mammals navigate by producing ultrasonic beeps which are not within the range of human hearing, but they also can screech in frequencies that anyone can hear. The screech begins in the ultrasonic range, but this high frequency quickly steps down into the sonic range that we hear. This program steps from 12,000 Hertz to 1400 Hertz in increments of 100, as is established at the beginning of the For-Next loop in line 20. Older readers may not

```
10 REM PHOTON TORPEDO FIRE
20 FOR X=4000 TO 100 STEP -150
30 SOUND X,.01
40 SOUND X/2+37,.01
50 SOUND X/3+37,.01
60 IF X<200 THEN SOUND 30000,.1:END
70 NEXT
```

Fig. 6-19. Photon torpedo fire.

```
10 REM MACHINERY
20 FOR X=400 TO 100 STEP -10
30 SOUND X,.01
40 SOUND X/2+37,.01
50 SOUND X/3+37,.01
70 NEXT
80 GOTO 20
```

Fig. 6-20. Machinery.

```
10 REM BAT SCREECH
20 FOR X=12000 TO 1400  STEP -100
30 SOUND X,.11
40 NEXT
50 GOTO 20
```

Fig. 6-21. Bat screech.

be able to hear 12,000 Hertz, but the sequence steps down so rapidly that this will not be detectable.

DRIPPING SPIGOT

The program in Fig. 6-22 will simulate a dripping spigot with the familiar "plop plop plop" sound of the droplets striking accumulated water in a sink. This is accomplished by using a series of three different medium-frequency audio tones of from 1000 to 1200 Hertz in increments of 100. This program is a continuous loop; line 50 is a time delay loop which adds periods of silence between each drip sound. I originally used this program in a graphics program which showed an on-screen spigot slowly spewing out droplets of water.

```
10 REM DRIPPING SPIGOT
20 FOR X=1000 TO 1200 STEP 100
30 SOUND X,.15
40 NEXT
50 FOR TD=0 TO 2000:NEXT TD
60 GOTO 20
```

Fig. 6-22. Dripping spigot.

This chapter has presented a number of different and quite interesting sound effects. Admittedly, some may not be immediately identified without explanation, but many are so obvious that persons will immediately recognize the sound. All may be used for demonstration purposes as shown and by slight modification may be incorporated into already existing programs to add a new dimension of sound. For the most part these effects are quite simple to generate and will not significantly slow an already established program run. As with all computer programming, you should make your sound effects routines as simple as possible, using a minimum of program lines. Reread the section in this chapter on modifying existing programs, so that you will be able to take advantage of already existing loops in a program to which sound effects are to be added.

If you have never attempted sound effects programming, here is an opportunity to play to your heart's content. You can add other Sound statements to the programs in this chapter to obtain different audio output. Modification of the minimum and maximum values of For-Next loops shown in these programs can also have a drastic and often pleasing effect on the output.

While it is true that microcomputers can do many things, some modes may require complex programs. This is usually not true of sound effects; much can be achieved with minimal programming time. These simple programs will require only a small amount of memory, so it is quite possible to program a hundred or more different sound effects and store the programs on a single disk. When these routines are added to existing programs which already require a large amount of memory, the added memory space will most likely be of little concern.

Music Programs...

Chapter 7

Music programming is generally quite simple in that it usually requires only a statement or two—followed by numeric or alphabetic designators to specify each note.

Although the Sound statement does have some application in music programming, time and efficiency can be greatly enhanced by using the Play statement, which allows you to use fewer commands and statements. Therefore a music program based upon Play statements will generally be far shorter than an equivalent program using Sound statements.

The Sound statement requires a frequency command and a duration command. The latter is given in clock cycles. This requires a great deal of interpolation when using this statement solely for the purpose of programming music. The exact frequencies for each musical note are given in Appendix B. For example, if you wanted to use the Sound statement to produce a middle C, the frequency command would be 523.250. This would be followed by the duration commands, which would be the most difficult to calculate, because you would have to convert clock cycles to the various note hold durations based upon tempo.

The Play statement avoids most of these problems. Several command options allow you to program music in different manners. A middle C would be programmed as a quarter note by simply typing "PLAY 03C4." The 03 command sets the octave in which middle C is located. The alphabetic designator C specifies the note C, and the 4 means the note is to be played as a quarter note. Subsequent notes can be added to this statement by typing their alphabetic designators (the note name) followed by their numeric designators, which specify hold times. As long as you stay in the middle octave range, no further 0 designators are required. Once a specific octave is named, all notes will be played in that octave until another 0 command causes a shift to occur.

Using the Sound statement, duration is specified in clock ticks. All duration commands are referenced to the clock cycle time, which is 18.2 times per second. However, using the Play statement, note duration is referenced to every other note. For example, a C8 (an eighth note) will be played for half the time of a C4 (a quarter note). Using IBM and its Advanced BASIC, duration may be as short as 1/64 of a whole note.

Although it is possible to program a complete tune using the Sound statement and separate frequency and duration commands for each note specified, increasing or decreasing the tempo would necessitate changing every duration command to reflect the new tempo. That would be a great deal of work. With the Play statement, however, all notes are entered in standard musical equivalents (whole, half, quarter, eighth, sixteenth and so forth).

The tempo command (T) is separate from these and ranges from 32 to 255. If no tempo command is given the default tempo is 120, *moderato* in musical terms.

Thus once the note has been entered the tempo may be changed in any way; each note will still be held for the proper duration in relationship to all other notes in the tune.

For example, let's assume a four-note piece consisting of C8, D4, F16, and B1. This is a string consisting of an eighth note, a quarter note, sixteenth note, and a whole note, respectively. If the whole note is held at one tempo for a total of one second, then the quarter note will be held for one-quarter second; the eighth note, for an eighth second; and the sixteenth note, for one-sixteenth second. Let's assume that the tempo is doubled by changing the tempo command. Assume also that the whole note is held for one-half second at this tempo. The eighth note will then be held for one-eighth of a half second (one-sixteenth second), and all other notes in this string will have equivalent shortened durations.

Using the Sound statement to produce the same tune would require four different statements followed by four different sets of frequency and duration commands. To increase tempo, it would be necessary to halve each of the four duration commands (for double time). Using the Play statement, however, it is only necessary to change the tempo command. Furthermore, less memory is required for storage, since in the former example this simple four-note song may be easily entered on one program line using a single play statement, whereas a minimum of four program lines would be required using the Sound statement in the latter.

Pauses or rests are specified in approximately the same manner as musical notes, but the letter P is used followed by a numeric designator to specify the pause length. A P4 is equivalent to a pause for the same duration as the hold time of the quarter note produced under the play tempo. You can see that this makes musical programming easier, since notes are named and their durations specified in exactly the same manner as in musical manuscripts. To play sharps and flats, the note is simply followed by the standard sharp symbol (#). Alternately, you may use a plus sign (+) after the note to specify a sharp and a minus sign (−) to specify a flat.

The IBM Personal computer goes a step further to help you write programs directly from musical manuscripts. In manuscripts one often sees a note followed by a dot or period. Musically, this means that the note is to be held for 1½ times the duration of an identical note without the dot. A half note followed by a dot is held for the equivalent of 1.5 times one half, or ¾ of a whole note. Using the Play statement, the same note (let's call it a C) would be specified as "C2." Many of the programs in this chapter include this type of designation. You should be absolutely certain you do not skip a dot while inputing a program.

Another method of specifying notes involves numeric designators only. These are used in conjunction with the N command. The numeric designators range from 0 to 84. A 0 is a rest; each succeeding number specifies individual notes over a seven-octave range. I don't use this style of programming very often, as I find the direct mode much easier. However, this can be put to good advantage when a Play statement using the N command is placed within a For-Next loop. The loop ouput (numerically) will then determine the note to be played.

Each of the musical pieces presented in program form was written directly from musical manuscript. It takes about one hour to become accustomed to this form of programming. Some songs are

```
10 REM "MARY HAD A LITTLE LAMB"
20 PLAY"MFT170GFE-FGGGP4FFFP4GB-B-P4GFE- FGGGGFFGFE-"
30 END
```

Fig. 7-1. "Mary Had a Little Lamb."

quite simple, others are complex. There are a number of musical programs reproducing the compositions of Johann Sebastian Bach, one of my favorite composers. His complex melody lines are especially suited to the microcomputer, in my opinion. You will also see popular songs, children's songs, and a program or two that combine the best of different types of music. I think you will find all of them pleasing and the programming exercise to be quite educational.

MARY HAD A LITTLE LAMB

The program shown in Fig. 7-1 will play the basic strain of "Mary Had a Little Lamb." It effectively uses only a single program line, in that the Rem statement and the End command are certainly not necessary for proper execution. This program uses the Play statement (in line 20) in conjunction with note commands, a tempo command, and the MF command, which places the music in the foreground mode. I chose a tempo of 170, which is fairly rapid, but you can adjust the tempo by changing the number sequence following the letter T. The alphabetic designators following the command are the actual notes that make up the song. There are three rest commands (P4) that create a quarter-note rest. Actually, the numeric designator is unnecessary, since the other notes are not followed by similar designators. Therefore, each is automatically played as the equivalent of a quarter note. You will note several minus signs occurring within the music command string. These identify flats.

If the program is inserted to complement an already existing program, only line 20 will be needed. This allows you to add music at the expense of a minimum amount of memory. This program is written from a child's music book; each note was read from the staff line and input as the same equivalent note in the Play statement commands. If you can read music, musical programming will be easier. If you can't read music you can learn to do so in a few days.

The microcomputer makes an excellent study tool. It may be difficult to decipher a complex musical passage in the mind, but the notes, input in a computer program, allow students to hear how the particular passage should sound. This can then be emulated using a musical instrument. The computer never makes a musical error. It will always play the specified note for the specified duration. The only possibility for error lies with the human being. The computer is totally dependent on him for input.

BLUE SKIES

Figure 7-2 shows another method of musical

```
10 REM "BLUE SKIES"
20 READ A$
30 IF A$="END" THEN 70
40 PLAY "XA$;"
50 GOTO 20
60 DATA C,G2,F8,E-16,F16,P8,G2,F8,E-16,F
16,P8,G3,C4,P6,C8,E-16,P8,C4,END
70 END
```

Fig. 7-2. "Blue Skies."

programming, which will produce the strains of the old standard "Blue Skies." This song has been around for a number of years, having been sung by Danny Kaye in the movie *White Christmas*. More recently, country music star Willie Nelson again made the song popular.

Instead of inserting the musical note designators directly in a Play statement, this program commits them to a Data statement. A subsequent Read statement pulls each note individually from the Data line. The Play statement in line 40 uses the X command to play a string statement. The Goto command in line 50 branches back to line 20, where the next element is read. In other words each note is pulled from the Data statement by a machine operation which is constantly repeated until the data runs out.

The variable A$ is composed of only one note, but the string is constantly refreshed by the Goto statement in line 50. Line 30 tests for the appearance of the last item in the Data statement.

I used the word "END", but anything will work as long as it is not one of the musical notes already read. Without building this feature into the program, the Read statement would still be trying to pull data elements from the Data statement after the line has been exhausted. That would result in an error message on the screen: "OUT OF DATA IN 20". This has no effect on the musical run of the program; however I always try to avoid error messages as these can confuse the beginning programmer.

Using this program all of the notes are pulled from the Data statement line. When the word "END" is encountered line 30 branches to line 70, which ends the program. To replay the song run the program again.

One might ask why such a method was chosen to play this simple song rather than the simpler method used previously. It is true that the latter method is more complex. It requires more program lines, and each note must be separated by a comma within the Data statement. It also requires several different branches. The reason this method is used is to demonstrate a different way of accomplishing the same result using the IBM Personal computer. In certain situations, this method is to be preferred over the former. The Name That Tune program in Chapter 3 made use of this song and nine others to produce a musical game. In this game program, the use of Read and Data statements was absolutely mandatory, as the direct programming method used with "Mary Had a Little Lamb" simply would not accomplish what was needed.

JINGLE BELLS

Figure 7-3 is identical to the Blue Skies program, except the data elements have been changed to produce the song "Jingle Bells." The same lines have been added as before to detect the end of the data string in order to stop the program run. One of the advantages of a program using Read/Data statements is that an original song can be expanded or more tunes added by simply adding further Data lines. Of course one must remove the word "END" from the first data line to prevent execution from

```
10 REM "JINGLE BELLS"
20 READ A$
30 IF A$="END" THEN 70
40 PLAY"XA$;"
50 GOTO 20
60 DATA E,E,E,P8,E,E,E,P8,E,G,C,D,E2,F,F
,F3,F8,F,E,E,E8,E8,G,G,F,D,C2,END
70 END
```

Fig. 7-3. "Jingle Bells."

```
10 REM "GO TELL AUNT RHODIE"
20 READ A$
30 IF A$="END" THEN 70
40 PLAY "XA$;"
50 GOTO 20
60 DATA A2,A4,G4,F2,F2,G2,G4,B-4,A2,F2,A
2,A4,G4,F2,F2,G4,F4,G4,A4,F3,END
70 END
```

Fig. 7-4. "Go Tell Aunt Rhodie."

being halted before the new lines can be read.

GO TELL AUNT RHODIE

The program in Fig. 7-4 is another example of this form of musical programming. The song has been changed to "Go Tell Aunt Rhodie" by substituting different data elements. Figure 7-5 shows a program which is the first program with the data lines from the next two added. This program will play all three songs, one after the other, before execution is halted. While a program that uses Read/Data statements to play one song may be more complex than one using the direct mode, if one program is used to play several songs, Read/Data statements often speed programming and certainly lessen program complexity. Using this method, you could write a single program to produce thirty or more different songs. Each song would be committed to a separate Data line. Therefore, a thirty-song program would include thirty Data statements. The remainder of the program could remain the same, regardless of the number of Data statements used. The last data line would end with the word "END", which would bring about a branch to line 1000, where the program halts. You can add more selections by merging other musical programs with the notes specified in Data statements.

```
10   REM "MULTISONG PROGRAM"

20   READ A$

30   IF A$="END" THEN 1000

40   PLAY "XA$;"

50   GOTO 20

60   DATA C,G2,F8,E-16,F16,P8,G2,F8,E-16,F16,P8,G3,C4,P6,C8,E-16,P8,C4

70   DATA E,E,E,P8,E,E,E,P8,E,G,C,D,E2,F,F,F3,F8,F,E,E,E8,E8,G,G,F,D,C2

80   DATA A2,A4,G4,F2,F2,G2,G4,B-4,A2,F2,A2,A4,G4,F2,F2,G4,F4,G4,A4,F3,END

1000   END
```

Fig. 7-5. Multisong program.

```
10 REM "MUSICAL PROGRESSION"
20 FOR X=1 TO 84
30 PLAY"N=X;"
40 NEXT
50 END
```

Fig. 7-6. Musical progression.

Notice that the information in some of these programs includes individual letters and also letters followed by numeric designators. Without the designator the note is played as a quarter note.. Therefore to speed programming time, I have often omitted the "4" (quarter note designation), since this is the default state. In other words an E4 within a Play statement will be output the same if the 4 is omitted.

MUSICAL FOR-NEXT LOOPS

Figure 7-6 shows a musical progression using the End command with the Play statement. Each note in a seven-octave scale is represented by a number. Line 20 begins the For-Next loop, which begins with 1 and ends with 84. This means that the entire range of notes will be played automatically. The End command is inserted in the Play statement in line 30, which specifies that N is equal to the value of X. I elected not to start with a 0 (FOR X = TO 84) because this value is always a pause or rest. The Next statement in line 40 allows the loop to recycle and step up by one place each time. The first note that is played is one, the next is two, then three and so on.

This program will allow for an output equivalent to starting at the bottom of the piano keyboard and playing every note in order to the very top... and then some. The last few notes will be so high as to be practically inaudible.

This type of designation and the use of For-Next loops are not very conducive to accurate musical programming. For creating certain types of musical sound effects, however, this mode may be ideal. Because of the recycling of the loop, an entire range of notes may be played with a minimum of programming time.

The program shown in Fig. 7-7 may be thought of as the previous program in reverse. The only change is in line 20, where the loop counts from 84 to 1 in steps of −1. The first program starts at the bottom of the IBM Personal computer's musical range and proceeds to the top. The latter program starts at the top and counts to the bottom, playing one note during each loop cycle. If you combine these two programs, the entire chromatic scale will be reproduced by the computer. This will start at the bottom of the range, go to the top, and then proceed to the starting point.

The fact that loop counts may be stepped in different increments allows for a specific series of notes to be selected. This can be put to advantage musically in some instances by committing a certain portion of a musical piece to a For-Next loop.

The program in Fig. 7-8 is identical to the first one, except the loop is not stepped in increments of one. The step command here causes the count to skip every other number; thus every other note is played. The first note will be a one, the second a three, the third a five and so on. With the proper step increments, many standardized musical scales can be produced using the same basic program under discussion in this section. You can randomize

```
10 REM "MUSICAL PROGRESSION - REVERSE OR
DER"
20 FOR X=84 TO 1 STEP -1
30 PLAY"N=X;"
40 NEXT
50 END
```

Fig. 7-7. Musical progression, reverse order.

```
10 REM "MUSICAL STEPS"
20 FOR X=1 TO 84 STEP 2
30 PLAY"N=X;"
40 NEXT
50 END
```

Fig. 7-8. Musical steps.

the step command to produce some unusual musical sound effects, none of which may be predicted in advance. The beginning and ending loop numbers may also be randomized for further effects.

The numeric designation system outlined here may also be used in a similar manner in programs discussed previously. Read/Data statements could be incorporated in a program and the numeric information included in the data lines. That would be identical to a previous programming method, but numeric designators would replace alphabetic ones.

Although most of us are accustomed to working with numbers on a microcomputer rather than letters, one must also remember that musical manuscript contains alphabetic and numeric designators. Therefore the ability to input various notes using an alphabetic and numeric format is much more convenient, especially for those who are more familiar with music than computers. Far less human interpolation and extrapolation are required in making the transition from manuscript to computer form, so this mode is to be preferred in most instances. However, a programmer who is more accustomed to working with computers than music may find that numeric-only designators are more to his or her liking.

Both can be used to accomplish the same thing, so choose the method you think most appropriate. The numeric method is limited in that it is inconvenient to specify different note lengths, something which is greatly simplified when alphabetic and numeric designators are combined. The numeric-only system is a shortcut for producing very simple songs in which each note is held for the same length as all others. It is possible to combine alphanumeric and numeric-only designations, but for the beginning programmer, this may become a bit confusing. Alphabetic-numeric designation will be used most of the time, but if one runs into a long series of quarter notes, one can immediately revert to the numeric-only style. The purpose of this discussion is to point out the available options. I think most programmers will choose the alphabetic-numeric mode of programming, as I have done throughout most of this chapter.

BACK TO BACH (J.S.)

Johann Sebastian Bach, a German composer of great renown, had the inborn ability to take simple melodies and combine them in such a manner as to produce a pleasingly complex interweaving of sounds. His pieces are often performed today on a single piano with little or no musical accompaniment. The harpsichord is often the instrument which communicates his delicate phrasings. Being a fan of Bach, it is only natural that I include some of his musical pieces in this chapter. I think of the audio output of the IBM Personal computer as being a delicate and quite precise musical form. I feel similarly about most of Bach's music. Therefore, the mating of Bach with the IBM Personal computer is only natural. If you're not a fan of the old classics, please bear with me and try some of the programs presented in this chapter. You may not like them as much as some of the more popular pieces, but you may find them eminently more interesting from a technical point of view.

How Gentle Is the Rain

You may think you've missed something or the publisher has omitted forty pages from this chapter, but this popular hit song from the sixties is based upon a piece that Johann Sebastian Bach wrote before the word "Beatles" meant anything more than a misspelling of the hard-shelled insect. I specifically chose this song to gently acquaint some of you to Bach, although I had to work out the song on a piano, since I didn't have the musical manuscript.

The song (Fig. 7-9) is produced by two Play statements in lines 20 and 30. I chose the music foreground mode (MF) because this song contains more than 32 notes, the buffer limit for the background mode. When songs are played in background

```
10 REM "HOW GENTLE IS THE RAIN"
20 PLAY "MF T130;O2;G2;L4;C8;D8;E8;F8;L2
;G;C;P16;L2;A;L4;F8;G8;A8;B8;O3;L2;C;O2;
C;P16;F;L4;G8;F8;E8;D8;E2;L4;F8;E8;D8;C8
;L2;O1;B;O2;L4;C8;D8;E8;C8;D2;O2;A;G;"
30 PLAY "O2;G2;L4;C8;D8;E8;F8;L2;G;C;P16
;L2;A;L4;F8;G8;A8;B8;O3;L2;C;O2;C;P16;F;
L4;G8;F8;E8;D8;E2;L4;F8;E8;D8;C8;L2;D;O2
;L4;E8;D8;C8;O1;B8;O2;C2;"
40 END
```

Fig. 7-9. "How Gentle Is the Rain."

all of the musical information is held in the buffer, which outputs it to the speaker on a programmed time basis. This effectively removes the processing from the main part of the computer, permitting it to tackle other problems. The buffer receives the musical information on a real-time basis (occurring in a fraction of a second) and then outputs it in a time which is based upon the tempo and the individual note durations, all of which are specified in the program information. This allows the computer to continue program execution past the music point; there is thus the capability of playing limited music while, for instance, information is being printed on the screen.

The notes in this program are too numerous to be fully committed to the background mode, so the foreground mode was chosen. The computer will continue processing after the song has been entered or until it has finished. The second command in line 20 specifies the tempo for the rest of the musical piece. Tempo may be changed by adding other T commands, but this is not necessary for this particular number. The rest of the commands specify notes, durations, and octaves. I will not discuss each command, but we will examine the first few.

Following the tempo command is an 02, meaning that all subsequent notes are to be played in octave 2, which begins with the note C (one octave below middle C) and ends with B. The next command specifies the note G as a half note. Then we come to C, D, and F, all of which are eighth-notes. Throughout the Play line you will see several octave changes. These are used to access higher or lower notes which fall outside of the second octave. In some pieces octave changes will be quite numerous, which confused me when I first began programming. If you remember that each octave begins with a C and ends with a B, you should have little difficulty.

Let's assume that you're in octave 2 and have just programmed a B. The next note is a C (above the B). This indicates that it will be necessary to go to octave 3 in order to accurately reproduce the C which begins a new octave. However, the reverse is true. If you've just input a C in one octave and then want to program the B which lies just below it (on the musical staff), it will be necessary to switch to the next lower octave (in this case, 01). After a bit of practice, the insertion of octave commands becomes almost automatic and will give you little trouble, especially if you're familiar with reading musical manuscripts.

Polonaise

The program shown in Fig. 7-10 is treated in approximately the same manner as the previous one, and for that manner, many of the programs that follow. Polonaise is a gentle piece composed by J.S. Bach.

This program commits the musical information to six program lines, all containing Play statements. The IBM Personal computer limits you to 64 characters per line, which may be one reason several Play statements are needed for a single song.

However, many musical pieces are written in different connective segments, and I will often use a separate Play statement when a new section in a piece takes effect.

Looking at line 20, you can see that this number is also played in the foreground mode, and the first note is in octave 3 (03). The first note is a G, a dotted eighth note. This means it will be held for 1½ times its normal duration. You can see that the command designation is "G8." This mathematically simplifies things, in that anytime you see a dotted note on a musical staff, you simply input the dot next to the commands that play that note. You will notice several octave changes in each program line. Part of Bach's magic is his use of closely spaced notes in different octaves. This gives the impression of constant and rapid movement, a trait with which Bach's music has long been associated.

I enjoy this piece so much that I built the program as an endless loop. As soon as the first playing has finished, the Goto statement in line 80 returns the program to its beginning and the song is heard again.

This program was written directly from the musical manuscript for piano and is completely accurate. Admittedly the score I used was a revised interpretation of Bach's piece, but it closely simulates the original work. The program took a total input time of about fifteen minutes including debugging. If you do much music programming, you will from time to time leave out a sharp or a flat, or even program an incorrect note. The same is true if you play a musical instrument. Sooner or later you're going to hit a "clam". If you are not familiar with Bach's music, you should not have much difficulty identifying a wrong note just by listening to the computer output. There is nothing especially dissonant about any of his pieces; a wrong note should stand out like a sore thumb. For those of you who are not very familiar with music and its many terms, dissonant means discordant. Some of the modern musical pieces may include a fair amount of dissonance, whch is intentional (or so the composers say), and identification of improper notes is more difficult. Bach's pieces, however, are quite logical. They are somewhat easier to debug and are more interesting than simple children's songs, which are also logical but are often quite boring.

Intrata

Figure 7-11 shows another composition by J.S. Bach, "Intrata". Each of the commands is separated by a semicolon, for note-by-note clarification. The semicolon has no effect on the program run. This is another intricate piece beautifully output by the IBM Personal computer. Placing semicolons between each note designation consumes more programming time, but makes debugging easier.

```
10 REM "POLONAISE" BY J.S. BACH
20 PLAY"MFO3G8.A16B-404C403A8A16B-1604C2
03B-8B-1604C16D8G8C8G803B-8A16B-16G2"
30 PLAY"B-8.04C16D4F4D8C1603B-16A16B-160
4C1603A16F4"
40 PLAY"04F8D803B804F8G16F16E-16D16E-8C8
03A804C8F16E-16D16C16D8C16D16E-8"
50 PLAY"D8C803B-8A16B-1604C1603A16B-402B
-404D4E-403G4"
60 PLAY"F#8F#16G16A8D8F8A8"
70 PLAY"04D4E-403G4F#8F#16G16A8D8F8A804D
8D16E-16D8D16E-16D8G803G8A16B-16G401G4"
80 GOTO 20
```

Fig. 7-10. "Polonaise."

```
10 REM "INTRATA" BY J.S. BACH
20 PLAY"MF O3 D4 G8;F#8;G8;D8;E8;F#8"
30 PLAY"G8;F#8;G8;D8;E8;F#8;"
40 PLAY"G8;F#8;G8;A8;B8;O4;C8;D2"
50 PLAY"O1;D4;G8;F#8;G8;D8;E8;F#8;G8;F#8
;G8;D8;E8;F#8;"
60 PLAY"G8;F#8;G8;A8;B8;O2;C8;D2;"
70 PLAY"O4;C8;D8;D8;C8;C8;O3;B8;O4;C8;O3
;B8;O4;C2;O4;D8;C8;C8;O3;B8;B8;A8;B8;A8;
B2;"
80 PLAY"O3;D4;G8;F#8;G8;D8;E8;F#8;G8;F#8
;G8;D8;E8;F#8;G8;F#8;G8;A8;B8;O4;C8;D2;O
3;G8;B8;A4;G4;O4;G8;B8;A4;G4;G8;F#8;E8;D
8;C8;O3;B8;A8;O4;D8;O3;B2;O1;G8;F#8;E8;D
8;C8;O0;B8;A8;O1;D8;O0;B2;O4;D8;C8;C8;O3
;B8;A8;G8;F#8;A8;G1;"
90 END
```

Fig. 7-11. "Intrata."

Debugging is best accomplished by inserting a very slow tempo command (T20). You can then follow each note on the musical score until the wrong one is identified, and then replay the piece while reading the Play command for each note. When all the glitches are found and corrected, the tempo can be increased to its original speed.

No tempo command is used in this program because the default tempo is 120, which is about right for this piece. If you want to have some real fun add "T255", the maximum tempo, and Bach is spewed forth at almost real-time speeds.

Minuet

By definition a minuet is a slow, graceful dance in three-quarter time. In purely musical terms a minuet is the music by which the dance is enacted. Bach's minuets cannot be classified as slow, but they do follow the three-quarter time format and are graceful, if a bit fast.

Figure 7-12 plays the Bach piece, "Minuet;" it is produced at a tempo of T120 (the IBM default tempo). You will see a number of sharps and flats and a profusion of octave changes, as there is a great deal of switching back and forth between octaves 3

```
10 REM "MINUET" BY J.S. BACH
20 PLAY"MS O4C4C4D4E-4E-4F4G4G4A-4G16F#1
6G16F#16G16F#16E16F#16G4G8A-8F8E8F4F8G8E
-8D8E-4C8O3B8O4C4D4O3G2."
30 PLAY"O3G4G4A-4B-8A-8G8A-8B-4C4E4G12A-
12B-12A-8G8F2F4F4G4A-8G8F8G8A-4O2B-4O3D4
F12G12A-12"
40 PLAY"G8F8E-2G4A-4A4B-4B4O4C4O3B4O4C4D
4E-4E4F4D4E-4E4F4F#4G4O3G4O4F8E-8D8E-8C2
."
```

Fig. 7-12. "Minuet."

```
10 REM "TEMPO DI MINUETTO" BY J.S. BACH
20 PLAY"MFO3A4O4F8E8D8C#8D4O3A4B-4C#8E8G
8B-8A8G8F4E8F8D4F4B-8A8O4D8C8F4E8D8C8O3B
-8A8B-16O4C16O3F4E4F2.A4O4F8E8D8C#8D4O3A
4B-4C#8E8G8B-8A8G8F4E8F8D4F4B-8A8O4D8C8F
4E8D8C8O3B-8A8B-16O4C16O3F4E4F2.O4A4O3F8
O4A8G8F8E16F16G8C2F4O3F8O4F8E8D8C#16D16E
8O3A2A8B8O4C#8
30 PLAY"D8E8F8G8E8C#8B-8A8G8F16E16D8E4C#
4D2."
40 PLAY"A4O3F8O4A8G8F8E16F16G8C2F4O3F8O4
F8E8D8C#16D16E8O3A2A8B8O4C#8D8E8F8G8E8C#
8B-8A8G8F16E16D8E4C#4D2."
```

Fig. 7-13. "Tempo Di Minuetto."

and 4. This is one of Bach's more pleasing features, and is highly enjoyable when produced by the computer.

Figure 7-13 produces Bach's "Tempo Di Minuetto." This is a more complex piece, and is characterized by sudden octave changes. You will see a number of sharps and flats specified in the Play statement lines.

ADDITIONAL NOTES

Many classical pieces include a number of what are commonly called "grace notes." The best way to describe grace notes is to say that they are more or less dispersed into a number with little or no specified mathematical patterns. The human performer is expected to play them very rapidly and make adjustments (in time) to the rest of the measure. For example, a whole note may be specified in one bar immediately preceded by a miniature series of grace notes. The whole note will normally consume the entire measure, but in this case the grace notes will consume a small amount of time. The performer will normally play the grace notes as quickly as possible, then hold the whole note for whatever time remains in that measure. Two different performers will probably play the grace notes a bit differently.

When programming grace notes on the IBM Personal computer, I usually specify them as 64th notes or 32nd notes. Many musical manuscripts will provide a hint for playing these notes; however, it is still necessary to instruct the machine as to the duration the main note or notes in that measure are to be held. When you start the musical programming on the IBM Personal computer, you may wish to eliminate the grace notes at first, then add them later when your musical programming proficiency has improved. You will have to calculate the total amount of time consumed by the grace note passage and then subtract that from the remaining note or notes in the single measure. If you are working with a fast tempo, you can probably drop a 32nd note or two and not be able to tell the difference in timing; but if you are a perfectionist, you will want all measures to be mathematically equivalent.

Some musical pieces require "trills," which are usually two notes played together very rapidly to produce a birdlike warble. These are often played as individual 64th notes and occasionally as 32nd notes. At rapid machine tempos, trills and complex grace note passages often seem to run together. For trills, this is desirable; but for grace notes, this may not be so. You may try slowing the tempo for better definition of each grace note. Alternately, you can specify each grace note with a slightly longer duration designator and make appropriate time adjustments later in the musical measure. Grace notes and the way they are played is pretty much left up to the musician, who will develop a feel for their presentation. The same applies to the musician who uses the computer as his instrument. The computer, however, cannot "feel" the phrasing of a certain passage. The programmer will have to perform this function for the computer mathematically.

A MORE COMPLEX MUSIC PROGRAM

Another section of this chapter presents a series of Christmas songs; two will be discussed here because of their intricacies. Figure 7-14 shows a program that will produce all the verses of "The Twelve Days of Christmas." This is a song nearly everyone is familiar with. Although there is much repetition, there are subtle differences in certain sections of verses. It is possible to use straight programming to produce this song, meaning that each verse will be given its own program line. It is not necessary to establish For-Next loops to repeat those bars that are constantly repeated in the song. Straight-line programming will take less forethought and planning, but will result in a very long program.

```
10 REM "THE TWELVE DAYS OF CHRISTMAS"
20 PLAY"MF T125 02C8C8C4F8F8F4E8F8G8A8B-
8G8A4.
30 PLAY"MF B-803C4D802B-8A8F8G4F2."
40 FOR X=1 TO 4
50 PLAY"MF T125 02C8C8C4F8F8F4E8F8G8A8B-
8G8A4.
60 GOSUB 80
70 NEXT X
80 FOR A=1 TO X
90 IF X=4 THEN 140
100 PLAY"MF 03C402G8A8B-4"
110 NEXT A
120 PLAY"MF A8B-803C4D802B-8A8F8G4F2."
130 RETURN
140 PLAY"MF 03C2D202B..03C1"
150 PLAY"MF C802B-8A8G8F4B-4D4F4G8F8E8D8
C4A8B-803C4D802B-8A8F8G4F2."
160 FOR X=1 TO 7
170 PLAY"MF02C8C8C8C8F8F8F4E8F8G8A8B-8G8
A2"
180 FOR A=1 TO X
190 PLAY"MF 03C8C802G8A8B-8G8"
200 NEXT A
210 PLAY"MF 03C2D202B..03C1"
220 PLAY"MF C802B-8A8G8F4B-4D4F4G8F8E8D8
C4A8B-803C4D802B-8A8F8G4F2."
230 NEXT X
240 PLAY"MF T75P402A8B-803C4D802B-8A8F8G
4F2."
250 END
```

Fig. 7-14. "The Twelve Days of Christmas."

The program takes advantage of For-Next loops and results in a relatively short program. Those verses which are repeated are committed to For-Next loops, and proper branches are inserted to pick up those verses which do not conform to the loop material.

Line 20 and line 30 play the first verse. A For-Next loop is then entered (line 40), and the first portion of that same verse is repeated. There is a Gosub in line 60 which causes the program to enter a nested loop. Line 100 plays the "Two Calling Birds, Three French Hens and Four Turtle Doves" song lines. Line 90 tests for the condition X = 4. When this occurs, there is a branch to line 140, which plays the "Five Golden Rings" portion of the song. Line 150 is the countdown verse to "A Partridge in a Pear Tree."

We are now at "Five Golden Rings." The next seven verses begin with the For-Next loop in line 160, which cycles seven times. Line 170 enters the "On The Sixth Day..." portion of the song, and another nested loop is then encountered in line 180 which plays the song line associated with "Six Geese A Laying" and the remaining verses. Notice that the loop starting in line 180 counts from 1 to X. When the loop times out, "Five Golden Rings" is played again in line 210. Line 220 is a repeat of line 150 and plays the verses which count down to the partridge again. The Next statement in line 230 branches back to line 160 for the next cycle of the loop. During this next cycle, X is equal to 2. Therefore, the nested loop will play the stanza in line 190 two times before reaching the "Five Golden Rings" sequence again in line 210. When this last loop has timed out completely, the finale is played in line 240. Notice that the tempo here has been slowed from 125 to 75. This gives us the needed retard for the final strains. This last portion is a repeat of the last few bars of the song, producing "And a Partridge in a Pear Tree."

The For-Next loops allow you to repeat repetitive stanzas without having to put in a separate Play statement for each one. The loops step the number of times corresponding to the number of times the verse is repeated in the song. There are two major internal verse repeats. One begins with the second day of Christmas and ends at the fourth day of Christmas; the other begins at the sixth day of Christmas and ends at the twelfth. The "Five Golden Rings" portion is a separate entity, but it must be inserted at the proper time, which is different as each day is encountered.

Admittedly, it took me longer to write this program in the form shown that it would have, had I used straight-line programming throughout. The program shows a more efficient method of producing this song and requires much less input time. There is less room for note errors as well, since there are fewer note commands and Play statements. If you do enter an incorrect note somewhere, it will probably crop up several times as it is accessed by the loops. Once you have identified and corrected this note, however, the correct version will also be repeated. I think this program will be much easier to debug than a straight-line version, and much less memory is required.

A SING-A-LONG CHRISTMAS SONG

Figure 7-15 shows a program combining music and text, similar to the bouncing ball sing-alongs you have probably seen on television. While it would be possible to duplicate the bouncing ball on the screen using graphics, this program does not go quite so far. It simply prints the words at the center of the screen as a particular musical verse is played. Locate statements are used to place the words at the center of the screen. As a new verse appears, it writes over the old one. Line 40 prints the first phrase line, "Joy to the World," and line 50 plays the music. Immediately after this Play line is completed, lines 60 and 70 print the next few words, followed by the music in line 80. This continues throughout the remainder of the program. You will notice in line 160 that the final word (sing) is followed by a number of spaces. This is because the phrase in line 160 is shorter than the one in line 130, so the spaces simply write over the previous line with screen blanks. In other words, the spaces cover up for the lack of length in the new line. The same method is used in line 250, which prints "Merry Christmas" at the end of the song.

This is a very simple program to write, since

```
10 REM "JOY TO THE WORLD" SINGALONG
20 CLS
30 LOCATE 14,30
40 PRINT "JOY TO THE WORLD"
50 PLAY "MF O3D4C#8.O2B16A4.
60 LOCATE 14,30
70 PRINT"THE LORD IS COME"
80 PLAY "G8F#4E4D4.
90 LOCATE 14,30
100 PRINT"LET EARTH RECEIVE HER KING
110 PLAY "A8B4.B8O3C#4.C#8D4.
120 LOCATE 14,30
130 PRINT"LET EV'RY HEART PREPARE HIM ROOM"
140 PLAY "D8D8C#8O2B8A8A8.G16F#8O3D8D8C#8O2B8A8A8.G16F#8
150 LOCATE 14,30
160 PRINT"AND HEAVEN AND NATURE SING                    "
170 PLAY " F#8F#8F#8F#8F#16G16A4.
180 LOCATE 14,30
190 PRINT"AND HEAVEN AND NATURE SING"
200 PLAY"G16F#16E8E8E8E16F#16G4."
210 LOCATE 14,30
220 PRINT "AND HEAVEN AND HEAVEN AND NATURE SING"
230 PLAY" F#16E16D8O3D4O2B8A8.G16F#8G8F#4E4D2"
240 LOCATE 14,35
250 PRINT"MERRY CHRISTMAS                               "
```

Fig. 7-15. "Joy to the World."

you first program the music line and then return to add the text. You will input this program as shown on a line-by-line basis.

I had originally intended to add an MB with the Play statements instead of an MF. The former places the music information in a buffer and will play it while other machine operations are taking place. My intentions were to have the text displayed while the music was being played. However, the write was so fast that the program was no more effective than the one shown here using Print statements ahead of the Play statements, the latter being in the foreground mode.

Nearly any song can be written in a program of the above type. Those which have short, choppy vocal portions that are clearly defined are especially applicable. You may choose not to write over previous lines. Each new vocal phrase will be printed below the old one. This program can be modified by removing all the Locate statements. You may also wish to use sophisticated color graphics to display something relevant to the music and/or words. A previous book of mine (same publisher) includes many programs which will draw color graphics on the IBM Personal computer. Christmas trees are usually quite easy to produce graphically. Circle statements can be used to produce Christmas ornaments, and multi-colored Point commands can produce an electrical lighting effect on the tree, which can be painted green (Paint statement). Some programmers have been successful in producing quite elaborate outdoor scenes, including snow-covered mountains and even horse-drawn sleighs. Such a scene would be very applicable to the seasonal song "Sleigh Ride."

Depending on what time of year you purchased this book, it may seem odd to be going into so much detail about Christmas songs. This book was written in late November. If you are reading these lines in the middle of August, be assured that in addition to Christmas songs, there are many other favorites included.

MORE CHRISTMAS SONGS

There is nothing especially difficult about programming music on your IBM Personal computer, but this does not apply if you cannot read music. The main difficulty is in deciphering the notes from the musical manuscript. Once that has been done, inputing the information to the computer via the keyboard is usually easy. The easiest way to program music is to copy an already existing program. The rest of this chapter is devoted to such programs; any may be directly input to your machine for a successful program run. Each of these programs was designed using the IBM Personal computer, and all have been completely debugged. Most were input while reading directly from musical manuscript. Those who are involved in music already know that manuscripts differ in quality and arrangement. I am delighted with many of these programs, but others can be improved by those with musical knowledge. Music arrangements, like books, are interpretations and will differ from author to author.

If you are reading this book in the spring or summer months, the following Christmas melodies may be of little practical use, but inputting them to the computer will certainly be good practice. The discussion surrounding each program will be helpful for future applications. Go ahead and input these Christmas programs and store them on a disk. When December arrives, you will be prepared.

God Rest You Merry, Gentlemen

Figure 7-16 will cause the computer to output the old Christmas carol, "God Rest You Merry, Gentlemen." The program requires only three lines, or only one (line 20), considering the fact that line 10 is not executed and the End statement in line 30 is not mandatory. Line 20 includes all of the musical information. I used a tempo of 160, which seemed to produce the most pleasing output. Notice that several L commands are used, because this particular piece has long series of quarter notes. Using the L4 command, all following notes will be played as quarter notes under the T160 tempo. When a note is encountered that is not a quarter note, there is a return to the alphabetical/numerical designations. I do not use the L commands unless I encounter a string of one type of note which includes four or more notes. Total programming time is approximately five minutes.

It may take you longer to type this program than it took me to input it directly from the musical manuscript, because it is necessary to double-check each number and letter command as it is being input. Since numbers and letters are strung together, this program may not be as easy to read as the information which came directly from the musical manuscript. This will apply to every other music program as well.

```
10 REM "GOD REST YOU MERRY,GENTLEMEN"
20 PLAY"MF T16003L4DDAAGFEDCDEFGA2.L4DDA
AGFEDCDEFGA2.L4AB-GAB-04CD03AGFDEFG2F4G4
A2B-4A4A4G4F4E4D2F8E8D4G2F4G4L4AB-04CD03
AGFED2."
30 END
```

Fig. 7-16. "God Rest You Merry, Gentlemen."

I Saw Three Ships

Figure 7-17 consumes three lines and outputs the carol "I Saw Three Ships." I found it desirable to avoid the L command in this program because of the constant mixture of note durations. No tempo command is specified in this program, since the default tempo (T120) was ideal. If you wish to speed up or slow down, insert a T command immediately following the MF command in the Play statement in line 20. You may wish to change the octave scale in this or any of the other programs. That is fine as long as you are consistent throughout the program. If you wanted to lower the frequency (octave) of a particular program, you might go through the Play statement and its commands in line 20 and subtract one from each octave command value. This would reproduce the entire song one octave lower than is obtained with the current program. You could also add one to each octave command to play the song an octave higher. Most programs presented here are played in the octave specified in the musical manuscript, but as with standard musical compositions, you can let your personality play its role. Programming music on the IBM Personal computer places one in the role of a conductor/arranger who has an entire orchestra at his fingertips.

What Child Is This

The program in Fig. 7-18 outputs "What Child Is This." You can call it "Greensleeves," the old English tune upon which the carol is based. The Christmas version has four separate verses; a For-Next loop is created to play one musical verse four times. The loop begins in line 20, causing a cycle of from 0 to 3. The Next statement in line 60 returns execution to the beginning of the loop. The musical information is contained in lines 30 through 50. The line number could be reduced from three to two by including more commands in each line. However, if there is enough memory, I would find it easier to use more lines. A new line begins at a logical point within the melody, possibly where one type of melody ends and another begins. This makes debugging much easier.

You may also notice that I use octave statements at the beginning of each line, often when they are not necessary, because the same octave is being referenced in a previous line. A good example of this can be seen in lines 30 and 40 of this program. The last command in line 30 is "02" and one of the first commands in line 40 (before any further notes are played) is also "02". The first octave command in line 40 is unnecessary since the octave command is specified in the previous line. Why is it present?

It is often necessary to debug music programs one line at a time. If I had detected a program error in line 40, I might have input the direct command "RUN 40", which would cause program execution to begin at line 40. Without the 02 command at the beginning, the default octave (03) would apply. Since the carryover octave command in line 30 would not be accessed by this particular debugging routine, the absence of the octave command at the beginning of line 40 would cause this particular line to be played an octave higher than originally specified in the program. When you debug by beginning execution at lines within the program past the original tempo statement, the default tempo will be in effect (T120). This can be circumvented by repeating tempo commands in each line. However, this adds to programming time and is not absolutely mandatory for effective debugging work. When I'm debugging a program that is played at a

```
10 REM "I SAW THREE SHIPS"
20 PLAY"MF O3C8F4F8F4O4D8C4O3B-8A4A8G8A8
B-8A4A8G8A8B-8A4C8F4F8F4O4D8C4O3B-8A4O4C
8D8C8O3B-8O3A8G8F8G4.F4"
30 END
```

Fig. 7-17. "I Saw Three Ships."

```
10 REM "WHAT CHILD IS THIS(GREENSLEEVES)
"
20 FOR X=0 TO 3
30 PLAY"MF  O2E8G4A8B8.O3C16O2B8A4F#8D8.
E16F#8G4E8E8.D#16E8F#4.O1B4O2"
40 PLAY"MF  O2E8G4A8B8.O3C16O2B8A4F#8D8.
E16F#8G8.F#16E8D#8.C#16D#8E4.E4."
50 PLAY"O3D4.D8.C#16O2B8A4F#8D8.E16F#8G4
E8E8.D#16E8F#4D#8O1B4.O3D4.D8.C#16O2B8A4
F#8D8.E16F#8G8.F#16E8D#8.C#16D#8E4.E4."
60 NEXT X
70 END
```

Fig. 7-18. "What Child Is This."

very slow tempo, I will often speed the tempo in order to access the notes more quickly. As your experience with music programming increases, you will undoubtedly arrive at a pattern best suited to your particular needs.

The Holly and the Ivy

Figure 7-19 shows a straight program (no For-Next loops) to reproduce the holiday strains of "The Holly and the Ivy." Each note is specified by an alphabetic/numeric command. No tempo command is given in the program lines, since the default tempo of T120 is best suited for this particular piece. The music is played in the foreground mode and in Music Normal (MN), the default play mode. Each note is held for seven-eighths of its specified value. This allows each note to be separated from all others. If you use the ML (Music Legato) mode, each note is played for its full value. Therefore, if you specified four successive quarter notes, the computer would output them as one continuous whole note. Other programs in this chapter use the legato mode and special programming considerations will be discussed regarding this mode later.

Go Tell It on the Mountain

The program in Fig. 7-20 outputs "Go Tell It on the Mountain," which is a Christmas song, a spiritual, and a religious work. The particular arrangement I wrote this program from had two verses, so a For-Next loop was established in lines 20 and 60 to repeat the basic musical verse twice. All musical information could have been included in line 30, but I separated the program into three play lines for ease of debugging. The music information in lines 30 through 50 is output twice because of the

```
10 REM "THE HOLLY AND THE IVY"
20 PLAY"MFO2F4F8F8F4O3D4C4O2A4.F8F8F4O3D
4C2C8O2B-8A8G8F4A8A8D8D8C4F8G8A8B-8A4G4"

30 PLAY"F2P8F8F8F8F4O3D4C4O2A4F8F8F8F4
O3D4C2C8O2B-8A8G8F4A4D8D8C4F8G8A8B-8A4G4
F2"
40 END
```

Fig. 7-19. "The Holly and the Ivy."

```
10   REM "GO TELL IT ON THE MOUNTAIN"
20   FOR X = 1 TO 2
30   PLAY "O2A4O3C4C4.D8C4O2A2F4G4G4F4G4A
2.F4A4O3C4C4.D8C4O2A2F4G4G4F4D4C2O3C2"
40   PLAY "O2A2A8.G16F8.D16C2F2G8G4F8G4F4
A8G4A8O3C2O2A2A8.G16F8.D16C2F4B-4A8A4."
50   PLAY "G8F8G4F1"
60   NEXT
70   END
```

Fig. 7-20. "Go Tell It on the Mountain."

cycling of the loop. When line 50 is played for the second time, the loop cycles out and the End statement in line 70 terminates the program run. Notice that no tempo or mode commands are used at the beginning of line 30. This will automatically bring in the default modes, which includes music normal, music foreground and a tempo of 120.

This piece runs very well on the IBM Personal computer. Generally speaking, songs that contain many short-duration notes and are played at a moderate to fast tempo sound better than those composed mostly of whole and half notes that are played at slow tempos. The reason for this is lack of *vibrato*.

Vibrato is the soft wavering or slight changing of frequency which is produced on a musical instrument or by the human voice. This is often used while sustaining whole notes or half notes to make them more pleasing to the human ear. When such notes are output from a computer, the lack of vibrato may not be consciously recognized by the average listener, but almost everyone senses that something is not quite right. These sustained notes (without vibrato) sound more like electronic tones than musical notes. True, a note is a tone and a tone is a note, but there are subtle differences as far as presentation is concerned when human beings are involved. In some instances you get away with it; in other cases the effect is not so pleasing. This particular piece moves along fairly rapidly and does not include many sustained notes; thus it sounds very good when played by the computer.

The First Noel

"The First Noel" also sounds very good on the IBM Personal computer. It is also played in the default mode. This program could very easily have been committed to a For-Next loop because there is repetition. However, I chose to use straight-line programming for demonstration purposes. You will notice a similarity in lines 40 and 50. Line 50 is the first part of the commands in line 40.

Line 50 produces the outro and was easily programmed after line 40 was originally written. To get the outro portion, I displayed line 40 and then changed its number to 50. When the entire program was redisplayed it was numbered 10 through 50, with lines 40 and 50 being identical. The unneeded commands in the new line 50 were then deleted, leaving what is shown in Fig. 7-21. This saved programming time by avoiding the necessity of duplicating commands contained in line 40 on a command-by-command keyboard input basis. Using a For-Next loop here would have involved more time, as it would have been necessary to exit the loop (using If-Then statements) at the appropriate time. Such an arrangement may have increased the difficulty involved in the debugging operation.

As is the case with most computer programs, there are several ways to arrive at the same machine output. It is the programmer's responsibility to determine the method which is most efficient and/or practical. Of course, different programmers use different methods, and any one may not be better than the others.

```
10   REM "THE FIRST NOEL"
20   PLAY "O2F#8E8D4.E8F#8G8A2B8O3C#8D4C#
4O2B4A2B8O3C#8D4C#4O2B4A4B4"
30   PLAY "O3C#4D4O2A4G4F#2F#8E8D4.E8F#8G
8A2B8O3C#8D4C#4O2B4A2B8O3C#8"
40   PLAY "D4C#4O2B4A4B4O3C#4D4O2A4G4F#2F
#8E8D4.E8F#8G8A2O3D8C#8O2B2B4A2.O3"
50   PLAY "D4C#4O2B4A4B4O3C#4D4O2A4G4F#2.
"
60   END
```

Fig. 7-21. "The First Noel."

Deck the Halls

Figure 7-22 outputs the robust Christmas song "Deck the Halls." The default tempo of 120 is too slow here. I used a tempo of 175 (T175), which is displayed in line 20. This moves the piece along at a moderately fast rate, making the computer reproduction very pleasing to the ear. I shortened programming time by duplicating the information originally contained in line 30 in line 50. The first three-quarters of the original line 30 were used because they contain the same note sequence. The end of the line was modified to produce a proper outro based upon the musical manuscript.

When converting musical manuscript information to a computer program, you will often see many repetitions of a series of musical bars throughout the piece. Many programmers like to commit these bars to For-Next loops; since there are often large numbers of repetitions, this can result in a program which becomes more complex than is really necessary. It is often easier (and less confusing) to duplicate these bars within straight Play statements. You may be typing ten or twenty extra commands, but this usually does not take much longer than establishing a For-Next loop and then inputting the lines which will enter and exit the loop at the appropriate sequence times. From a debugging standpoint, a large number of For-Next loops with an equally large number of If-Then statements for ingress and egress can often increase the total time required to input, test and debug a program in order to end up with a usable product.

This program may run a little faster than some people would prefer. If you want to slow it up, lower

```
10 REM "DECK THE HALLS"
20   PLAY "MFT175O3C4.O2B-8A4G4F4G4A4F4G8
A8B-8G8A4.G8F4E4F4P4"
30   PLAY "O3C4.O2B-8A4G4F4G4A4F4G8A8B-8G
8A4.G8F4E4F4P4"
40   PLAY "O2G4.A8B-4G4A4.B-8O3C4O2A4A8B-
8O3C4D8E8F4E4D4C4P4"
50   PLAY "O3C4.O2B-8A4G4F4G4A4F4O3D8D8D8
D8C4.O2B-8A4G4F2"
60 END
```

Fig. 7-22. "Deck the Halls."

the value associated with the T command. The musical designation of the tempo specified would probably be allegro, which is in the "fast" category. When performed by orchestras and choral groups, this piece is often presented at an allegro tempo; occasionally it will be heard at *moderato* or even *andantino* (medium to medium-fast). Having worked in commercial radio for fifteen years, I know that one person's taste in music is rarely identical to another persons. The IBM Personal computer will allow you to make desired changes in a few seconds, so that the musical output will conform to your idea of how the song should sound.

Good King Wenceslas

Figure 7-23 outputs another old Christmas favorite "Good King Wenceslas." This song moves along at a medium-fast tempo and is generally restricted to the second and third octaves. The piece will also play quite well on the IBM computer if you lower the octaves by one step. The lower frequency output of the computer closely simulates the sound of a clarinet or a bass clarinet. You may also wish to insert an MS mode command following the tempo command to give the notes a more staccato ring. Since this particular song consists of a large number of sequential quarter notes, a number of L commands are used to avoid having to inset a numeric designator with each alphabetic note command.

This song plays very well on the computer and lends itself well to a number of personal adaptations, modifications and interpretations. As a starting point, try decreasing every *other* octave command in this program by one. This will produce an answering or echo effect, with one strain played two octaves below the next. Once you have the basic program input to the computer and have checked to make sure it is running properly, you are free to make the changes which will tailor the song to your liking.

Christmas Is Coming

The program in Fig. 7-24 is the computer version of an old English Christmas ditty which is not heard much today. I came across the manuscript in an obscure store in New York City, and after making a few changes, committed it to the IBM machine. The tempo is fairly rapid (T175), and the song includes a number of high notes which are accessed by 03 octave statements. The song has two verses, so a For-Next loop is established in lines 20 and 50 to repeat the first verse a second time. Any of these programs can be committed to an endless loop by replacing each End statement with "GOTO 10". Each song will then play completely through and be repeated over and over again until program execution is manually halted with a "CTRL-BREAK" keying sequence.

We Three Kings

Figure 7-25 reproduces another Christmas standard "We Three Kings." I think of this as a drab but pleasing song. Its strains are almost tortuous and remind me of the "Volga Boat Song," a Russian favorite. The tempo is rather slow (*andante*) and is keyed up by the T100 command in line 20. For good note separation, pause or rest commands (P) have been included. This will shorten some notes while apparently lengthening others (by comparison). When debugging a program that plays at a fairly

```
10  REM "GOOD KING WENCESLAS"
20  PLAY "MFT150O2L4GGGAGGD2L4EDEF#G2G2L
4GGGAGGD2L4EDEF#G2G2O3D4C4"
30  PLAY "O2B4A4B4A4G2L4EDEF#G2G2L4DDEF#
GGA2L4O3DCO2BAG2O3C2"
40  PLAY "O2G1"
50  END
```

Fig. 7-23. "Good King Wenceslas."

```
10  REM "CHRISTMAS IS COMING"
20  FOR X = 1 TO 2
30  PLAY"MFT17503C202G4.G803C4C2C4C4C402
B4A4G103C4.02C8C4D4"
40  PLAY "E4C4E4G4A2G4F4E1E4.F8E4D4C403C
402G4E4F2G401B402C1"
50  NEXT X
60  END
```

Fig. 7-24. "Christmas Is Coming."

slow tempo, it is often advantageous to temporarily increase the value of the tempo commands. This will allow you to go through the entire piece, noting any difficulties very rapidly. When the debugging operation is complete, the tempo command can then be changed to its final value.

Some musical compositions may be executed at maximum machine tempo (T255). You may have to reverse the tempo/debug technique, especially if you are following the note pattern on the musical manuscript. At very rapid tempos, the computer notes may be produced too fast to accurately follow them on the manuscript. The tempo command can be decreased considerably to allow for a run that is slow enough to follow each note on paper. You can use the "TRON" function, which is accessed by Soft Key F7 on the keyboard. This will cause the screen to display the program line which is currently being executed.

When a problem develops, immediately note the last displayed number on the screen, then search that line for the error. Alternately, you can run the program without the "TRON" feature and hit "CTRL-BREAK" when an error occurs. The screen will then display "BREAK IN LINE ____". This will tell you in which line the error has occurred. You have to be fast, however, in order to stop the run on the line where the error has occurred. Once you know the number of the suspect line, you can double-check it by beginning execution of the program starting at this line. This is accomplished by typing "RUN" followed by the line number.

O Tannenbaum

Also known as "Oh Christmas Tree," "O Tannenbaum" is an old German Christmas carol and is produced by the program in Fig. 7-26. I elected to play each note in the staccato mode, specified by the MS command in line 20. In this mode of output, each note is held for three-quarters of its specified time. This produces a pleasing effect for this number, but you can also try the music normal (MN) mode for a

```
10  REM "WE THREE KINGS"
20  PLAY "MF T10002B4A8G4E8F#8G8F#8E4P8B
4A8G4E8F#8"
30  PLAY "G8F#8E4P8G8.P16G8A8.P16A8B8.P1
6B803D8C802B8A8B8A8G4"
40  PLAY "F#8E4P8F#4A2.G8.P16G8P32G4D8G4
E8G4P8G8.P16G8P32G4D8G4E8G4P8G8.P16G8"
50  PLAY "A4B803C402B8A4B8G8.P16G8P32G4D
8G4E8G4."
60  END
```

Fig. 7-25. "We Three Kings."

```
10   REM "O TANNENBAUM"
20   PLAY "MS O2C4F8.F16F8.G8A8.A16A4.A8G
8A8B-4E4G4F4P8"
30   PLAY "O3C8C8O2A8O3D4.C8C8O2B-8B-4.B-
8B-8G8O3C4.O2B-8"
40   PLAY "B-8A8A4C4F8.F16F4.G8A8.A16A4.A
8G8A8B-4E4G4F4"
50   END
```

Fig. 7-26. "O Tannenbaum."

change of effect. The music normal mode plays each note for a total of seven-eighths of the time specified. The staccato mode, then, plays the note for a length of time which is one-eighth of the specified time shorter than MN. This is straight-line programming as no For-Next loops are used. The standard default tempo (T120) is keyed up here in the absence of a tempo command. I wrestled with the tempo for a few minutes before arriving at 120. One can increase the tempo up to as much as 175, according to one's musical taste.

Adeste, Fideles

"Adeste, Fideles" or "Oh Come All Ye Faithful" is a standard Christmas carol and is produced by the program in Fig. 7-27. This program differs from some shown previously in that it is output in music legato mode (ML). Each note is held for the full duration of its specified length. This produces a smooth output because there is no noticeable space between notes, as is the case in other modes of operation. This mode produces some very nice musical sounds, but special programming requirements are often encountered when several notes of the same frequency are arranged sequentially. When this occurs, it is necessary to break up the notes with short-duration pauses or rests. Fortunately, this is not necessary very often with this piece, because the rests were already indicated on the musical manuscript. You will see instances where I have purposely shortened some notes, making up the difference with a P command. The pause forms the break between notes. For instance, in line 20 following the 02 command, you will see a "G8." followed by a "P8" and the "G2". The "P8" separates the "G8." and the "G2," and the rest was originally included in the manuscript. However, at the end of line 50 you will see a "G16.P32G2.".

```
10   REM "ADESTE, FIDELES" (OH COME ALL Y
E FAITHFUL)
20   PLAY "ML O2G8.P8G2D4G4A2D2B4A4B4O3C4
O2B2A4G8.P16G2F#4E4F#4"
30   PLAY "G4A4B4F#2E4.D16.P32D2.P4O3D2C4
O2B4O3C2O2B2A4B4G4"
40   PLAY "A4F#4.E8D4G8.P16G4F#4G4A4G2D4B
8.P16B4A4B4O3C4O2B2"
50   PLAY "A4B4O3C4O2B4A4G4F#2G4O3C4O2B2A
4.G16.P32G2."
60   END
```

Fig. 7-27. "Adeste, Fideles."

Originally, the manuscript called for simply a "G8" followed by a "G2.". If these notes had been programmed in the manner specified by the manuscript, no space would have been heard between the two notes, and the effect would have been the note G continuously sustained for an eighth note plus a half note. To overcome this problem, I changed the eighth note to a dotted sixteenth and made up the difference with a rest for 1/32nd of a beat. Then the next G was encountered. This produced the note separation desired without affecting the timing of the piece.

I could have used another method with this situation. Preceding the first G, I could have changed operating mode by inserting an MN (music normal). Then the note commands could have been programmed as "G8G2." The music normal mode would have caused the computer to produce the eighth note for seven-eighths of the specified duration. There would have been a short pause following the playing of this note before the second G was output.

The problem of note separation applies only when two notes of the same frequency are to be repeated in succession. This is something you have to notice when programming in the legato mode. It is usually necessary to subtract a portion of the total length from the first note and make up the difference with a rest of the appropriate length to make the timing come out right. That often involves some mathematics, but this problem is overcome in the next program.

O Little Town of Bethlehem

Figure 7-28 plays "O Little Town of Bethlehem" in the smooth legato mode. Notes of the same frequency played in succession are input exactly as they occur on the musical manuscript, but are separated by P64 pause commands. The time these commands require is not considered with respect to the remainder of the measure in which they are used. Assume a measure contains two half notes which, for the sake of discussion, are middle C. In the music normal mode I would simply input "C2C2". The total measure would consist of two half notes, which is the equivalent of four quarter notes (in duration) of 4/4 time.

However, when programming in music legato mode, I would input "C2P64C2". This means that each half note is separated from the other by a rest equal to 1/64th of the total time devoted to that measure. The result is that the measure's total time is equal to 4/4 plus 1/64th. This throws off the timing slightly, but in most applications it is not humanly detectable. One measure is a very small fraction longer than another of the proper length. However, if there is a long series of, say, quarter notes, all of which are the same, it is necessary to insert more 1/64th rests. This further throws off the timing, but not too much when quarter notes are involved. When there are eighth notes and sixteenth notes, the 1/64th rest becomes a larger fraction in relationship to the length of time which the notes are to be sustained; this can create real problems, especially at the faster tempos.

```
10  REM "O LITTLE TOWN OF BETHLEHEM"
20  PLAY "O2B4P64B4P64B4A#4B4O3D4C4O2E4A
4G4F#8G8A4D4"
30  PLAY "B2.P64B4P64B4P64B4O3E4D4P64D4C
4O2E4A4G4F#8"
40  PLAY "G8B4A4G2.B4P64B4P64B4A4G4F#2P6
4F#4P64F#4E4"
50  PLAY "F#4G4A4B2.P64B4P64B4P64B4A#4B4
O3D4C4O2E4O3"
60  PLAY "E4D4O2G4B4.A8G2."
70  END
```

Fig. 7-28. "O Little Town of Bethlehem."

This program is run at the T120 default tempo, so I was able to get away with a larger number of P64 commands without throwing off the timing to a noticeable extent. This piece was mostly whole notes, half-notes and quarter notes, so the 1/64th rest was not a very large relative fraction. If I had encountered a large number of sequential eighth or sixteenth notes of the same frequency, it would have been necessary to switch to the MN mode to avoid throwing off the timing. Remember, the music normal (MN) mode shortens each note by a factor of one-eighth of its specified time. Therefore the measure will always come out with correct timing and the separation between notes will be maintained. The purpose of using the legato mode is to establish smooth transitions between notes.

In other instances when the music normal mode is used for programming, it may be necessary to switch to the legato mode in order to accurately program notes which are of the same frequency but are connected by a musical "slur". This is demonstrated by the sample musical measures shown in Fig. 7-29. The first measure contains a whole note which is connected to the first half note in the second measure by the slur symbol overhead. This means that the whole note is to be held for its full measure duration and also for half the duration of the next measure *without* a break in between. If you were programming this measure in the music normal mode and input "B1B2", the output would sustain the note B for a full count of 4 times ⅞ths, followed by a pause of ⅛th of the entire measure count; then the half note would be output. The musical manuscript indicates that the note is to be held for a measure and a half, not a measure, a space, and then a half.

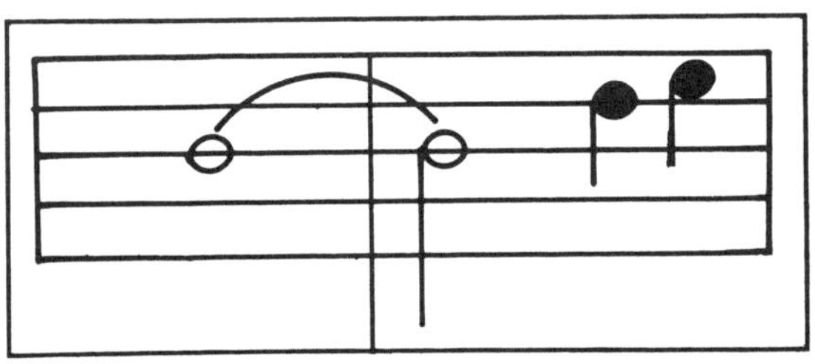

Fig. 7-29. Sample musical measures.

There are two ways of overcoming this problem. First, you can stay with the music normal mode of operation and input the two measures mathematically. The two note combination may be successfully played by inputing "B1." The dot following the numeric designator indicates that the note is to be held for 1½ times the indicated value. However, this notation (on the computer) does not follow the notation on the musical manuscript, and you could encounter some debugging problems because of this difference. To make the note commands conform more closely with those found in the musical manuscript, you could leave the music normal mode and switch to music legato (ML). You would then input "B1B2" and return to MN. In the ML mode the output would be the first whole note, immediately followed by the second half note, with no space in between. The end result is a sustained B, held for a measure and a half.

Obviously the mathematics involved in programming these two notes in music normal mode is not difficult, but suppose the whole note was connected to a quarter note, an eighth note, or even a sixteenth? What would you do then? In the latter instance, the only answer would be to switch to the legato programming mode.

I Heard the Bells on Christmas Day

Figure 7-30 shows another example of legato programming using the Christmas carol "I Heard the Bells on Christmas Day." A more rapid tempo (T150) is used, but the addition of an occasional (and extra) 1/64th rest does not seem to throw the playback out of kilter. The additional rests are inserted only between identical notes in the same octave which are to be played back to back, but are to be separated by a short but definite pause. Remember, as the tempo increases, each note is held for a shorter period of time. Therefore any additional rests that are included become a larger fraction of the whole measure. You can get away with these additions as long as they are relatively few and far between and the tempo permits. The only other alternative is to omit the extra rests and switch to MN or MS programming mode.

```
10  REM "I HEARD THE BELLS ON CHRISTMAS
DAY"
20  PLAY "ML T150G4P64G4D4G8A8B4O3C8O2B8
A4G4P64G4P64"
30  PLAY "G4D4G8A8B8O3C#8D4C#4D4P64D4C4O
2B4O3E4.D8C4"
40  PLAY "O2B4A4P64A4B4.O3C8D4O2A4B4A4G2
"
50  END
```

Fig. 7-30. "I Heard the Bells on Christmas Day."

It Came Upon a Midnight Clear

Figure 7-31 takes us back to music normal programming. "It Came Upon a Midnight Clear" is another old Christmas standard and plays quite well on the IBM Personal computer. P64 rests are included to accentuate the pauses between notes. These rests are not mandatory, as separation will be maintained anyway by this mode of programming. However, the additional pauses help to retard certain lines and are used here more for effect than out of necessity.

Angels We Have Heard on High

Figure 7-32 uses the legato mode of programming, along with a moderate tempo (T140) to produce the strains of "Angels We Have Heard on High." I originally began with a much slower tempo, but found that the song dragged too much. I increased the tempo in steps of twenty until I finally arrived at the tempo shown in line 20. The program was also originally written in music normal mode, but the lack of smooth transition between notes detracted from the song. Therefore I switched to the legato mode and inserted the necessary short-duration rests where required. This is one of my favorite Christmas music programs, and runs very nicely on the IBM Personal computer.

Silent Night

No selection of Christmas songs would be

```
10  REM "IT CAME UPON A MIDNIGHT CLEAR"
20  PLAY "MF T100O2F8O3D4C8P64C8O2B-8G8F
4G8F4P64F8G8"
30  PLAY "A8B-8P64B-8O3C8D8C4.C4O2F8O3D4
O2A8O3C8O2B-8"
40  PLAY "G8F4G8F4P64F8G4P64G8A8G8F8B-4.
B-4O3D8P64D4O2D8"
50  PLAY "P64D8E8F#8G4A8B-4O3D8C8O2B-8A8
G8A8G8F4.F4P64"
60  PLAY "F8O3D4O2A8O3C8O2B-8G8F4G8F4P64
F8G4P64G8A8G8F8B-1"
70  END
```

Fig. 7-31. "It Came Upon a Midnight Clear."

```
10  REM "ANGELS WE HAVE HEARD ON HIGH"
20  PLAY "ML T14002A4P64A4P64A403C4P64C4
.02B-8A2"
30  PLAY "P64A4P64A4P64A403C402A4.G8F2A4
P64A8.G16"
40  PLAY "A4P64A803C8P64C4.02B-8A2P64A4P
64A8.G16"
50  PLAY "A4P64A803C802A4.G8F2ML03C2D8C8
02B-8A8B-2"
60  PLAY "03C802B-8A8G8A2B-8A8G8F8G4.C8P
64C2F4G4A4B-4"
70  PLAY "A2G203C2D8C802B-8A8B-203C802B-
8A8G8A2B-8A8G8F8"
80  PLAY "G4.C8P64C2F4G4A4B-4A2G2F1"
90  END
```

Fig. 7-32. "Angels We Have Heard on High."

complete without "Silent Night." The program in Fig. 7-33 produces this in the legato mode. "Silent Night" is traditionally played at a slow tempo, and the T70 tempo command causes the song to be played back in adagio. This is a short program and will most likely require minimal or no debugging. However, for the first couple of runs you may wish to increase the tempo to 170 in order to get through it rapidly. Once all of the bugs have been worked out, you can then revert to the T70 tempo.

Wassail Song

The last Christmas song in this series is called the "Wassail Song." While this has nothing to do with programming, it might interest you to know that a wassail was an early English toast to someone's health. It was also a liquor that was made of wine or ale and included spices and even baked apples. The entire melange was served in a large bowl, usually at Christmas time. At this period the term wassail was often used to refer to revelry, riotous drinking and all kinds of non-Christmas-like activity. Today, a wassail is most often thought of as a Christmas Carol (which it is), and the "Wassail Song" in Fig. 7-34 is a fine old English melody that has survived the ravages of time.

```
10  REM "SILENT NIGHT"
20  PLAY "ML T7002F8.G16F8D4.F8.G16F8D4.
03C4P64C8"
30  PLAY "02A4.B-4P64B-8F4.G4P64G8B-8.A1
6G8F8.G16F8"
40  PLAY "D4.G4P64G8B-8.A16G8F8.G16F8D4.
03C4P64C8E-8."
50  PLAY "C1602A8B-4.03D4.02B-8F8D8F8.E-
16C801B-2."
60  END
```

Fig. 7-33. "Silent Night."

```
10  REM "WASSAIL SONG"
20  PLAY "ML T15002D4E8F#4E8D4E8F#4E8D4A
8P64A4P64A8"
30  PLAY "P64A4.A4P64A8B4P64B8A4F#8A4.G4
F#8E4D8E4F#8"
40  PLAY "G4.T175MSF#4G4A203D402B4A2F#4G
4A4A403D402B4A2"
50  PLAY "MLF#4G4A2B4F#4G4E4D4C#4D4.E8F#
4D4G2F#4G4"
60  PLAY "A2B4F#4G4E4D4C#4D2.D2"
70  END
```

Fig. 7-34. "Wassail Song."

This program runs not only in legato mode, but also in staccato. Lines 20 and 30 are played at a tempo of T150 and in legato mode, but when the musical bridge is encountered there is a tempo change and the notes revert to staccato mode. This is set up in line 40, where the tempo is increased to T175 and the MS command is issued to revert to the staccato mode. In line 50, the legato mode is reentered but the tempo remains at the new and faster setting. This is an excellent example of mixing both mode and tempo commands to cause the desired musical effects.

WHATEVER WILL BE, WILL BE

This song and the ones that follow present a tremendous variety of non-Christmas songs. Some are old standards; others are fairly modern. The point to remember is that any piece of music can be programmed on the IBM Personal computer. The programs shown in this chapter concentrate on the melody lines, but musicians may also choose to input the harmony lines. The two cannot be run simultaneously, as the machine is restricted to a single tone output at any time. However, the inputing of different melody and harmony lines from a single piece can aid the composer and the student who must dissect an entire piece of music to understand its intricate functionings properly.

Bridging the gap from Christmas carols that are hundreds of years old to the semimodern, the program in Fig. 7-35 is known by two names, "Whatever Will Be, Will Be" and "Que Sera Sera." Rosemary Clooney had a hit with this song in the middle fifties.

The program is run in legato mode at a moderate tempo of T150. This was an ideal tune to input in the legato mode, since it was not necessary to insert a string of P64 separation rests because of the note sequence. I prefer the mode of legato programming for most songs because of the smooth output. The music normal mode often brings about an unwanted choppiness and does not differ in highly noticeable form from staccato mode programming.

This song has been performed at extremely fast and extremely slow tempos, so I chose a point somewhere in between. The Play statement information is included in lines 20 through 70. It is possible to arrange all of this information in two lines; my method was used for easy debugging purposes. The total range of notes spans only two octaves, so 02 and 03 statements are used throughout. The manuscript from which this program was written came from a student piano book. I incorporated a few subtle changes to make the piece sound better. Those persons who are heavily involved in composition and arranging may spend hours on a simple song to custom-tailor it. Admittedly, I did not have this amount of time, but I think you will find this program quite enjoyable and capable of bringing back memories associated with this song when it was popular in the fifties.

```
10  REM "WHATEVER WILL BE, WILL BE" (QUE
 SERA SERA)
20  PLAY "MF ML T150 O2C4D4E4G2E4G2E4G2.
"
30  PLAY "E4G4E4A4G2A4G4E4F2.F2.B4O3C4D4
C4O2B2"
40  PLAY "O2A4B4O3C4O2B2.F4G4A4G2F4E2."
50  PLAY "F4O3C4.O2B-8A2F4A2.A2B4O3D4C4O
2A4"
60  PLAY "O2G2C4E2.E2F#4A4G4E4G2D4G2.G4D
4E4F2O1B4O2C2.C2.C4"
70  PLAY "O2D4E4F2O1B4O2C2.C2.C2"
80  END
```

Fig. 7-35. "Whatever Will Be, Will Be."

VAYA CON DIOS

The program in Fig. 7-36 causes the IBM Personal computer to output what can certainly be classified as an old standard, "Vaya Con Dios." This song precedes my birth, so I can't say when it reached its height of popularity. You can still hear this song occasionally on records and radio stations.

The song plays through the main theme twice and then enters the musical bridge to its conclusion. Therefore the main melody lines are committed to a For-Next loop in lines 20 and 90, respectively. The intro to the bridge is a modification of the last few bars of the initial verse, so it was necessary to include the detection line found in line 70 of the program. During the second cycle of the loop, execution will branch to line 100 after line 60 is completed. Line 100 contains the musical intro to the bridge, while lines 110 through 190 include the bridge notes themselves.

This program is run in legato mode. Therefore, you will notice an occasional P64 rest in several portions of the program. The outro is actually a repeat of the opening verse, so lines 30 through 60 are repeated in lines 130 through 180, until the final outro in line 190. It would have been possible to reenter the loop at the desired point, but for the sake of understanding (both from the reader's and the author's standpoint), straight-line programming was used for the final portions of the song. This piece is normally performed at a medium-slow tempo, and the T100 tempo command produced the desired speed.

WINDY

The program shown in Fig. 7-37 brings us up to the sixties and a big hit for the musical group known as The Association. The song is called "Windy" and is output by the IBM Personal computer in staccato mode programming, which closely simulates the original song.

The first portion of the song, the main verses, is committed to a For-Next loop which begins in line 20. The detection line at 90 exits the loop at the proper point to access the outro lines at 130 and 140. Since the staccato mode of programming was used, it is unnecessary to use P64 dividers in the first few lines. However, beginning at line 60 there is a switch to legato mode. This occurs during the middle of the first two verses. During the first verse play, line 120 recycles the loop and the staccato mode is again entered in line 30. When the final loop exit is made from line 90 to 130, the legato mode is maintained until the end of the piece. Therefore you will see several P64 dividers beginning below line 60.

The switch from staccato to legato programming mode was not mandatory, but allowed me to more acurately reproduce the song in its original style. If you are familiar with the tune, you already know what I am talking about. If not, you will find out as soon as you run the program. Musical switches from staccato to legato and back are quite common in many modern pieces, though not with older songs. The duration mode capabilities of the IBM Personal computer will greatly aid you in accurately reproducing many of these modern pieces. To really be able to hear the difference, input the program and run it as shown. When you have finished debugging, display line 60 and temporarily change the ML command to MS. When the modified program is run, you will be able to see the difference made by the mode change. You certainly will want to switch back to the ML command in line 60 after completing this test run.

EVERYTHING IS BEAUTIFUL

A popular entertainer of the sixties and seventies, Ray Stevens, wrote and sang "Everything Is Beautiful", which was a bit hit around 1970. This song reminds me of a small town in Virginia, and to

```
10   REM "VAYA CON DIOS"
20   FOR X = 1 TO 2
30   PLAY "MF ML T100 O2C8D8E8D#8E8D#8E4E
8D#8E4.F8E4D2"
40   PLAY "D2P64D8E8F8E8F8E8F4F8E8F4.D8D#
4E2E2."
50   PLAY "O3C4P64C4.P64C8P64C4O2B4.A8P64
A4G2G2."
60   PLAY "O2P64G4P64G4.P64G8P64"
70   IF X = 2 THEN 100
80   PLAY "G4F4G4E2.E2"
90   NEXT X
100  PLAY "O2G4F4O1B4O2C2.C2P64C4"
110  PLAY "O2B-8O3C8O2B-8A8B-4B-8A8B-4.O
3C8"
120  PLAY "O2B-4A2A2C4G8A8G8F#8G8A8G2A4F
2.F2D4"
130  PLAY "O3C8D8C8O2B8O3C4C8O2B8O3C4.D8
C4O2B2B2"
140  PLAY "O2D4A8B8A8G#8A8G#8A2B4G4.F#8F
8E8D2"
150  PLAY "O2C8D8E8D#8E8D#8E4E8D#8E4.F8E
4D2"
160  PLAY "D2P64D8E8F8E8F8E8F4F8E8F4.D8D
#4E2E2."
170  PLAY "O3C4P64C4.P64C8P64C4O2B4.A8P6
4A4G2G2."
180  PLAY "O2P64G4P64G4.P64G8P64"
190  PLAY "O2G4F4O1B4O2C2.C2"
200  END
```

Fig. 7-36. "Vaya Con Dios."

```
10  REM "WINDY"
20  FOR X = 1 TO 2
30  PLAY "MF MS T170 02A403C802A8G4F403D
8D8C402A403C402A4"
40  PLAY "03C802A8G4F403D8D8C402G2A403C8
02A8G4F4"
50  PLAY "03D8D8C402A403C402A403C802A8G4
F4G4F2.01F4F4F2"
60  PLAY "ML 02F4F4A803C8F4D202B-403C4C4
02F4A803C8F4"
70  PLAY "03D202B-4G4G4E4F8A803F4D202B-4
03C4C402A4"
80  PLAY "02F64A8F64A4."
90  IF X = 2 THEN 130
100  PLAY "02G4.03F8F64F8F64F4.C4.D8F64D
8F64D4.C4.F64C8"
110  PLAY "D8F4.G1"
120  NEXT X
130  PLAY "02G4.03D8F64D8F64D4.F64D4.F64
D8F64D8F64D4."
140  PLAY "C4.D8F64D8F64D4.F2."
150  END
```

Fig. 7-37. "Windy."

an even smaller AM radio station where I was employed when this song was popular.

This is an unusual song, in that it begins with children singing "Jesus Loves the Little Children." When that has been completed, the main melody line of Steven's composition begins. The melody line is then repeated twice before entering the musical bridge. Line 20 begins the intro part and contains the tempo and mode designations for the remainder of the song. The intro is completed in line 50. At this point the main melody line begins. Since this is to be played twice, a For-Next loop is established in line 60, with the main melody note information found in lines 80 through 120. During the second cycle of the loop, line 110 creates a branch to line 140 where the second melody strain begins. When this portion is exited at the conclusion of line 210, the original melody line is repeated in lines 220 through 260. It would have been possible to reenter the original loop, but it was much easier to renumber original lines 70 through 100 with 220 through 250. Line 260 plays the final outro to this number.

This program is longer than most of those presented thus far, because it includes three separate melody sections. By efficiently utilizing an additional For-Next loop the program could be shortened to about twenty lines; this would result in little savings of time for programming and for input and would probably add to the debugging.

The basic program is executed in legato mode. However, I have often switched to music normal mode rather than include a larger number of P64 separation rests between identical notes. The first switch occurs toward the end of line 20, where a series of G notes must be produced. The switch back to legato mode occurs near the center of line 30. You will see instances where I elected to use

```
10  REM "EVERYTHING IS BEAUTIFUL" (BY RA
Y STEVENS)
20  PLAY "MF ML T120 O2A4P64A4P64A8.G16F
8.D16C2F2MNG8.G16G8.G16"
30  PLAY "O2A8.G16F8.A16MLG2.C8.O1B-16A8
.O2C16F8.G16F4P64"
40  PLAY "O2F8.E16D8.E16F8.D16C4A8.G16F8
.E16F8.D16E8.C16E8.G16"
50  PLAY "F1F4P4T160A8O3C8P64C8O2A8O3"
60  FOR X = 1 TO 2
70  PLAY "O3D4.C8P64C2C2"
80  PLAY "O2A8B-8A4P64A8G8G2.G2"
90  PLAY "O2D8E8F8G8A4.G8P64G4O3C4D4C8P6
4C8"
100  PLAY "O2A8G8F8G8"
110  IF X = 2 THEN 140
120  PLAY "O2A1P2A8O3C8P64C8O2A8"
130  NEXT X
140  PLAY "O2D8C8D8F2.F2P2P4A8P64A8B-4A4
"
150  PLAY "O2P64A4G2C4D4F4G8A4.G8F8F2.P4
"
160  PLAY "O3C8P64C8P64C4P64C8P64C8P64C8
O2A8G2C8P64C8D4F4G4.A8G8F8F2."
170  PLAY "O3P8C8F8P64F8P64F2P8C8E8P64E8
D4C4"
180  PLAY "O2P8F8O3D8C8D8C8O2A8MNC8C8C8"

190  PLAY "MLO2A8G8F2.P8F8O3C8O2A8O3C8P6
4C8D4"
200  PLAY "O2P8A8O3C8O2A8P64A4MNC8C8MLD8
F4.P8F8G8A8"
210  PLAY "O2G8F4.P2P2A8O3C8P64C8O2A8"
220  PLAY "O3D4.C8P64C2C2"
230  PLAY "O2A8B-8A4P64A8G8G2.G2"
240  PLAY "O2D8E8F8G8A4.G8P64G4O3C4D4C8P
64C8"
250  PLAY "O2A8G8F8G8"
260  PLAY "O2D8C8D8F2.F2"
270  END
```

Fig. 7-38. "Everything Is Beautiful."

P64 separators rather than switch modes. In these cases the identical note strings were short, and I felt this form of separation was more advantageous than switching to the music normal mode. You may elect to do otherwise, but the program will run quite satisfactorily as shown here.

SNOWBIRD

Figure 7-39 outputs another song which was popular around 1970. As I recall, Anne Murray had a big hit with "Snowbird". As with most popular songs, a main verse repeats at least twice, with an exit near the end of the second repetition playing to an appropriate outro. The For-Next loop established at lines 20 and 100 contains the main verse data. The detection portion in line 80 exits the loop at a specific point in the second run by branching to lines 110 and 120, where the outro data is located.

The original version of this song was treated very delicately by Ms. Murray and included smooth transitions from note to note at a fairly rapid tempo. A T150 command was an appropriate tempo; it was necessary to use the legato play mode to bring about smooth transitions. As before, I used a combination of P64 rest separators between identical notes and switched to music normal mode for the longer, identical note lines. The last notes of the outro are all run in music legato mode. In this program I relied heavily on P64 separators and not much on mode transitions.

WIPEOUT

In the middle sixties I surprised my family and especially my band director by becoming very involved in the rock and roll scene, which was given new life by the Beatles. Their popularity generated hundreds of other rock groups, who enjoyed varying degrees of success. Most groups relied heavily on vocal ability and not much on instrumental backup. An exception was the Surfaris, who were famous for their guitar instrumentals rather than their vocals. Their most popular hit was called "Wipeout" and is still performed by bands today.

"Wipeout" was built mostly from staccato eighth notes at a very fast tempo. Figure 7-40 presents the IBM computer version performed mainly

```
10  REM "SNOWBIRD"
20  FOR X = 1 TO 2
30  PLAY "MF ML T150 O3F4P64F4E4P64E4D4P
64D4C4P64C4O2F4G1"
40  PLAY "O2G2.O3C8P64C8P64C4O2B-4P64B-4
A4P64A4G4P64G4A4B-4"
50  PLAY "O3C4O2A4G4C1C2.P8"
60  PLAY "O3F8P64F4E4P64E4D4P64D4C4P64C4
O2F4G1G2."
70  PLAY "O3C8P64C8P64C4O2B-4P64B-4A4P64
A4G4P64G4A4B-4P64B-4A4G4"
80  IF X = 2 THEN 110
90  PLAY "O2F1F2."
100  NEXT X
110  PLAY "O2F1F2O3E8D8C4MNE8E4.E4D4C4C4
O2B-4O3C4MLD1D1"
120  PLAY "P4MNF4F4F4MLF1F1F2."
130  END
```

Fig. 7-39. "Snowbird."

```
10 REM "WIPEOUT" BY THE SURFARIS
20 PLAY"MF MS T200 O2G8B-8B8O3C8C8C8O2B-
8G8G8B-8B8"
30 PLAY"O3 C8C8C8O2B-8G8G8B-8B8O3C8C8C8O
2B-8G8G8B-8B8"
40 PLAY"O3C8C8C8O2B-8G8O3C8E-8E8F8F8F8E-
8C8C8E-8E8"
50 PLAY"O3F8F8F8E-8C8O2G8B-8B8O3C8C8C8O2
B-8G8G8B-8B8"
60 PLAY"O3C8C8C8O2B-8G8O3C8E8F8G8G8G8F8D
8D8G8G8"
70 PLAY"O3F8F8F8E-8C8O2G8B-8B8O3C8C8C8O2
B-8G8G8O3C8O2B-8"
80 PLAY"O3C8C8C8MLC8C8"
90 PLAY"MF MS T200 O2G8B-8B8O3C8C8C8O2B-
8G8G8B-8B8"
100 PLAY"O3 C8C8C8O2B-8G8G8B-8B8O3C8C8C8
O2B-8G8G8B-8B8"
110 PLAY"O3C8C8C8O2B-8G8O3C8E-8E8F8F8F8E
-8C8C8E-8E8"
120 PLAY"O3F8F8F8E-8C8O2G8B-8B8O3C8C8C8O
2B-8G8G8B-8B8"
130 PLAY"O3C8C8C8O2B-8G8O3C8E8F8G8G8G8F8
D8D8G8G8"
140 PLAY"O3F8F8F8E-8C8O2G8B-8B8O3C8C8C8O
2B-8G8G8O3C8O2B-8"
150 PLAY"O3C16P16O2B-8G8MLO3C1"
160 END
```

Fig. 7-40. "Wipeout."

in staccato mode at a rapid tempo of T200. In musical terms this tempo would be described as presto or prestissimo.

This program is straight line; lines 90 through 150 mostly repeat lines 20 through 80. Programming time was not greatly lengthened by using this method, because after I completed line 80 I returned to line 20 and renumbered it 90. Line 30 became line 100, and so on. I did this after the first eight lines had been debugged. Therefore, I was certain that the "copy lines" would be accurate. Line 150 is the outro and differs greatly from line 80, which would be its match if the copied line sequence were maintained throughout.

I have made a few transitions from staccato mode to legato, as shown in lines 80 and 150. It was only at these two points that sustained legato mode was necessary. The switch from staccato to legato in line 80 is reversed at the beginning of line 90, which repeats line 20. The ending note in line 150 is sustained in legato mode.

This type of program is ideally suited for the IBM Personal computer. Each note is distinct, although the tempo is quite rapid. This is the type of program ideal to run during a programming pause, after long hours behind the computer have made you sleepy. The output from this program should pep you up and allow a few more hours of programming.

BLUES IN F

The program in Fig. 7-41 is entitled "Blues in F" and will slow things down after the panic strains of the previous program. This piece is fairly old and was designed to be plated at a slower tempo than that keyed by the T100 command in line 20. I originally tried T50, but it was too slow to be enjoyable on the computer.

The program is run entirely in legato mode and is input without the need for P64 dividers because of the note transitions. In some cases I lengthened or shortened a note and made up for the difference with a longer duration rest, but each of the bars should come out mathematically correct. In some instances I had difficulty with the math, so you will see a P64 or two, but these are used very rarely in this program.

For programming this blues number the legato mode was mandatory to cause the "lazy" sliding effect common to these types of pieces. Because of the single melody line and the note transition, there was no point within this piece where a For-Next loop would have been practical. Therefore straight-line programming was used throughout. Since the program plays through only once, this might be an ideal situation to introduce an endless loop by replacing the End statement in line 100 with a Goto 20 statement. This is not the type of program you will want to play when you are tired or sleepy. The output will make you feel even drowsier and will probably put you in a bad mood. (That's why they call it the blues.)

SOMETHIN' STUPID

During the last half of the sixties, Frank Sinatra's daughter Nancy became an exceedingly popular entertainer in her own right. Many of her songs did not receive highly favorable reviews, but a few are still heard in smooth instrumental form today. One of these, "Somethin' Stupid", is presented in Fig. 7-42. I never liked this song, but I'm probably in the minority.

You will see many transitions from music normal to music legato mode. The note structure is exceedingly simple (from a musical standpoint) and involves the sequential playing of a series of identical quarter and/or eighth notes. I switched to music legato whenever possible, but many sections re-

```
10 REM "BLUES IN F"
20 PLAY"MF ML T100 O3 C1C8O2F8A8B-8O3C4O
2B-8O3C8O2A2."
30 PLAY"O2F8E8E-2.F8O3F8P64F1F8O2B-8O3D8
E8F4D4C2.D8C8"
40 PLAY"O2A2P8F8A8O3C8E8C4.C8O2E8G8O3C8D
8O2B-4.B-8"
50 PLAY"O2D8F8B-8O3C8O2F4.F2P1"
60 PLAY"O2A2O3C2C2.O2B-8O3C8O2A2.F8E8E-2
F8O3F8"
70 PLAY"O3D2F2F2.D4O2A2O3C2C2P8O2F8A8O3C
8E8C4.C8"
80 PLAY"O2E8G8O3C8D8O2B-4.B-8D8F8B-8O3C8
O2F4."
90 PLAY"O3C8O2F8G8F8A2"
100 END
```

Fig. 7-41. "Blues in F."

```
10 REM "SOMETHIN' STUPID"
20 PLAY"MF MN T160 O1 A8O2C8C8C8C8D8D8D8
D8E8E8E8E8"
30 PLAY"O2F8F8E8C8D8D8F4MLE2E2.MNP8C8C8C
8C8C8D8D8D8D8"
40 PLAY"O2 E8E8E8E8F8F8E8C8D8D8E4MLD2D2.
MNP8C8"
50 PLAY"O2 F8F8F8F8G8G8G8G8A8A8A8A8O3C8O
2B-8A8B-8"
60 PLAY"O2A4G8MLG8G2G2.MNP8D8F8F8F8D8E8E
8E8D8"
70 PLAY"O2F8F8F8D8E8E8E8A8G2MLF2MNF2.F8F
8"
80 PLAY"O2F8F8F8F8G8G8G8G8A8A8A8A8O3C8O2
B-8A8B-8"
90 PLAY"O2A8G8MLG2.G2MNP8F8G8G8G8G8A8A8A
8A8B8B8B8B8"
100 PLAY"O3D8D8D8E8D8C8MLC2.C2.MN"
110 PLAY"MF MN T160 O1 A8O2C8C8C8C8D8D8D
8D8E8E8E8E8"
120 PLAY"O2F8F8E8C8D8D8F4MLE2E2.MNP8C8C8
C8C8C8D8D8D8D8"
130 PLAY"O2 E8E8E8E8F8F8E8C8D8D8E4MLD2D2
.MNP8C8"
140 PLAY"O2 F8F8F8F8G8G8G8G8A8A8A8A8O3C8
O2B-8A8B-8"
150 PLAY"O2A4G8MLG8G2G2.MNP8D8F8F8F8D8E8
E8E8D8"
160 PLAY"O2F8F8F8D8E8E8E8A8G2MLF2MNF2."
170 END
```

Fig. 7-42. "Somethin' Stupid."

quired the normal mode to avoid destroying measure timing. A good example of this is shown in line 50, where four Fs played as eighth notes are followed by four Gs played as eighth notes and four eighth note As. If I had inserted P64 between each one, I would eventually have an extra measure at the end. Running this sequence in music normal mode causes the same effect at the audio output end, greatly shortens programming time, and keeps me mathematically correct with the original manuscript. The music legato mode was used mainly to play certain identical notes over several sustained measures.

For Nancy Sinatra fans, please don't become angry over my remarks about this particular song. I liked her version of "You Only Live Twice," the theme song for the James Bond movie of the same name. Unfortunately I couldn't find a manuscript for this song, so it's not included here.

KING OF THE ROAD

The biggest hit for a country music entertainer named Roger Miller, who made the transition to the pop charts, was "King of the Road." The program in Fig. 7-43 offers an especially nice run on the IBM Personal computer. This program combines

```
10  REM "KING OF THE ROAD"
20  FOR X = 1 TO 2
30  PLAY "MF MN T150 O3P4C4O2G4E4D4E8MLF
8F2P4B4MNB8G8A8G8C4"
40  PLAY "O2C8MLC8C2MNP4O3C4O2G4E4"
50  PLAY "O2D4E8MLF8F2MNP8G8G4B4O3C4"
60  PLAY "O3D4C8MLO2B8B8MNG8A4P4O3C4O2G4
E4"
70  PLAY "O2D4E8MLF8MNF4F8D8P4MLB4B8MN"
80  PLAY "O2G8A8G8C4C8MLC8C8MNE8G4"
90  PLAY "O3P4E2D4MNC4C4C8O2A4.P2"
100  PLAY "O3D8C8O2B4"
110  IF X = 2 THEN 140
120  PLAY "O3C1"
130  NEXT X
140  PLAY "O3C2MNP8C8C4C8C8C4C8C8C8O2B8"

150  PLAY "O2A8O3C8O2A4F4P4B8B8B4A8G4G8"

160  PLAY "O2A8O3C8O2A4G4P8G8O3G8G8E4D8C
4"
170  PLAY "O2A8O3C8O2A8O3C4O2A4P8A8G8G8G
8G8"
180  PLAY "O2B8B4B8O3D8D8D8MLF8MNF8E8D4"

190  PLAY "O3P4C4O2G4E4D4E8MLF8F2P4B4MNB
8G8A8G8C4"
200  PLAY "O2C8MLC8C2MNP4O3C4O2G4E4"
210  PLAY "O2D4E8MLF8F2MNP8G8G4B4O3C4"
220  PLAY "O3D4C8MLO2B8B8MNG8A4P4O3C4O2G
4E4"
230  PLAY "O2D4E8MLF8MNF4F8D8P4MLB4B8MN"

240  PLAY "O2G8A8G8C4C8MLC8C8MNE8G4"
250  PLAY "O3P4E2D4MNC4C4C8O2A4.P2"
260  PLAY "O3D8C8O2B4"
270  PLAY "O3C2."
280  END
```

Fig. 7-43. "King of the Road."

straight-line programming with a For-Next loop at the beginning. Some of the main melody lines are repeated in the latter portion of the program.

Line 110 allows the For-Next loop to be exited at the proper point. The bridge lines are contained in program lines 140 through 180. The main melody appears in straight-line programming form again beginning at line 190 and executing through line 270, which contains the outro.

You will see a lot of transitions from music

normal to music legato modes and then back. This allows the song to be reproduced in much the same manner as the original, which included some choppy note sections, along with those which offered smoother transitions. I had originally programmed for a faster tempo, but later decided to slow it to a moderate speed with a T150 command. I also tried varying the tempo at different sections, but the final version shown here produces the best effect (in my opinion).

Whenever possible I have tried to program the various songs presented in this chapter close to their original style. There is much to be said for taking a popular song and creating a special arrangement designed to take advantage of all the computer has to offer. The computer offers much less than a full orchestra, so certain changes are warranted to create the best run possible using the limited musical abilities of the microcomputer. It may sound like I am contradicting a previous statement alluding to the excellent musical capabilities of the IBM Personal computer. However, that statement was in relation to the musical capabilities of other computers, which are sometimes nonexistent. The musical output of the IBM Personal computer is produced by a flexible, single-tone generator. The single tone output is a major disadvantage. The computer may be interfaced with an electronic organ or a synthesizer to control hundreds of different tone generators (offering simultaneous output), to form a highly versatile and efficient musical instrument. This book concentrates on the abilities of the computer along and does not take into account the unlimited possibilities of the musical peripherals that are available.

JEAN

"Jean," written by Rod McKuen, was another big hit at the beginning of the seventies and is shown in program form in Fig. 7-44. This piece was performed very delicately and at a moderate tempo; hence, the legato programming mode and the T120 tempo. The T120 command is unnecessary, since this is the default tempo. If the tempo command is not included, the speed will still be the same. The main melody lines are committed to a For-Next loop in lines 20 and 80, respectively. By now you have probably noticed a "rhythm" (pardon the pun) to my musical programs, in that there is an exit from the loop during the second cycle, which enters the bridge lines found in program lines 90 through 120. The outro is a repeat of the main melody lines and begins at line 130. Lines 130 through 150 are copies of lines 30 through 50 at the beginning of the program. Line 160 gives the final outro notes.

You will also notice that I have switched between legato and normal modes of programming, and have combined these transitions with P64 separation commands when it was not convenient to exit the legato programming mode. The P64 separators are used only at program positions where the short, extra bar duration cannot be practically detected.

FIVE HUNDRED MILES

"Five Hundred Miles" was a big hit for the folk group, Peter, Paul and Mary, in the late sixties. The program to reproduce this song, mostly in legato mode, is shown in Fig. 7-45. Construction-wise, this program is very similar to many others which repeat the opening verse and then move into a bridge and an outro. The same pattern is used here as with similar programs and includes an opening For-Next loop. You will notice a separate Play line in program line 15. This is the intro to the opening melody line and is not repeated during the second repetition of the loop. The opening is placed outside of the loop and plays the two quarter notes that form the intro before entering the loop. There is an intro to the main melody line which is different from the first; it begins the second playing, which is composed of two quarter note Gs, found at the end of line 70. When the loop repeats, line 60 branches to line 90, which enters the bridge strains. In modern songs you will often find a one-time intro to the main melody. In these cases it is desirable to keep these few notes outside of your major melody loop.

SUPERCALIFRAGILISTICEXPIALIDOCIOUS

One of the major musical hits of the sixties was the movie *Mary Poppins*. One of the many musical numbers performed in this movie was "Supercali-

```
10  REM "JEAN" (BY ROD MCKUEN)
20  FOR X = 1 TO 2
30  PLAY "MF ML T120 O2F2.O3C2.D4.C8O2B-
4O3C2.P2MNO2F8F8"
40  PLAY "MLO2F4.D8F4D4C2C2A8O3C8D2C8O2A
8O3C2O2A8F8"
50  PLAY "O2G4F4.D8F2.P4P8G8A8F8P64F8P64
"
60  IF X = 2 THEN 90
70  PLAY "MLF4P64F2P64F2.P1"
80  NEXT X
90  PLAY "MLO2G2F8G8F2.F4P4O3MNF8F8ML"
100  PLAY "MLO3D2P64D8E8F4E4.D8E2C4P64C2
MNF8F8MLD2P64D8E8F4E4D8"
110  PLAY "MLO3E2C8O2A8O3C2E8F8D2P64D8E8
"
120  PLAY "MLO3F4E2P4F8C8D8C8O2A-4G2F4P6
4"
130  PLAY "O2F2.O3C2.D4.C8O2B-4O3C2.P2MN
O2F8F8"
140  PLAY "MLO2F4.D8F4D4C2C2A8O3C8D2C8O2
A8O3C2O2A8F8"
150  PLAY "O2G4F4.D8F2.P4P8G8A8F8P64F8P6
4"
160  PLAY "MLO2G2F8G8F2.F2"
170  END
```

Fig. 7-44. "Jean."

fragilisticexpialidocious." This was termed a comical, nonsense song and was quite popular among children as well as adults.

The program in Fig. 7-46 reproduces this song using staccato mode programming throughout. The major verse is repeated four times before entering the outro section. Therefore the For-Next loop established around the melody line segment cycles four times before an exit occurs in line 60, branching to line 150.

The staccato mode programming was ideal for this song, as each note was to be short and choppy. You will also notice that maximum machine tempo (T255) is used to play the notes at the fastest possible pace. Because of the staccato mode programming, each note is clearly defined. Legato mode programming would be very difficult here, since there are many sequences which repeat the same note up to seven times. At these speeds a P64 separator would throw off the timing to a very noticeable degree.

You may wish to slow the tempo; this will probably be mandatory during the debugging procedure. This piece should be executed very rapidly, so don't slow the final version too much. The notes in this song span three octaves. You will see designations in octave commands of 01 to 03. The broad range of note frequencies makes this song especially interesting when played at a rapid tempo on the IBM Personal computer.

THEME FROM LOVE STORY

Americans fell in love with tragedy, based partially upon the hit movie *Love Story*, starring Ryan

```
10  REM "FIVE HUNDRED MILES"
15  PLAY "MF ML T100 O2D4G4"
20  FOR X = 1 TO 2
30  PLAY "O2B4.P64B8A8G4.B2A4G4"
40  PLAY "O2A4.B8A4G4E2.P64E8G8A4.B8A8G4
."
50  PLAY "E8D4.D8P64D8E8G8P64"
60  IF X = 2 THEN 90
70  PLAY "G1MNG4.G8G4G4ML"
80  NEXT X
90  PLAY "MLO2G1MNG2G4G4.ML"
100  PLAY "MLO2B2A8G4.B2A4G4A4.B8A4G4E2.
P64E8G8A8B4.A8G4."
110  PLAY "O2E8D4.D8P64D8E8G8P64G1MNG4.G
8G4G4"
120  PLAY "MLO2B4.P64B8A4G4B4.P64B8A4G4A
4.B8A8G4."
130  PLAY "O2E2.P64E8G8A8B4.A8G4.E8D4.D8
P64D8E8G8P64G1G2"
140  PLAY "P64MNO2G4G4O3MLE4.D8C4O2B4A4.
G8E4G4G1G2."
150  END
```

Fig. 7-45. "Five Hundred Miles."

```
10  REM "SUPERCALIFRAGILISTICEXPIALIDOCI
OUS"
20  FOR X = 1 TO 4
30  PLAY "MF MS T255 O2L4EGGGAGGEGGAGG2F
2"
40  PLAY "O2L4GGGGAGGDGGAGG2E2L4GGGGAGGG
"
50  PLAY "O3L4CCDCC2O2A2L4AO3CO2BAL4O3CO
2GGE"
60  IF X = 4 THEN 150
70  PLAY "O2L4GG#ABO3C2C4P4O2G4L8GGGGGGG
4G8G8G4P4"
80  PLAY "O1G4L8GGGGGGG4G8G8G4"
90  PLAY "O2L4GEGGGAGGEGGAGF2.G4"
100  PLAY "O2L4GGGGAGGDGGAGE2.L4GGGGG"
110  PLAY "O2L4AGGGO2CCDCA2.A4"
120  PLAY "O2L4AAAABAAAO3DCO2BA"
130  PLAY "O2G4P4F2"
140  NEXT X
150  PLAY "O2L4GG#ABO3C2C4":END
```

Fig. 7-46. "Supercalifragilisticexpialidocious."

O'Neal and Ali McGraw. The haunting theme from this movie still endures and is still performed by many orchestras. The program in Fig. 7-47 reproduces this song using a fairly slow tempo and a legato format. P64 separators are used in conjunction with mode changes in music normal for long sequences of identical notes. At the slower tempo, the P64 separators and the measure imbalance they cause are not audibly detectable.

After the main melody line is played through twice, there is a branch to the bridge lines beginning at line 100. When the bridge is complete (line 160), the main melody line is again entered, and this carries through to the outro. Lines 170 through 200

```
10  REM "THEME FROM LOVE STORY"
20  FOR X = 1 TO 2
30  PLAY "MF ML T100 O3C8O2E8P64E8O3C8P64C2C8O2E8"
40  PLAY "O2P64E8O3C8P64C8O2E8F8E8MND8D8D8B8MLB2B8"
50  PLAY "O2D8P64D8B8P64B8D8E8D8MNC8C8C8A8A2P8C8C8A8"
60  PLAY "MLA8C8D8C8MNO1B8B8B8O2G#8MLG#2G#4"
70  IF X = 2 THEN 100
80  PLAY "O2A4B4F4E1E2.P4"
90  NEXT X
100  PLAY "O2A4B4G#4O3C#1P4D4E4O2A4"
110  PLAY "MLO3F2F8O2A8O3F8O2A8P64"
120  PLAY "O2A8B8P64B4B8O3D8F8D8E2E8O2G8O3E8O2G8P64G8A8"
130  PLAY "O2P64A4A8O3C8E8C8D2D8O2B8O3D8O2B8O3C4.D8"
140  PLAY "O3E8O2A8O3C8E8F2F8O2G8A8O3C8"
150  PLAY "O3P64C4O2B4B8O3C8D8O2F8E2E8P64E8F8G8"
160  PLAY "O2B4A4A8P64A8G12F12E12D#2D#8F#8A8F#8G#1G#1"
170  PLAY "MF ML T100 O3C8O2E8P64E8O3C8P64C2C8O2E8"
180  PLAY "O2P64E8O3C8P64C8O2E8F8E8MND8D8D8B8MLB2B8"
190  PLAY "O2D8P64D8B8P64B8D8E8D8MNC8C8C8A8A2P8C8C8A8"
200  PLAY "MLA8C8D8C8MNO1B8B8B8O2G#8MLG#2G#4"
210  PLAY "O2A4B4G#4A1A1"
220  END
```

Fig. 7-47. "Theme from Love Story."

```
10  REM "TIJUANA TAXI"
20  PLAY "MF MS T225 O2A8O3C4F4E4D8C4.O2
B-2P8G8B-4O3E4D4C8O2B-4.A2"
30  PLAY "O2P8F8A4O3D4C4O2B-8A4.G2P8G8A4
O3C8C8C4P2"
40  PLAY "O2P4B-4A4G4MLF1F4MSP4P8A8O3C4"

50  PLAY "O3F4E4D8C4.O2B-2P8G8B-4O3E4D4C
8O2B-4."
60  PLAY "O2A2P8F8A4O3D4C4O2B-8A4.G2P8G8
A4O3C8C8C4P2"
70  PLAY "O2B-8B-8B-4P2A8A8A4P2G8G8G4P2F
8P8O1C8MLD8D8MSC8O0A4F4P4O3F8"
80  END
```

Fig. 7-48. "Tijuana Taxi."

are repeats of lines 30 through 60. Line 210 plays the notes which form the final outro.

TIJUANA TAXI

Herb Alpert and the Tijuana Brass were another hit instrumental group in the sixties and early seventies when vocal groups were usually considered king. Alpert's group combined the sounds of a Mariachi band with the style of jazz ensembles. They had many hit songs, one of which was "Tijuana Taxi", produced by the program in Fig. 7-48. This is a very fast number and is played at T225 tempo. Most notes are played in staccato mode, although there is an occasional change to legato mode to create the needed slurs indicated in the musical manuscript. There is straight-line programming all the way. The music runs so rapidly that you may wish to insert a For-Next loop beginning at line 15, with the Next statement at line 75. If the loop counts from 1 to 2, then the entire song will be played twice, but you can increase the upper end of the loop to play it through any number of times. Alternately, you can leave the program as is, but replace the End statement in line 80 with a "GOTO 20". This will form an endless loop, and the song will play continuously until manually halted at the keyboard.

SPANISH FLEA

Another of Alpert's big hits (possibly his biggest) was "Spanish Flea," and is run on the IBM Personal computer using the program in Fig. 7-49. This runs in music normal mode; there is an intro line (line 20) which is placed before the beginning of the For-Next loop, which contains the main melody information. The intro notes are played and the For-Next loop is then entered. During the second go-round there is an exit at line 80, which branches to line 1000. This line contains the final outro information.

I slowed this piece quite a bit. The T150 tempo should accurately reflect the playing of the original version of the song. Other versions done by different orchestras have been played at different tempos, and depending on which version you like, you may or may not wish to modify the tempo command found in line 20.

COTTON CANDY

Another trumpet player who enjoyed popularity to the mid-sixties was "Mr. Mardi Gras," Al Hirt. Whereas Herb Alpert brought a blend of Mariachi/jazz to the American public, Al Hirt gave us modified Basin Street sounds. One of his hits was "Cotton Candy", produced by the program shown in

```
10  REM "SPANISH FLEA"
20  PLAY  "MF MN T150 O2D8E-8E8F4O3D4D8C
4."
30  FOR X = 1 TO 2
40  PLAY "O2B2P8G8G-8F8E4O3C4C8O2B-4."
50  PLAY "O2A2P8F8E8E-8D8F8B-8MLG8MNG8B-
8O3C4"
60  PLAY "O2F8A-8O3D-8O2MLB-8MNB-8O3D-8E
-4MLF1MNF4"
70  PLAY "O3MNF8F8G8F8D-8C8"
80  IF X = 2 THEN 1000
90  PLAY "O2MNB-4O3D4D8C4."
100  NEXT X
1000  PLAY "O2MNB-4F8F8P4F8F8P4F4P4F4P4F
8F8P4F8F8P4F4B-8"
1010  END
```

Fig. 7-49. "Spanish Flea."

Fig. 7-50. The song is run in staccato mode at maximum machine tempo (T255).

Musically the tempo may be classified as prestissimo. This arrangement involves a number of sharps; be careful you make note of each when inputting the program to your machine. I have used the standard musical sharp symbol throughout these programs (#); you may also use a plus sign (+) to indicate a sharp.

When debugging this program it might be best

```
10  REM "COTTON CANDY"
20  FOR X = 1 TO 2
30  PLAY "MF MS T255 O2G4P8G8G8E8G4A4P8F
8A4O3C4"
40  PLAY "O2G4P8G8G8E8G4A4P8F8A8A8O3C4"
50  PLAY "O2G4G8E8G8E8G4A4P8A8B8A8B4A4P8
A8B8A8B4"
60  PLAY "O2O2A4G2.
70  NEXT X
80  PLAY "O2A4P8A8L8G#G#G#G#A4P8A8G#2A4P
8A8L8G#G#G#G#F#1"
90  PLAY "O2A4P8A8L8G#G#G#G#A4P8A8G#2"
100  PLAY "O2A4P8A8L8G#G#G#G#F#2.F#4G#1"

110  PLAY "O2B4G#4G#4G#4"
120  PLAY "O3C1C4O2F8F8A8A8O3C4O2B4E8E8G
8G8B4"
130  PLAY "O2A4D8E8F8G8A8B8O3C2."
140  END
```

Fig. 7-50. "Cotton Candy."

to use a test tempo of 155, since there are so many notes. Once you have debugged each line, you can revert to the faster speed.

ALLEY CAT

Most readers will remember the popular song "Alley Cat," which was originally played as a solo piano instrumental. The version in Fig. 7-51 is a solo computer instrumental. This song moves rapidly with a T220 tempo command. Music normal mode is used throughout; the intro line (line 20) lies outside of the main melody line. The latter is contained in the For-Next loop between lines 30 and 80. Lines 100 and 110 form the musical bridge between the intro melody and the outro melody, which begins in line 120. Lines 120 and 130 are identical to lines 40 and 50. Line 140 is the final outro. You may also wish to run this program in staccato mode. It will be completely different from the original version, but at this speed it becomes a very novel arrangement. You can also convert to legato mode programming, but it will be necessary to insert some P64 separators or switch to the music normal mode for identical note progressions.

I originally used a much lower speed with this program. The original song was played at moderato; however this was not too pleasing to the ear in the computer version so I increased the speed by 50 percent.

IT WAS A VERY GOOD YEAR

Frank Sinatra fans, take heart! The program in Fig. 7-52 will play "It Was A Very Good Year," a big hit in the late sixties. This song followed Frank Sinatra's hit "That's Life," by one year.

The program runs in legato mode, although there are numerous changes to music normal mode to accommodate the note spacing. The tempo chosen is faster than the version Frank Sinatra sang, but this produces the most pleasing output from the computer.

```
10   REM "ALLEY CAT"
20   PLAY "MF MN T220 O2D#8E12G12A12"
30   FOR X = 1 TO 2
40   PLAY "O3L4CO2BAA-GG#AP4G8G8G#4A4A#4B
2.P4"
50   PLAY "O3C4O2B4A4A-4G4G#4A4P4G8G8G#4A
4B4"
60   IF X = 2 THEN 90
70   PLAY "O3C2P8O2D#8E12G12A12"
80   NEXT X
90   PLAY "O3C2P4C4D4D2O2C#4D2.O3C4"
100   PLAY "O3D4D2O2C#4D2.O3C4D4D2O2C#4D2
."
110   PLAY "O3C4D4C4O2B4A4G4G-4F8D#8E12G1
2A12"
120   PLAY "O3L4CO2BAA-GG#AP4G8G8G#4A4A#4
B2.P4"
130   PLAY "O3C4O2B4A4A-4G4G#4A4P4G8G8G#4
A4B4"
140   PLAY "O3C2P4O2E8C8D8D8P4D#8D#8P4E4G
4B4.A8O3E4C8O2A8O3E-4D4C2"
150   END
```

Fig. 7-51. "Alley Cat."

```
10  REM "IT WAS A VERY GOOD YEAR"
20  PLAY "MF ML T120 O1B8O2C#8D#8"
30  FOR X = 1 TO 2
40  PLAY "O2E4B4P64B2B2P8G8A8B8"
50  PLAY "O2MNA8A8F4MLF2F2P8F8G8F8"
60  PLAY "O2MNE8E8B4MLB4.O3C#8D4O2B4"
70  PLAY "O2P64B4.O3D8O2B4MNA8A8MLA2A2"
80  PLAY "O3P4C4O2B4MNG#8G#8MLG#2G#2.MNB
8B8"
90  PLAY "O2MLA4F#4P64F#2F#2P8F#8G#8A8G#
4E4P64E2E2"
100  PLAY "O2MLF#4E8F#8O1B4P4O2F#4E8F#8G
8F#8E4F#4"
110  PLAY "O2MLE8F#8D4P64D4D#2P8O1B8O2C#
8D#8"
120  PLAY "O2E4B4P64B2B2P8G8A8B8"
130  PLAY "O2MNA8A8F4MLF2F2P8F8G8F8"
140  PLAY "O2MNE8E8B4MLB4.O3C#8D4O2B4"
150  PLAY "O2P64B4.O3D8O2B4MNA8A8MLA2A2"

160  PLAY "O3P4C4O2B4MNG#8G#8MLG#2G#2.MN
B8B8"
170  PLAY "O2MLA4F#4P64F#2F#2P8F#8G#8A8G
#4E4P64E2E2"
180  PLAY "O2MLF#4E8F#8O1B4P4O2F#4E8F#8G
8F#8E4F#4"
190  IF X = 2 THEN 220
200  PLAY "O2MLE8F#8D4P64D4D#2P8O1B8O2C#
8D#8"
210  NEXT X
220  PLAY "O2MLE8F#8D4P64D4D#1"
230  END
```

Fig. 7-52. "It Was A Very Good Year."

The main melody line is in two nearly identical parts. The second portion is nearly a repeat of the first, but there are subtle differences. I originally thought I could use a For-Next loop that would count from 1 to 4; because of the differences in the second portion of the first melody line, I had to straight-line program the entire sequence. When these two similar melodies are coupled together, they are contained within a For-Next loop which counts from 1 to 2. This takes you from age 17 to the "Autumn of My Life". The exit line (If-Then statements) is at 190. This causes a branch to the final outro line in 220. Some readers may wish to slow the tempo marginally to 90 or 100. I feel the default tempo of T120 produces the best musical effect.

I LEFT MY HEART IN SAN FRANCISCO

While Frank Sinatra may rate first as the most popular male vocalist of all time, Tony Bennett has to rate a close second, and to many might even end up tied for first. The program shown in Fig. 7-53 produces one of his biggest hits on the IBM Personal computer, "I Left My Heart in San Francisco."

The program is a shortened version of the song, since it only plays through one complete chorus. This is an unusually simple program and uses straight-line techniques throughout, with no For-Next loops. I was able to slow the tempo to T100, which closely matches the tempo in the original song. I was not delighted with the musical manuscript used to program this song, so the better musicians among my readers may want to "dot a few eights" to match the original version more closely.

You may perhaps use music normal mode, but the legato programming mode used is the most pleasing. At no point was it necessary to switch to music normal mode, as P64 statements were used only sparingly as identical note separators.

AMERICA THE BEAUTIFUL

I came across a pleasing arrangement of "America the Beautiful" in a music manuscript book written in 1937. The program in Fig. 7-54 reflects the most pleasing parts of this manuscript.

Legato programming is used throughout to accurately reproduce the solemn strains. I elected to go with the default tempo (T120), which is automatically activated because there is no tempo command included in any of the eight program lines. The moderate tempo allows me to use the P64 commands without any noticeable effects detrimental to the timing of this piece.

Like the previous program, this is a one-verse version. You can play all the verses by using For-Next statements in new lines 15 and 75, if desired. This song is often performed at a faster tempo; however the default tempo in this program closely matches the speed of the 1937 arrangement. This was a very basic manuscript, and you may wish to use this program as a starting point for a more modern version. This gives much leeway to the musicians among the readers who might like to add grace notes and other refinements.

ME AND BOBBY MCGEE

Modern composer and singer Kris Kristofferson enjoyed one of his biggest hits with "Me and Bobby McGee", shown in program form in Fig.

```
10  REM "I LEFT MY HEART IN SAN FRANCISC
O"
20  PLAY "MF ML T100 O2D4E-4G4F1F4G4A4B-
4"
30  PLAY "O2G4C2.C4P64C4O1B4O2C4G1G4B-4A
4.F8D1D8P8D4E-4E4"
40  PLAY "O2F8E-8D8E-8F2F2.G4"
50  PLAY "O2A8G8F8G8A2A4P64A4G#4.A8B-1B-
4"
60  PLAY "O3C4O2A4.C8F2.G8F8E-4D4E-4G4F1
F4G4A4B-4"
70  PLAY "O2G4C2.C4P64C4O1B4O2C4A1A4P64A
4B-4O3C4"
80  PLAY "O3D1D8P64D4C#4D4E-2.D4O2B2O3C4
D4C4O2G2.G8"
90  PLAY "O2P8G4F#4G4O3E-2.O2G4O3D2P64D2
O2B-1B-2."
100  END
```

Fig. 7-53. "I Left My Heart in San Francisco."

```
10   REM "AMERICA THE BEAUTIFUL"
20   PLAY "ML O2G4P64G4.E8P64E4G4P64G4.D8
P64D4E4"
30   PLAY "F4G4A4B4G2.P64G4P64G4.E8P64E4G
4P64G4."
40   PLAY "D8P64D4O3D4C#4D4E4O2A4O3D2.O2G
4O3E4.P64"
50   PLAY "E8D4C4P64C4.O2B8P64B4O3C4D4O2B
4A4G4O3C2."
60   PLAY "P64C4P64C4.O2A8P64A4O3C4P64C4.
O2G8P64G4"
70   PLAY "P64G4A4O3C4O2G4O3D4C2."
80   END
```

Fig. 7-54. "America the Beautiful."

7-55. The most popular version was probably performed by the late Janis Joplin. She sang the blues rock-style, but the version shown here is more like the original as sung by Kristofferson. Unfortunately, songs by this writer do not play very well on the IBM Personal computer, mainly because they

```
10   REM "ME AND BOBBY MCGEE"
20   PLAY "MFLT200O2G4P64G4P64G4P64G4P64G
4F4E2G4P64G4P64"
30   PLAY "G4F4E2.P4E4G4P64G4E4F4E4D4C4D1
D1P4F8E8F4E4F4E4D4D4"
40   PLAY "P4F8E8F4E4D1P4F8E8F4P64F4E4D4C
4D4E1E2.P4G4P64G4"
50   PLAY "P64G4P64G4P64G4F4E4F4G4P64G4P6
4G4P64G4F4E4P64E4"
60   PLAY "F4G4P64G4P64G4A4B-4P64B-4G4E4F
1F4P4A4B4O3C4P64"
70   PLAY "C4P64C4P64C4P64C4O2B4A4F4G4F4E
4F4G4E4F4E4D4P64"
80   PLAY "D4P64D4E4F4D4C4O1B4O2C1P2.O3C8
P64C8P64C4P64C4P64"
90   PLAY "C4O2B4A4P64A4G4F4E4F4G1P4F8P64
F8P64F4P64F4E4D4C4D4E1E4"
100   PLAY "P2.O3C8P64C8P64C4P64C4P64C4O2
B4A4F4P4G8F8E4F4G1"
110   PLAY "P8D8P64D8P64D8P64D4E4F4D4P64D
4P64D4O1B1B2P2P4"
120   PLAY "O2F8P64F8P64F4E4D4.P64D8P64D8
C4O1B8O2C1C4"
130   END
```

Fig. 7-55. "Me and Bobby McGee."

entail many sequentially-run identical notes. His songs depend on the phrasing of the artist rather than the manuscript notes themselves. To overcome some of the difficulties in programming this song, I speeded the tempo considerably using a T200 command. Because there are long series of identical quarter notes, I was able to use large numbers of P64 rest separators, evenly spaced, which has the effect of stretching the entire song fairly evenly. In most instances these separators would completely destroy a song at this tempo. It would probably be simpler to use the music normal mode and switch to legato during different portions of the song which required this mode.

OH YOU CAN'T GET TO HEAVEN

Figure 7-56 shows a music program for a novelty song I first heard at 4H Camp. Some versions of "Oh You Can't Get to Heaven" have only two or three verses; others have ten or more. I elected to program the basic single verse. You can use appropriate For-Next statements to cause the desired number of play-throughs, assuming you or your children would like to sing along with the computer. I detest the song, but it has been around for many years and is bound to be popular in some quarters. The song itself is nothing much; it's really the words that give it audience appeal.

I played with this song, attempting to make it more interesting from a programming standpoint. The first line is output in legato mode. Then in line 30 I switch to staccato, back to legato, then to staccato. The first staccato command occurs at the end of line 20, therefore most of line 30 is played in this mode. The song varies in tempo. The fast portion is near the end of line 50, where I have switched to legato mode and increased the tempo one third by using the T200 command. This tempo is maintained to the end of the song. Feel free to increase or decrease the tempo at any portion of the song where these changes are useful. A tempo command is valid anywhere within the Play statement line, but remember that this new tempo will be in effect for all notes until a new tempo command is encountered.

MOCKINGBIRD

Also known as "Daddy's Gonna Buy Me a Mockingbird," the song produced by the program shown in Fig. 7-57 has been around for a long time,

```
10  REM "OH YOU CAN'T GET TO HEAVEN"
20  PLAY "ML T150O2F8.G16A4F8.P64F16C8P6
4C8MS"
30  PLAY "F8.G16A8P8F8.P64F16C8P64C8MLF4
D4F4C4"
40  PLAY "MSF8P8D8P8F8P8C8P8MLF8P64F8E4F
4G4MSF8P64F8"
50  PLAY "E8P8F8P8G8P8MLG4F4G4A4MSC8P8F8
P8G8P8A8P8MLT200F8.P64"
60  PLAY "F16G4A8.P64A16B-8P64B-8P64B-4P
64B-4"
70  PLAY "P64B-4P64B-4P64B-8.P64B-16F4G4
A4P64"
80  PLAY "A4P64A4P64A4P64A4P64A4O3C4O2A8
P64A8"
90  PLAY "G1G4B-4A4G4F1F4"
100 END
```

Fig. 7-56. "Oh You Can't Get to Heaven."

```
10   REM "MOCKINGBIRD"
15   FOR X = 1 TO 2
20   PLAY "ML T10002C8A16P64A16P64A8B-8A8
G16P64"
30   PLAY "G16P64G4C16P64C16G16P64G16P64G
8P64G16A16G8F8P64F8.C16P64C16A8P64A8"
40   PLAY "B-8A8G8P64G4C16P64C16G16P64G16
P64G8P64G16A16G8F8P64F8."
50   NEXT X
60   END
```

Fig. 7-57. "Mockingbird."

but was made especially popular by the version sung by Carly Simon (and husband, James Taylor) in the early seventies. The program, like the song, is short, sweet and to the point.

The program runs entirely in legato mode. All Play lines are contained in a For-Next loop that causes the main verse to be output twice. The moderate tempo closely reflects the Carly Simon version; to produce this in its traditional form, switch to T150 or T175.

THE CAMPTOWN RACES

The program in Fig. 7-58 will play "The Camptown Races" by Stephen Foster. This is another song that I detest (no reflection on Mr. Foster), but my musical tastes are not necessarily yours.

The output from this program is treated in what I call a "rinky-dink" style, produced by using staccato mode programming through the entire piece. You can make it even more rinky-dink by speeding up the tempo with a T255 command. Alternately, you can remove some of the rinky-dink effect by running the song in music normal mode and leaving the tempo at the default setting (T120), as in the program shown. There are some sharps in this piece; make certain you do not omit a period after the numeric designators.

```
10   REM "THE CAMPTOWN RACES"
20   PLAY "MS T12002A8A8A8F#8A8B8A8F#8P8F
#8E4."
30   PLAY "F#8E4A8A8A8F#8A8B8A8F#8P8E4F#8
E8D4P8A8A8A8F#8A16"
40   PLAY "A16B8A8F#8P8F#8E4.F#8E4A8A8A8F
#8A8B8A8F#8P8"
50   PLAY "E4F#8E8D4.P8T150D8.D16.F#8A803
D4.P802B8.B16"
60   PLAY "03D802B8A4.F#16G16A8A8F#16F#16
A16A16B8A8F#4"
70   PLAY "E8F#16G16F#16E8E16D4."
80   END
```

Fig. 7-58. "The Camptown Races."

MISTY

Erroll Garner fans would never forgive me if I omitted the old standard "Misty," still performed almost everywhere. This is a haunting piece of beautiful music; the version in Fig. 7-59 gives a pleasing reproduction on the IBM Personal computer. This is a delicate composition. Perhaps my choice of a T100 tempo was an error; however, this produced the best effect, even though the tempo may be fast for some people or slow for others.

The main melody lines are in lines 30 through 80. Most of this section is output twice by the For-Next loop which contains it. The bridge is encountered in lines 100 through 120; then the main melody line is repeated one more time, from line 130 to line 150.

Music legato mode is used throughout this piece, although there are several changes to music normal mode in order to produce a series of identical notes. A good example of this switch is shown in line 50, where I converted to music normal in order to play the three eighth note Cs required. Following the playing of the last eighth note C, there is an octave change; I have then returned to legato mode programming. In other instances I used rest separators rather than switch from legato mode.

In many pieces there is a difference in sound produced in the output when P64 separators are used instead of music normal mode. In the latter mode each note is held for ⅞ths of its specified length. Using legato mode and P64 separators, the spaces between notes are much shorter; this gives a smoother overall effect, even though identical notes are definitely separated. In some instances switching to music normal for a few bars does not drastically alter the sound of the song, so I have elected to make such a switch in situations where this mode is usable. In other instances I create

```
10 REM "MISTY" BY ERROLL GARNER
20 FOR X=1 TO 2
30 PLAY"T100 ML O3C8O2A8E2.C8D8E-8O3D8P6
4D8P64D8P64D8C8O2A8F8D2."
40 PLAY"P8O1A16B-16O2F8A8"
50 PLAY"O3MN C8C8C8O2MLB-8O3C4.O2B-8A4B-
8O3C8O2F4G8A8"
60 PLAY"O2B-8D4P64D8E8F4G8"
70 IF X=2 THEN 100
80 PLAY"A1A2P4"
90 NEXT X
100 PLAY"MLF1P4O2F8G8A8O3C4D8E-4P64E-8P6
4E-8P64E-2E-4P64E-8"
110 PLAY"F8G-4F8E-8D4P64D8P64D8P64D2D4O2
F8G8B-8O3C4D8"
120 PLAY"O3E8P64E8P64E8D8E2E8P64E8P64E8D
8G4E8D8C1C2P4"
130 PLAY"O3C8O2A8E2.C8D8E-8O3D8P64D8P64D
8P64D8C8O2A8F8D2.P8O1A16B-16O2F8A8"
140 PLAY"O3C8P64C8P64C8P64O2B-8O3C4.O2B-
8A4B-8O3C8O2F4G8A8B-8D4P64D8E4"
150 PLAY"F8G8F2P2O3C4O2A4E2."
160 END
```

Fig. 7-59. "Misty."

spaces by inserting the short-duration rests. Admittedly, a professional musician will be quite critical of this practice, since it does throw off the timing slightly. The purpose of this book, however, is partly to provide ready-to-run musical programs that will be generally pleasing to the averge ear. In this respect I do not think the slight timing errors create any problems.

MOON RIVER

Andy Williams fans and those followers of Henry Mancini should both be satisfied with "Moon River", since Andy had a hit with it and Henry Mancini wrote it. This song has become a modern classic and is produced by the program in Fig. 7-60.

I chose a moderately slow tempo and kept the notes near the middle octave. You can decrease all octave commands by one and arrive at a bassy-sounding version, but I would not recommend increasing all notes by one octave, because the higher-pitched notes become quite annoying after the first few plays. As you can see by the ML command in line 20, this is another example of legato mode programming. This piece of music is especially easy to program in legato mode, because in no instance is there a back-to-back repetition of a note. Therefore the timing will be correct. Few musical pieces will be so easy to handle, however, in legato mode. If you decide to play this song an octave lower, your IBM Personal computer will sound very much like a clarinet (in the lower range). The lower-pitched outputs sound more mellow. The pleasing timbre is partially a product of the machine, but mostly can be attributed to the human ear. It is not possible to reproduce the same quality effect at higher frequencies.

NIGHT TRAIN

The next song was a challenge. "Night Train" is an old standard that was performed by the big bands and also became a popular song in striptease clubs. It is not a gentle song and is often performed with a lot of interior improvisation. The manuscript I had to work from was fair; the problems associated with producing some of the necessary effects on the computer were quite numerous.

At the beginning of the song there is a sustained whole note, followed by a half note at the same frequency, which is randomly slurred down to a low frequency. This is sometimes known as a "gliss". In an attempt to reproduce this, I programmed mostly in legato mode; the gliss was still a problem. The first gliss occurs near the beginning of line 20. You will see a whole note E (E1) followed by a P64 separator and a half note E. This latter note includes a gliss at its end. To simulate this on the machine I used an L32 command, which specifies the following notes to be played as 32nds. I then built in a descending chromatic scale, starting with F and trailing off to A. The same method is used

```
10 REM "MOON RIVER"
20 PLAY"MF ML T100 O2 G2.O3D4C2O2B4.A8G8
F8G2C4"
30 PLAY"B4.A8G8F8G2C4D2.D2E4C2.G4E4.D8C2
.G4E4.D8"
40 PLAY"C4E4G4O3C4O2B4.A8B4A4.G8A4A2G2.O
3D4C2O2B4.A8G8F8"
50 PLAY"G2C4B4.A8G8F8G2C4D2.D2E4C2.E2G4O
3C2.D2C4O2G2."
60 PLAY"G4B8A8G8F8G2.G8C8B8A8G8F8G2.C2.F
4D2D2E4C2.O3C2."
70 END
```

Fig. 7-60. "Moon River."

```
10 REM "NIGHT TRAIN"
20 PLAY"MF ML T170 O3E1P64E2L32E-FEDCO2B
B-AP8O3C8E8D8C8O2B-8G8F8E-8D8D1"
30 PLAY"O3E-1P64E-2L32FEDCO2BB-AGG-P8O3C
8E8D8C8O2B-8G8F8E-8D8D1"
40 PLAY"O3E-1P64E-2L32FEDCO2BB-AGG-P8O3C
8E8D8C8O2B-8G8F8E-8D8D1"
50 PLAY"P8O2G8O3MNC8.C16E-8.E-16C8.C16O2
A8.G16"
60 PLAY"O3C8.C16E-8.E16C8.C16O2A8.G16"
70 PLAY"O3C8MLC4.C2P64C4.P64C8C4P8"
80 PLAY"O2G8O3MN C8.C16E-8.E-16C8.C16O2A
8.G16"
90 PLAY"O3C8.C16E-8.E-16C8.C16O2A8.G16O3
C8MLC4.C2P64C4."
100 PLAY"P64C8C4P8O2G8O3MNC8.C16E-8.E-16
C8.C16O2A8.G16"
110 PLAY"O3C8.C16E-8.E-16C8.C16O2A8.G16O
3MNC8MLC4.C2"
120 PLAY"O3E1P64E2L32E-FEDCO2BB-AP8O3C8E
8D8C8O2B-8G8F8E-8D8D1"
130 PLAY"O3E-1P64E-2L32FEDCO2BB-AGG-P8O3
C8E8D8C8O2B-8G8F8E-8D8D1"
140 PLAY"O3E-1P64E-2L32FEDCO2BB-AGG-P8O3
C8E8D8C8O2B-8G8B-8B8O3MLC8C1."
```

Fig. 7-61. "Night Train."

near the beginning of line 30 and in line 40 to produce the same effect.

How does it sound? Not too bad. Anyone who listens will certainly identify the song, though I still am not satisfied with the gliss effect. The problem lies in the fact that in the actual performance, the gliss is randomly timed within a certain set of parameters. This might mean that the first three notes of the gliss string are held for slightly longer than the succeeding notes, according to musical interpretation. Moreover, when a true glissando is played (such as on a trombone), the trail-off involves frequencies which fall between established musical notes. For example, a middle F is a frequency of 698.460 Hertz and a middle E is 659.260 Hertz. Any value between these two frequencies is not considered to be a true musical note. But in the glissando, the frequency theoretically decreases linearly, which means you would have a series including 698.460 (F), 698.450, 698,440, and so forth to 659.260, which is middle E. These between-note frequencies could certainly be reproduced on the computer (using For-Next statements), but the speed control would be almost unattainable in this particular case. This program does give a reasonably good simulation of "Night Train".

RAINDROPS KEEP FALLIN' ON MY HEAD

The program in Fig. 7-62 plays the hit songs "Raindrops Keep Fallin' on My Head" from the movie *Butch Cassidy and the Sundance Kid.* A Burt Bacharach composition, this program switches between staccato mode and legato mode programming. The main melody line is played in staccato,

```
10 REM "RAINDROPS KEEP FALLIN' ON MY HEA
D" BY B. BACHARACH
20 FOR X=1 TO 2
30 PLAY"MF MS T160 O2 A4A8A8B-8A8G8F8A2.
P4O3C4C8C8D8C8O2B-8A8"
40 PLAY"O2A4B-4G4F4O3E2D8C8O2A8E8O3E2D2"

50 PLAY"O3C4C8O2A8B-8O3C8O2B-8A8O3C4C8O2
A8B-8O3C4.O2F4"
60 PLAY"O2P4F4F4G4
70 NEXT X
80 PLAY"MLA2.O3C4O2G2P4A4B-8A4G8G4F4A8G4
.A4B-4"
90 PLAY"O3D8C4.C4P8O2A8O3D8C4P64C8C4P8O2
A8"
100 PLAY"O3 E8D4C8C4O2A4F4P64F8A8A8G4G4"

110 PLAY"O2F8G8G2P4F8G8G2"
120 PLAY"MF MS T160 O2 A4A8A8B-8A8G8F8A2
.P4O3C4C8C8D8C8O2B-8A8"
130 PLAY"O2A4B-4G4F4O3E2D8C8O2A8E8O3E2D2
"
140 PLAY"O3C4C8O2A8B-8O3C8O2B-8A8O3C4C8O
2A8B-8O3C4.O2F4"
150 PLAY"ML O2 P4F4P64F4G4A1P4F8P64F8O3D
8C8O2F4A8G8F2."
```

Fig. 7-62. "Raindrops Keep Fallin' on My Head."

whereas the bridge is played mostly in legato. You will notice several P64 separators in bridge lines 80 through 110. Line 120 and most of those which follow are repeats of the first three lines. The final outro line (150) has another switch to legato mode programming, which is in effect for the remainder of the song.

While the staccato mode is useful, I feel the notes are still held for too long. Although not shown in this program, you can get a more pronounced staccato effect by changing all quarter notes in the staccato string to dotted eighth notes, followed by a P8 rest. Likewise, all original eighth notes can be changed to dotted sixteenths, with a P16 rest after each. If you follow this logical progression with all types of notes in this original program, you will obtain a much more pronounced staccato effect. If each note is too short, try switching to music normal mode using the same note conversion technique. You may find it necessary to increase the tempo when the dotted note conversion is used. If so, you probably will have to decrease the tempo should you switch to legato mode. It would be nice to see a future music command added to the Play statement such as MSS, for an abbreviated staccato play mode.

PUT ON A HAPPY FACE

From the popular musical, *Bye Bye Birdie*, the program in Fig. 7-63 will play "Put on a Happy Face". This is a very bright, cheerful number and is played at a rapid tempo (T200). The staccato programming mode is used along with a For-Next loop to play the opening lines twice. There is an early branch midway through the second playing of the opening verse. This causes the outro line (100) to be executed. This is a fairly short piece, but you can extend its play time by changing the maximum value of X in line 20 go 3, 4, or a larger value. The main melody line will be repeated the specified number of times. You will also have to change line 50 to let the value of X represent its maximum value in line 20.

You will see several switches to legato mode, which is used to hold notes for longer than one measure or to tie a note in one measure to an identical note in another. Make certain you note the appropriate mode changes. If you should accidentally insert a change to staccato mode, several of the notes which should be played separately will be run together at the output. If you notice this occurring, it is nearly certain that an MS command has been inadvertently omitted during the input phase of programming.

BASIN STREET BLUES

Undoubtedly, some readers won't recognize the name of this song, but "Basin Street Blues" has been around for a long time; even if you don't know the name, you will probably recognize the melody.

Figure 7-64 shows the program. Notice that in line 20, there is a two note intro which is played before the For-Next loop containing the main melody lines is entered. This latter melody is played twice before the bridge is entered in line 100.

The original version of this song was played at a much slower tempo than the computer version. One reason for this change is the particular arrangement I had, which was far more simplistic than the original version. This arrangement sounds better at a T150 tempo. Music normal mode is used throughout most of this program, but there are several changes to legato mode when the song requires such an effect. This song sounds good as is, but can accept many modifications to be adapted to your individual taste. There are many dotted eighths and quarters in this program. For some reason, many persons who input music programs will inadvertently omit a dot or two. This can create tragic but temporary consequences, as this piece depends heavily upon dotted notes for the Basin Street effect.

```
10 REM "PUT ON A HAPPY FACE"
20 FOR X=1 TO 2
30 PLAY"MS T200 O2C8D4F8A4O3C4D8MLD4.D2P
64MSD8C4O2B-8G4E4"
40 PLAY"D2.P4C8D4F8A4O3C4D8MLD4.D2P64MSD
8C4O2B-8G4E4"
50 IF X=2 THEN 100
60 PLAY"E-2.P4D8F4B-8O3D4D4C#4O2A8O3C4D8
C4P4"
70 PLAY"O2B4B-4O3C4O2A2.E-4P4D8F4B-8O3MS
D4D4C#4O2A8O3C4D8C4O2B4G4B4O3"
80 PLAY"MLC4C2.MSP4"
90 NEXT X
100 PLAY"O2MLE-2.F4O3D1P64D4C2F4C4O2B-2O
3C4O2A2O3D2E4D2O2A4O3C2D2F1F2"
110 END
```

Fig. 7-63. "Put on a Happy Face."

```
10 REM "BASIN STREET BLUES"
20 PLAY"MN T150 O2 G8.G16"
30 FOR X=1 TO 2
40 PLAY"MNT150 O2 E8.E16F4F#8G4.O3E4F4F#
8G4."
50 PLAY"O3C8.C16O2B-8.A16G8G4O1C8.C16O0B
-8.A16G8A4."
60 PLAY"O2G8O3C4O2G8O3C4O2G8G8O3C4C8MLD8
D2"
70 IF X=2 THEN 100
80 PLAY"MNC4O2B-8A8G8E8F8F#8G8G4.C4G4"
90 NEXT X
100 PLAY"MN O3C4O2B-8A8G4O3C8D8E-8D4.C2"

110 PLAY"O2E8E4MLE8E2P64MNE8E4MLE8E4.P64
MNE8E8B4MLE8E2MN"
120 PLAY"B8B4MLC8C4MNE4E8E4MLE8E2P64MNE8
G4MLE8E4MNG4"
130 PLAY"O3D8.D16C8.C16O2B8.B16A8.A16O3C
8.C16O2B8.B16A8.A16G4E8E4"
140 PLAY"MLE8MNE2B8B4MLG#8MNG#4E4E8B4MLA
8MNA2F8F4MLE8MNE4E4E8B4"
150 PLAY"MLA8MNA2P4E4G8E8D4C1"
160 END
```

Fig. 7-64. "Basin Street Blues."

BABY ELEPHANT WALK

John Wayne fans will like this song. No, the "Duke" was never noted for his singing ability, but this is a popular theme song from the movie "Hatari", in which John Wayne starred.

The program in Fig. 7-65 produces an especially pleasing output. This is one of those songs that is easily adapted to a computer run. The piece is bright, fairly fast, and includes many 8ths and 16ths.

The T150 tempo is a tradeoff: some portions of the song drag a trifle because of this speed; but because of the number of sixteenth notes, a more rapid tempo might create problems for human perception. There are also a few 32nd notes in this program, and their amazingly fast staccato runs can be well appreciated at T150 tempo.

The program run begins in staccato mode and switches among staccato, legato and music normal modes. This is the first program in this chapter which uses all three length modes in a single piece.

You may have already noticed that there is no exit line from the For-Next loop. I have taken my own advice and written a single song which is repeated three times. Lines 30 through 70 play the song through once. The For-Next loop established in lines 20 and 80 causes the melody to be repeated three times. I did this because I like the computer version and was not content to hear it played through only once. I could have accomplished the same thing by changing the End statement to a Goto branch back to the beginning of the program. Endless loops are often useful, but I like most of my programs to have a definite beginning and ending. The For-Next loop accomplishes this.

DOMINIQUE

"Dominique" was the hit song of the movie *The*

```
10 REM "BABY ELEPHANT WALK"
20 FOR X=1 TO 3
30 PLAY"T150 MS O2F8.A16O3C8F8MLA8MSG8F8
D8O2B8O3C8P4P2O2F8.A16O3C8F8"
40 PLAY"MLA8MNG8F8D8C2.D8O2MLA-8A-2.MSA-
8O3D8O2G32A-8F8P4P2"
50 PLAY"O2F8.A16O3C8F8MLA8MSG8F8D8O2B8O3
C8P4P4P8"
60 PLAY"MNO3C8G4G4D#32E8C8P8C8F4F4E-16F1
6E-16C16O2B8G#8B4B4"
70 PLAY"B-16B16O2B-16A-16F8C8E-8F8P2."
80 NEXT X
90 END
```

Fig. 7-65. "Baby Elephant Walk."

Singing Nun and is often heard today in instrumental versions. This song is very pleasing to the ear, and it reproduces nicely on the IBM Personal computer. The program is in Fig. 7-66.

The T200 tempo command will produce a tempo that is equivalent to the original version. I first chose staccato mode programming but later switched to music normal mode, as that produced a slightly better effect. This is another version of a program that repeats all music lines three times to match the three verses (in French) that accompany the song. For sing-a-long purposes the speed may be too rapid, so if that is the ultimate goal of your program, try T120 or T150.

JAVA

"Java," produced by Fig. 7-67, was another big instrumental hit for trumpeter Al Hirt. The main melody line is repeated in the For-Next loop at the beginning of the program and again following the bridge in lines 130 through 160. These latter lines are carbon copies of lines 30 through 60, with the exception of an outro command section at the end of line 160.

This program is run in staccato mode, though I was was not pleased with the duration of these shortened notes. You can experiment with this program by using the dotted note and additional rest method discussed earlier. The tempo is quite rapid, and can safely be increased to the maximum of T255. If you slow the tempo appreciably below T200, the song loses much of its bright effect.

MIDNIGHT COWBOY

From the movie of the same name, John Barry's "Midnight Cowboy" is a haunting piece of

```
10 REM "DOMINIQUE"
20 FOR X=1 TO 3
30 PLAY"T200 MN O2 G4G4O3C4.E8G4E4C4C4O2
B4O3C4C4."
40 PLAY"O2A8A4A4A2.O3C4C2.O2G4G2O3C2O2B1
.G4G4O3C4C4C4D4C2C4O2B4A4A4A4G4"
50 PLAY"F2E4F4G2E2D2D2C1P2"
60 NEXT X
70 END
```

Fig. 7-66. "Dominique."

```
10 REM "JAVA"
20 FOR X=1 TO 2
30 PLAY"MS T200 O2A8G#8A4F4D4C4D8F8D8C8D
4D8C8D4D8C8D4D8C8"
40 PLAY"D8F8D8C8D4A8G#8A4F4D4C4D8F8D8C8D
4D8C8D4D8C8D4D8C8"
45 PLAY"O2D8G8D8C8D4A8G#8A4F4D4C4D8F8D8C
8D4A8G8A-4F4D4C4"
50 PLAY"D8F8D8C8D4A8G#8A4F4D4C4O3D8O2D8O
3D8D8C4O2D8C8D4D8"
60 PLAY"C8D4D8C8D8F8D8C8F4"
70 NEXT X
80 PLAY"O2G8G#8F8F4F8F8F4F8D8D4D8D8D4D8F
8F4F8F8F4F8"
90 PLAY"O2D8D4D8D8D4D8G8G4G8G8G4G8C8C4C8
C8C4C8G8G4G8G8G4G8"
100 PLAY"O2C4C4C4"
130 PLAY"MS T200 O2A8G#8A4F4D4C4D8F8D8C8
D4D8C8D4D8C8D4D8C8"
140 PLAY"D8F8D8C8D4A8G#8A4F4D4C4D8F8D8C8
D4D8C8D4D8C8D4D8C8"
145 PLAY"O2D8G8D8C8D4A8G#8A4F4D4C4D8F8D8
C8D4A8G8A-4F4D4C4"
150 PLAY"D8F8D8C8D4A8G#8A4F4D4C4O3D8O2D8
O3D8D8C4O2D8C8D4D8"
160 PLAY"C8D4D8C8D8F8D8C8F4P4O3MSD4D4O2A
4A4D4D4A2D8D8D8D8C4C4F4"
```

Fig. 7-67. "Java."

music. The original version used many sorrowful harmonicas to bring out a nostalgic effect.

The computer version in Fig. 7-68 runs at a moderately slow tempo (T100) and switches equally between legato and normal length modes. There is straight-line programming all the way; most of line 80 is borrowed from the program information contained in line 20. It was necessary to delete the latter portion of this line in order to obtain a sustained ending, which is accomplished by playing the whole note G. The T100 tempo is about right, but you may wish to decrease the tempo. Because there is no vibrato (which cannot be produced by the IBM Personal computer), it is often necessary to play slower tunes at a slightly faster tempo to keep them from sounding droll. When a note is sustained for a relatively long period without vibrato, it begins to sound more like an electronic tone than a musical note.

THIS TRAIN

The best known old-time folk singer has to be Woody Guthrie. The program (Fig. 7-69) gives the computer version of one of his biggest hits, "This Train". Although I like Woody Guthrie, I'm not particularly pleased with the way his music reproduces on the computer. This version switches from normal to legato mode and includes many identical eighth notes toward the finish. These can be seen at the end of line 40, where ten successive eighth note

```
10 REM "MIDNIGHT COWBOY" BY JOHN BARRY
20 PLAY"ML T100 O3 D4C4O2B4G4B-4A4G4F4O3
D4C4O2B4G4B-4A4G4F4O3D4C4O2B4G4B-4A4G4"
30 PLAY"F4O3D4C4O2B4G4B-4A4G4F4"
40 PLAY"G2MNG8G8A8G8G4F8E8F2O2MLO3C2MNO3
C8C8C8C8C4D-8C8O2B4.G8"
50 PLAY"MLG2MNG8G8A8G8G4F8E8F2O3MLC2MNC8
C8C8C8C4D-8C8D2"
60 PLAY"O3 ML E2MNE8C8C8C8C2D2MLE-2MNE-8
C8C8C8C2O2B2MLG2MNG8"
70 PLAY"O2G8A8G8G4F8E8F2G2.P8F8G1G2.P8F8
G1"
80 PLAY"ML T100 O3 D4C4O2B4G4B-4A4G4F4O3
D4C4O2B4G4B-4A4G4F4G1"
```

Fig. 7-68. "Midnight Cowboy."

Gs are inserted. There is a quarter note G preceding this string, three quarter note Gs following it, and a half note G at the very end, thus a total of fifteen G notes in one string. Such a song must necessarily depend on the mastery of the artist in order to sound interesting. You will see a large number of eighth notes (mostly G) throughout this piece. The program run is only fair, but it is a good exercise for readers who might like to try exotic programming techniques.

JACKHAMMER BLUES

Another Woody Guthrie song, "Jackhammer Blues," is not too well known but is still popular among his followers. The same problems associated with the previous song apply equally here. Both arrangements were taken from the same musical manuscript collection; again there is a long series of eighth note Gs with occasional quarter or whole notes. As can be seen in Fig. 7-70, straight-line programming techniques are used throughout. It is important to point out that the music of this era and in this genre is extremely simple. Performers in those days often depended strongly on their personal styles to make a song popular, rather than the music itself. Certainly there are many who will argue with this statement, but one must remember that just because a piece of music is simple does not mean it is of poor quality.

```
10 REM "THIS TRAIN" BY WOODY GUTHRIE
20 PLAY "MN T200O2G4G2A4B4.G8E4D4G4MLG2.
G4P4P2"
30 PLAY"MN B4O3D2D4E4D8O2B4G4A4O3MLD2.D4
"
40 PLAY"P4P2MNO2B4O3D2D4E4E4D4O2B4G4G8G8
G8G8G8G8G8G8G8G8G4G4G4G2"
50 PLAY"A4B4.G8E4D4G4MLG2.G4"
60 END
```

Fig. 7-69. "This Train."

```
10 REM "JACKHAMMER BLUES" BY WOODY GUTHR
IE
20 PLAY"MN O2F8G8G8G8B8B8O3C8C8C8O2G8G8G
8B-8G8G8C8F4.E8"
30 PLAY"C1P2F8G8G8G8B4B8B8B8G8O3C8O2B8"
40 PLAY"G8F8E-8C8F4.E8C1P2P4F8G8"
50 PLAY"A8G8A8G8A8F8F8G8G8F8E8C8F4.E8C1"

60 PLAY"P2.P8F8G8.F16G8G8G8.F16G8G8G8L8D
D2F8E8"
70 PLAY"F8.G16G8D8F4.E-8C2P4L8B-BO3C4.O2
B-8G8C4."
80 PLAY"A4.F8G4.E8F8.G16G8D8F4.E-8C2."
90 END
```

Fig. 7-70. "Jackhammer Blues."

DEEP PURPLE

The old standard "Deep Purple", written by Peter De Rose, has special meaning to me since this is the first solo piece I ever performed in public (when I was a high school musician). The computer version (Fig. 7-71) runs entirely in legato mode, so you will see an occasional P64 spacer. I chose to use the default tempo (T120), which is why a tempo command is not used in any of the Play statement lines. This is somewhat faster than most versions, but I think it is necessary to get the best rendering on the computer. This is another example of a program which uses a For-Next loop to play the main melody portion, exiting the loop at the proper point to produce the outro.

SUNDAY MORNIN' COMIN' DOWN

This is another Kristofferson composition. Both he and Ray Stevens performed different versions of this song, and both enjoyed moderate success. Straight-line programming is used throughout; the Tempo is increased to T160 to make the

```
10 REM "DEEP PURPLE" BY PETER DE ROSE
20 FOR X=1 TO 2
30 PLAY"ML O2C4D4O3C2O2C4D4E-2C4C#4D4G4B
-4O3D4C2O2G#4A4O3G4"
40 PLAY"F4C4O2A4G4G#4A4O3D4O2D1D4D8P8C#4
D4O3C2O2B4B-4A4A-4G2"
50 IF X=2 THEN 80
60 PLAY"P64G2F#4F4E4E-4D2P64D2D-4C4O2G2G
#4O3D4O2A1.P4"
70 NEXT X
80 PLAY"O2P64G2G-4F4O3E4E-4D2P64D2D-4C4G
2G#4A4F1"
90 END
```

Fig. 7-71. "Deep Purple."

song more interesting. The run begins in music normal mode, then switches to legato at the beginning of line 40 to sustain a B flat for a measure and three-quarters. There is a return to music normal for most of the rest of the song. Many of Kristofferson's songs do not play well on the computer. Many of the kinks have been ironed out of this one, however, so the run is fairly successful. The program is shown in Fig. 7-72.

AVE MARIA

One of the most beautiful pieces of religious music is Schubert's "Ave Maria". A few problems are associated with committing this to the computer, since the song has a fairly large number of sustained notes played at very slow tempo. Figure 7-73 shows the program. Note that a T70 command specifies the tempo at a very slow adagio. I worked with this program for quite some time, dotting a few quarter notes and inserting a few rests, and arrived at a highly acceptable version that will run nicely on your IBM Personal computer. Naturally, this piece is played in legato mode to effect the smooth note changes necessary with a delicate song such as this.

The manuscript I used to help write this program did not include any grace notes, which are quite important for the performance of this piece. You will see these added in line 60 as 32nd notes. This simple chain adds significantly to the piece. Grace notes are especially pleasing on this computer, because they are played delicately as well as with great speed. I am presenting this program with the T70 tempo. I tried several faster tempos and was not satisfied. I am still unsure about this issue, so I'll leave it up to the reader to choose an appropriate speed.

A TIME FOR US

From the movie *Romeo and Juliet,* "A Time For Us" (Fig. 7-74) by Nino Rota has established itself as a modern classic. This is another song that must be output at a very slow speed. A T80 tempo command is used, which places the speed musically in the lower andante range. Legato programming is used throughout along with the necessary P64 separators, although there are only a few of these.

```
10 REM "SUNDAY MORNIN' COMIN' DOWN" BY K
RIS KRISTOFFERSON
20 PLAY"MN T16001B-8B-802B-8B-8B-8B-8A-8
G8F8G8A-8.A-16A-8A-8G8F8E-8F8"
30 PLAY"G1P2.01B-8B-802B-8B-8B-8G8A-8G8G
8F8E-8.C16E-8F8G8E-8D8.C16"
40 PLAY"01 MLB-1B-2.P8MN02G16A-16B-8B-8B
-8B-803C802B-8G8E-803C8.C16C8D8E-802A-40
3C1602B-8"
50 PLAY"B-1P2.G8G8A-8A-8A-8A-8G8F8F8G8A-
8A-8A-4G8G16F16F8.E-16E-1"
60 PLAY"P4G8B-803E-8E-8E-8D8D4C2.P4E-8E-
8D8.02A-1603C8C802B-1"
70 PLAY"P4G8A-8B-8B-8A-8G8G4F2.P4A-8A-8G
8F8E-8.F16G1"
80 PLAY"P4G8B-803E-8E-8E-8D8D4C2P4E-8E-8
D8D8C8C802MLB-1B-4"
90 PLAY"MNG8A-8B-8B-8A-8G8G4F2.P4A-8A-8G
8F4E-16D16MLE-1E-1"
```

Fig. 7-72. "Sunday Mornin' Comin' Down."

```
10 REM "AVE MARIA" BY FRANZ SCHUBERT
20 PLAY"MF ML T70 O2 F2.F4.E4F8A2.A4.G4.
F2.F2.G4.G8A8G8F4E8"
30 PLAY"O2D4E8F2.F4.A4.P64A4.A8G8F8E4D8A
4B8"
40 PLAY"A2.G#4.E4.G4.G4F8E8G8A8B-8G8E8F2
.F4."
50 PLAY"A4G8G4.G4E8D8F#8A8O3C8O2A8F#8"
60 PLAY"O2G2.P8D8E8F8A32F32E8D8C2.C4.P64
C4.G4.G4P64G8P64G4F#8"
70 PLAY"G4A8G4A8F4.F4.P64F4.G4.G4P64G8P6
4G8F#8G8B-8A8G8F2."
80 PLAY"F4.P64F4.G4.G4P64G8A4P64A8P64A8G
8A8O3C4.O2B-4.B-4.D4.A4.G4.F8E8"
90 PLAY"O2F8A-8G8F8G2.G2.F2.F4.E4F8A2.A4
.G4.F2.F2.P64F4.P64F8A8O3C8F2."
100 END
```

Fig. 7-73. "Ave Maria."

This is a beautiful piece of music which plays moderately well on the IBM Personal computer, although one sometimes loses touch with the music during some of the longer sustained portions. The computer is best suited to faster tempos and to those pieces which do not contain a large number of sustained note sections.

AMAZING GRACE

The religious song "Amazing Grace" became a popular hit in the late sixties when it was sung by Judy Collins acappella, which means "without accompaniment", or without any instrumental backup.

The program (Fig. 7-75) outputs this piece at a moderate tempo of 100 beats per minute (T100). The main melody line is committed to a For-Next loop which is exited on the third cycle in order to play the outro line. All of the information found within the For-Next loop could have been commit-

```
10 REM "A TIME FOR US" BY NINO ROTA
20 PLAY"ML T80O2A8O3C8O2B8E4.P64E8G8E8A4
.P64A8G8F8G4.P64G8F8E8D4.E16D16C8D8E4.A8
O3C8O2B8E4.P64E8G8E8A2A8P64A8O3D2."
30 PLAY"O2B2B8E8O3C4.O2B8A8G8O3C8O2B8A4G
4A2P8O3C8"
40 PLAY"O3E2E8C8D2D8E8F2F8D8E2E8C8D2D8O2
B-8O3C2C8O2A8B2B8G8A4.P64A8O3C8O2B8"
50 PLAY"ML O2E4.P64E8G8E8A4.P64A8G8F8G4.
P64G8F8E8D4.E16D16C8D8E4.A8O3C8O2B8E4.P6
4E8G8E8A2A8P64A8O3D2."
60 PLAY"O2B2B8E8O3C4.O2B8A8G8O3C8O2B8A4G
4A2."
```

Fig. 7-74. "A Time For Us."

```
10 REM "AMAZING GRACE"
20 FOR X=1 TO 3
30 PLAY"T100 MLO2D4G2B8G8B2A4G2E4D2P64D4
G2B8G8B2A4O3D2D4P4O2B4O3D4.O2B8O3D8"
40 IF X=3 THEN 70
50 PLAY"O2B8G2D4E4.G8P64G8E8D2P64D4G2B8G
8B2A4G1P4"
60 NEXT X
70 PLAY"O2B8G2D4E4.G8P64G8E8D2P64D4G2B8G
8B2A4G1G1"
```

Fig. 7-75. "Amazing Grace."

ted to a single Play statement line, but then it would not have been possible to insert the If-Then line at the appropriate point.

SHENANDOAH

Since I live in the Shenandoah Valley, it is only appropriate that I include a local song that has reached national prominence. "Shenandoah" is another slow number which is output from the computer at the rate of 80 beats per minute. The T80 tempo command can be seen in line 30 of the program displayed in Fig. 7-76. The For-Next loop plays all of its information twice. When the loop is exited, a whole note F is played as the finale in line 60. The tempo closely reflects the speed of the original version, but the output sounds much better when increased to the default tempo of 120 beats per minute.

CHIM CHIM CHER-EE

We pick up the tempo with another hit from the movie *Mary Poppins*. "Chim Chim Cher-ee" is output at a tempo of 200 beats per minute and is run entirely in staccato mode to achieve a very bright effect. All notes are found near the middle octave. You will see a pattern of identical eighth notes in several different portions of the program in Fig. 7-77.

There are several verses to this song, but the program plays through only once before execution is terminated. You can use For-Next statements surrounding these program lines to have the computer output the music for many verses.

CAST YOUR FATE TO THE WIND

Figure 7-78 produces a very popular hit of the mid-sixties, "Cast Your Fate To The Wind". Unfor-

```
10 REM "SHENANDOAH"
20 FOR X=1 TO 2
30 PLAY"MNT80O2CF8F8F4.G8A8B-8O3D8C4.F8E
8D4.C8D8C8O2A8O3C4.C4"
40 PLAY"D8D8D4.O2A8O3C8O2A8G8F4.G4A4.F8A
8O3D8C2.O2F8G8A4.F8G4MLF2"
50 NEXT
60 PLAY"F1"
70 END
```

Fig. 7-76. "Shenandoah."

```
10 REM "CHIM CHIM CHER-EE"
20 PLAY"MS T200 O2D4A8A8A4A4A8A8A4A4B-4.
A8G2G4"
30 PLAY"G4A4G4F8G4.F4E8D#4.E4A2."
40 PLAY"D4A8A8A4A4A8A8A4A4B-4.A8G2G4"
50 PLAY"G4A4G4F2G8F8E4F4.E8D4P4O3D4D4C4O
2B-4O3D2O2A4O3C#4D4E4D1"
60 END
```

Fig. 7-77. "Chim Chim Cher-ee."

tunately, one very rarely hears this song anymore. It's a beautiful piece which was originally performed as a piano instrumental.

Straight-line programming is used all the way; because of the legato mode, you will see an occasional P64 separator. The song is played very slowly (80 beats per minute), but there are enough eighth notes to make the song run very well at this relatively slow speed.

DIDN'T WE

Probably the hottest composer of the late sixties and early seventies was a man named Jimmy Webb. His hits include "Up Up and Away", "Wichita Lineman" and "MacArthur's Park". Figure 7-79 outputs another Webb hit, "Didn't We." A moderate tempo is used along with an overall legato effect, although there are several excursions into the music normal realm. A For-Next loop is used to play the main melody lines and to exit to the outro lines, which begin at line 110. The original version was played slightly slower than the tempo used here. This song runs very well on the computer.

CLOSE TO YOU

One of the most precise modern singing groups to appear in the sixties was the Carpenters, a brother-sister team of Karen and Richard Carpenter along with several other excellent musicians. One of their biggest hits is played by the program in Fig. 7-80, "Close to You." I originally used the default tempo but later lowered it slightly

```
10 REM "CAST YOUR FATE TO THE WIND"
20 PLAY"ML O2 E8O3E4C8O2G8G4P8O1A8O2A4F8
C8C4P8E8"
30 PLAY"O3E4C8O2G8P64G4B-8F8D2."
40 PLAY"P8E8O3E4C8O2G8G4O1A8P64A8O2A4F8C
8"
50 PLAY"C8O1A8O2C8F8D4F8D8D4E8G8F2D8P64D
4."
60 PLAY"G2D8P64D4.F2D8P64D4.G2D8P64D4E8O
3E4C8O2G8G4P8O1A8O2A4"
70 PLAY"F8C8C4P8E8O3E4C8O2G8P64G4B-8F8D2
.P8E8O3E4C8O2G8G4P8O1A8O2A4F8C8C8"
80 PLAY"O1A8O2C8F8D4F8D8E8P64E8G8E8F2."
90 END
```

Fig. 7-78. "Cast Your Fate To The Wind."

```
10   REM "DIDN'T WE" (BY JIMMY WEBB)
20   FOR X = 1 TO 2
30   PLAY "MF ML T100 O3P4L4CO2AFMNE4E4E4
.E8MLE8F8G2."
40   PLAY "O2F8G8A4P64A2P4O3C4O2A4.G8"
50   PLAY "O2MNF4.F8F4.F8MLF8G8A2.G8A8B4P
64B2P1"
60   PLAY "O3MNP4C4C4.C8C4.C8C8MLO2B4."
70   IF X = 2 THEN 110
80   PLAY "O3C8O2B8O3C8D8"
90   PLAY "O3E2E2C4D4MNE4E4E2MLF4E4C4.P64
C8D1"
100   NEXT X
110   PLAY "O3MLC4D4E2E1P4C4P64C4.O2B8"
120   PLAY "O3MNC4C4MLC4D4G2E4O2G4A4O3C2.
"
130   PLAY "O3MLD8E8MNF4F4F4MLF4D2P64D4C1
C2."
140   END
```

Fig. 7-79. "Didn't We."

to 110 beats per minute. The note commands use many dotted eighths. It is extremely important to include each one, to obtain a program output as precise as the original version. The Carpenters were noted for their excellent harmony, but of course, we cannot accomplish this with the computer alone.

SOMETHING

Unlike most of the original hits by the Beatles, "Something", produced by Fig. 7-81, was written by George Harrison rather than Lennon and McCartney. I went to extra lengths to demonstrate the method of exiting a For-Next loop with a Gosub statement, and returning at the appropriate time to perform the final verse at the end of the bridge. Previous programs which involve songs in a two-verse, bridge, third-verse format have committed the first two verses to a For-Next loop. The bridge strains and the final verse are in straight-line programming form.

In this program the For-Next loop cycles three times. The main melody line is exited near the end of the second playing, where the bridge is performed. As soon as the bridge has been completed, the Return statement in line 180 branches back to line 100, where the loop cycles for the third and final time. Writing this type of program usually involves more of the programmer's time than when the former method is used. Inputing this finished program to your machine will take slightly less time than if it were written using the previous format.

The song is played in music legato at a fairly slow tempo of 100 beats per minute (T100). Two detection statement lines are used in program lines 90 and 100. During the second cycle of the loop, line 90 causes the bridge branch with a Gosub statement. This branch to line 120 plays the outro of the second verse. Another For-Next loop contains the repeated bridge lines in program lines 140 and 150. When this loop times out, the bridge outro occurs in program line 170. The Return statement in line 180 causes the loop to cycle for the third time. Line 100 detects the third cycle and causes the final outro note to be played. The second statement on this line terminates the program run.

```
10   REM "CLOSE TO YOU"
20   PLAY "MF ML T110 O2C4E-4"
30   FOR X = 1 TO 2
40   PLAY "O2MLB-2P64B-8.A-16B-8.O3C16O2G
2.P64G8B-8"
50   PLAY "O3D2.O2G8B-8O3E-2.P4"
60   PLAY "O2C8E-4.B-2C8E-4O3C8O2B-2"
70   IF X = 2 THEN 100
80   PLAY "O2C8E-4.B-2B-2C4E-4"
90   NEXT X
100   PLAY "O2C8E-4.B-2B-1"
110   PLAY "MNO2E-8.E-16F8.F16G8.G16F8.F1
6E-8.E-16F8.F16G8.G16"
120   PLAY "O2F8.F16B-8.B-16O3C8.C16D8.D1
6C8.O2B-16O3D2."
130   PLAY "O3MNC8.D16E-8.E-16E-8.E-16E-8
.E-16E-8.E-16"
140   PLAY "O3MNE-8.E-16E-8.E-16E-8.E-16D
8.E-16F1"
150   PLAY "O2P2C4E-4"
160   PLAY "O2MLB-2P64B-8.A-16B-8.O3C16O2
G2.P64G8B-8"
170   PLAY "O3D2.O2G8B-8O3E-2.P4"
180   PLAY "O2C8E-4.B-2C8E-4O3C8O2B-2"
190   PLAY "O2MLC8E-4.B-2B-2"
200   END
```

Fig. 7-80. "Close to You."

There is nothing unusual about exiting a loop with a Gosub statement and then returning at a point further along in the execution. However, while many modern songs repeat the main melody verse two, three, four or more times, each repeat may be slightly different. This is the reason for the additional play lines which lie outside of the loop, or are coupled at the end of If-Then statements to be played at a certain preset time. In music programming this can take more time to write the original-program, but the result usually involves fewer lines than are encountered in straight-line programming of the final verse following the loop exit and the playing of the bridge.

BUTTERFLY TIME

"Butterfly Time" is a beautiful piano exercise that involves mostly sixteenth notes. The musical strains are supposed to aurally emulate the flitting patterns of a butterfly in flight. This can be a fairly difficult piece for beginning pianists, but is a simple program on the IBM Personal computer.

I originally wrote this program with a much faster tempo, but the speed was too much for a listener to fully appreciate the intricacies. There are several grace notes in the program, so a slower tempo allows each to be fully recognized. This program is written in the straight-line format as shown in Fig. 7-82. Because of the nature of this piece, the establishment of For-Next loops was neither mandatory nor desirable to arrive at the most efficient program. You may try running this song in staccato or normal mode. However, the up-down bars are a little more enjoyable when using the legato mode.

The piece programs very well in this mode, and it is not necessary to constantly use P64 separators or to switch between legato and normal mode.

BUGLE CALL

The program shown in Fig. 7-83 is treated in a different manner from previous programs. The For-Next loop plays the entire sequence through twice, but the octave command is assigned to the variable X (line 40). During the first cycle of the loop, the output is in octave 2. This is established in line 20 by assigning the value of 2 to the variable X. However, line 50 is encountered just before the loop repeats itself for the second and final time. Here the variable is reassigned, having been given a value of 3. During the second playing the output will be an octave higher than the first.

This bugle call is programmed in staccato mode with a rapid beat of 120. Previous programs have used the default tempo, which was considered to be a moderate speed. Because of the presence of many eighth notes (as opposed to quarters, halfs and wholes), this piece moves at a very rapid pace. This may be confusing unless you remember that music tempo and detected tempo are often different; it depends on how many notes are in a single measure. At T120 tempo, a measure consisting of four quarter-notes would "sound" (to the listener) twice as slow as a measure consisting of four eighth notes and a two-beat rest. In the latter

```
10  REM "SOMETHING" (BY GEORGE HARRISON)

20  FOR X = 1 TO 3
30  PLAY "MF ML T100 O2B-8P64B-8P64B-8P6
4B-8P64B-4P64B-4A1P8"
40  PLAY "O2A-8P64A-8P64A-8P64A-8B-8O3C8
O2B-8P64B-8G8G4P2"
50  PLAY "O3C8P64C8P64C8P64C8O2B-4O3C4O2
A8F8F4P4P8.F16"
60  PLAY "O2G16B-16G16O3C16C16O2G16B-8B-
8.P4"
70  PLAY "O2G16O3D16C16O2B-16O3C16C16D16
O2B-16G16G4P4"
80  PLAY "O2F8G8B-8G8A-4A4"
90  IF X = 2 THEN GOSUB 120
100  IF X = 3 THEN PLAY "O2B-1":END
110  NEXT X
120  PLAY "O2B1"
130  FOR Y = 1 TO 2
140  PLAY "T180O2F4P8B8P64B4P64B4P64B4P6
4B8O3D8E2O2B1B2O3D8E4."
150  PLAY "O3F64E2C4F4F2.E4D1D1"
160  NEXT Y
170  PLAY "T50"
180  RETURN
190  END
```

Fig. 7-81. "Something."

```
10  REM "BUTTERFLY TIME"
20  PLAY "MF ML T120 O2P16L16CDCP16CDCP1
6CDCA4L16P16O3CDCP16CDC"
30  PLAY "O3P16CDCA4P16CDCGEDCP16CDCAFDC
P16CDCP16CDCP16CDCO4C4."
40  PLAY "O2P16CDCP16CDCP16CDCA4P16O3CDC
P16CDCP16CDCA4"
50  PLAY "O4P16FGFP16DEDP16CDCP16O2ABAP1
6FGFP16DEDP16"
60  PLAY "O3CDCP16O2AB-AP16FGFP16DEDP16C
DCA4"
70  PLAY "O2P16CDCO3C4P16O2FGFO3F4."
80  PLAY "O1P16AB-AP16AB-AP16AB-AO2F4P16
AB-AP16AB-AP16AB-AO3F4"
90  PLAY "O2P16AB-AO3EC#O2B-AP16AB-AO3FD
O2B-A"
100  PLAY "O2P16AB-AP16AB-AP16AB-AO3A4"
110  PLAY "O1P16AB-AP16AB-AP16AB-AO2F4P1
6AB-AP16AB-AP16AB-AO3F4"
120  PLAY "O3P16DEDP16O2B-O3CO2B-P16O3CD
CP16O2AB-A"
130  PLAY "O3P16CDCP16CDCP16CDCO4C2."
140  END
```

Fig. 7-82. "Butterfly Time."

example the four notes would be played in half a measure, whereas in the former the four would span the entire measure. Both are played in the same musical tempo, but tempo relates more to musical timing than it does to actual speed. The latter depends on the timing allotted to each individual note.

TAPS

Figure 7-84 reproduces the most recognizable bugle call, "Taps". This is run in legato mode at an extremely slow tempo of T50. This program will faithfully reproduce the lulling sounds of sleep often associated with military barracks. If you are an

```
10 REM BUGLE CALL
20 X=2
30 FOR I=1 TO 2
40 PLAY"MF MS T120 O=X;C8C24C24C24C8C8E4
C8E8G8G24G24G24G8E8G8E8C4C8C24C24C24C8C8
E4C8E8G8G24G24G24G8E8C4P4"
50 X=3
60 NEXT I
```

Fig. 7-83. "Bugle Call."

```
10 REM "TAPS"
20 PLAY"MF ML T50 O2G8.P64G16O3C2.O2G8.O
3C16E2.O2G8O3C8E4"
30 PLAY"O2G8O3C8E4O2G8O3C8E2.C8.E16G2E4C
4O2G2.P64G8.P64G16O3C2."
40 END
```

Fig. 7-84. "Taps."

ex-serviceman, this program may be handy in allowing you to drift off at the end of the day.

REVEILLE

In the same vein, the program in Fig. 7-85 might be used to wake you up in the morning. This program plays the rapid strains of "Reveille," which is associated with the universal wakeup call of all United States servicemen. This call is run in staccato mode, although there are occasional switches to legato in order to effectively execute the needed slurs. There are many eighth notes and a fair number of sixteenths in this piece, so when run at the T180 tempo it is bound to cause startling effects. This program uses two For-Next loops. One begins in line 30, the other in line 90. Lines 50 and 110 exit the loops at the appropriate times.

In an earlier chapter a program was discussed which simulated a ticking alarm clock. It also caused the monitor to display the time digitally and allowed for the input of an alarm trigger time. When this time is reached, a whooper siren goes off as a wakeup call. To give this program a military flair, you can simply substitute the "Reveille" program for the whooper sound effect line in the alarm clock program. The program will run as before, but when the alarm time is reached, instead of a whoop you will be awakened to the strains of "Reveille". If this

```
10 REM "REVEILLE"
20 PLAY"MF MS T180 O2G8"
30 FOR X=1 TO 3
40 PLAY"O3C8MLE16MSC16O2G8"
50 IF X=3 THEN 80
60 PLAY"O3E8"
70 NEXT
80 PLAY"O3C8MLE4MSC8O2G8"
90 FOR X=1 TO 3
100 PLAY"O3C8MLE16MSC16O2G8"
110 IF X=3 THEN 140
120 PLAY"O3E8"
130 NEXT
140 PLAY"O2G8O3C4."
150 PLAY"O3MSL8EEEEEMLG4MSE8C8L8ECECMLE4
MSC8"
160 PLAY"L8EEEEEMLG4MSE8C8L8ECO2GGO3C4."

170 END
```

Fig. 7-85. "Reveille."

is too startling a way to start your day, you can substitute any of the other music programs in this chapter.

SONG OF THE BRIDESMAIDS

The program in Fig. 7-86 is obscure; one of my music teachers gave me his personally written manuscript for this song to be played at a recital when I was young. It moves quickly and is fairly difficult for beginning music students. It is shown here in program form because the song is very interesting when output by the IBM Personal computer. I originally began to program this piece using a For-Next loop, but the subtle differences in the main melody lines turned out to be too much, so I elected to program line-by-line with no branch statements. The speed is a little faster than was intended by the manuscript. The piece still sounds good at slower tempos, but at this speed the complexities of the song are enhanced. All notes are held to the second or third octave, so the range is not too large. This song is composed mostly of eighth notes, so it may remind one of Johann Sebastian Bach.

PIANO CONCERTO #1

No book of musical programs would be complete without one of the many compositions of Peter Ilich Tschaikovsky. Figure 7-87 is a program for his "Piano Concerto #1", which is lesser known than some of his other compositions but is a favorite of mine. Run in legato mode at T130 tempo, the program reproduces very well on the computer. Notice that when programming older forms of music, one doesn't see many For-Next loops in my programs. Repetition of a main melody line is more a product of modern music. The older forms may almost repeat a melody line, but there are significant differences in the second playing. This causes real headaches when using loops.

This program is written in straight-line form; the speed is similar to that which is appropriate for the original version. You will see an occasional P64 separator command, but not as many as might be the case with more modern songs. Another characteristic of the older forms of music is a lack of repetition of the same note through several bars. This may be related to the fact that many types of older music were instrumentally performed, whereas much modern music is concentrated on the vocals.

THE RIDDLE SONG

"The Riddle Song", produced by the program in Fig. 7-88, has been popular for a long time; recently you may have heard these strains sung by a guitar player in the movie *Animal House.* You didn't

```
10  REM "SONG OF THE BRIDESMAIDS"
20  PLAY "MF ML T165 O2G4O3C8O2B8O3C8D8E
4O2G4"
30  PLAY "O3C8O2B8O3C8D8E4P64E4D4.E8D8C8
O2B8A8G8F8E2"
40  PLAY "G4O3C8O2B8O3C8D8E4O2G4O3C8O2B8
O3C8D8E4P64E4"
50  PLAY "O3D4.E8D8C8O2B8A8G4B8A8G4P4O3C
2E2G2E2"
60  PLAY "O3D8C8O2B8O3C8D4E4C1D8O2G8P64G
4O3D8O2G8P64G4"
70  PLAY "O3C8D8E2.G4F8E8D8C8O2B8A8G8F8E
2O3G8E8F64E8C8F64"
80  PLAY "O3C8O2G8P64G4O3E8D8C2."
90  END
```

Fig. 7-86. "Song of the Bridesmaids."

```
10   REM "PIANO CONCERTO #1"
20   PLAY "MF ML T130 O3G4.D4A8G2.C8O2B8A
8O3D4P64D8"
30   PLAY "O2G2.P64G8A8O3C8D4P64D8C8D8E8F
4P64F8"
40   PLAY "O3E8F8G8A-4P64A-8"
50   PLAY "O2A-4.A-4G8O3G4.D4A8G2."
60   PLAY "O3C8O2B8A8O3D4P64D8O2G2."
70   PLAY "O2P64G8A8O3C8D4P64D8"
80   PLAY "O3C8D8E8F4P64F8"
90   PLAY "O3E8F8G8A8O4C8O3B8P64B2.B4.B4P
8"
100   PLAY "O2G4.D4G8P64G2.O1E-8G8B-8"
110   PLAY "O2G4.D4G8P64G8O3G8E8C8O2G8E8"

120   PLAY "O2C8G8E8C8O1G8E8C4P8.O3C8P4O2
C2"
130   END
```

Fig. 7-87. "Piano Concerto #1."

hear much of this song, because the late John Belushi promptly removed the guitar from the musician and smashed it into the wall.

A For-Next loop is used in order to play the song completely through three times to perform the three verses with which I am familiar. This program runs mostly in legato mode, although there are many switches to music normal in order to properly space repeated identical notes. I chose a tempo at random, since performance tempos have bridged the gap between very slow and very fast. The T130 command produces a medium tempo with this song.

LONESOME ROAD

"Lonesome Road" was a hit many decades ago; I believe it was popular in its revised form in the late fifties or early sixties. Shown in Fig. 7-89, this

```
10   REM "THE RIDDLE SONG"
20   FOR X = 1 TO 3
30   PLAY "MF MN T130 O2C4C4.C8C4MLC4D4F2
G4F2D2C2.F4"
40   PLAY "MNO2G4.G8G4MLG4A4O3C2D4C2O2A2G
2.P64"
50   PLAY "MNO2G4G4.G8G4MLG4A4O3C2D4C2O2A
2G2."
60   PLAY "O2A4MNC4.C8C4MLC4D4F2G4F2D2F2.
"
70   NEXT X
80   END
```

Fig. 7-88. "The Riddle Song."

```
10  REM "LONESOME ROAD"
20  PLAY "MF ML T100 O2E4G2.A4E4C2P64C4"

30  PLAY "O2F2.P64F4P64F4A-2P64A-4G2.E4"

40  PLAY "O2D2.E4C1C2P4E4G2.A4E4C2P64"
50  PLAY "O2C4F2.P64F4P64F4A-2P64A-4G2.E
4D2.E4C1C2."
60  END
```

Fig. 7-89. "Lonesome Road."

program produces a melancholy strain in legato mode at a medium-slow speed (T100). There is nothing unusual about this program, and it closely matches the programming style of many others in this chapter. Each program produces a unique and usually interesting audio output. The real challenge comes when you go back through the Play statement lines and make modifications, so that the result can be honestly classified as your own arrangement.

I have alluded to the fact that you can take any piece of music and program it directly on the IBM Personal computer. However, the programs shown in this chapter all have a touch of myself in them. This involves the pure programming on a theoretical level and the arranging of the music as well. When writing a program from a musical manuscript, I find myself constantly making changes to the input information, which causes the output to be a bit different from a performance which sticks strictly with the manuscript notes. Some manuscripts are excellent and require little or no changes, but others are simply horrible, having oversimplified a very beautiful piece. In the latter instances, you can use the manuscript solely as a basic guide and then make the appropriate embellishments when you feel they are warranted. If you fail the first couple of times, so what? It's not like you're performing your music at Carnegie Hall.

The IBM Personal computer can be a great aid to serious musicians who will take the time to learn the simple programming steps that will allow them to input any piece of music. To beginning or amateur musicians, programming music on the IBM Personal computer is an education in computer programming and also in music itself. Again, music is a mathematical language, and if you intend to pursue a serious musical career, the computer can aid you in firmly establishing the mathematical relationship (both in frequency and time) of one note with all of the others in a given piece. Music, then, complements the computer world. This is fair exchange, because the computer also complements the music world.

Talking Programs...

Chapter 8

You should think of the speech output of a synthesizer as just another means for the computer to convey information to the human operator. The speech synthesizer is no different from a printer, a monitor screen, or even the tone generator within the IBM Personal computer. Each of the music programs which have been presented allowed the computer to communicate or convey information to human beings by means of an audio output. If you program a whole note A on the keyboard, the computer will communicate this input to you by outputing the musical note A for the equivalent of a whole measure. Certainly human extrapolation is necessary to equate the output frequency with the note A, with its mathematical length in musical manuscript or with the command which originally causes the output.

Another type of extrapolation is necessary when a word is printed on the monitor screen or in hard copy form on the IBM printer. Our human eyes must visualize each character and compare it with the data stored in our massive memory banks. The brain does most of the extrapolation subconsciously. With a musical audio output, the various forms of extrapolation are handled on a conscious level at first, but eventually a portion of this work may be consigned to the subconscious.

When someone speaks to us, the same type of subconscious extrapolation takes place as was the case with printed words. Our audible senses feed the information to the brain, and through repetition the subconscious extrapolation process occurs very quickly. However, if someone speaks a word that is not repeated constantly or that you have never heard before, your thinking processes immediately go into overdrive, mostly in the conscious mode. You will search your memory banks for the meaning of the word; or if you've never heard it before, for a familiar word whose meaning is known to you. After a new word is heard many times, the subconscious takes over and you don't have to consciously search for a meaning. While scientists are still bickering over exactly what the differences are between the conscious and subconscious mind, one might be fairly accurate in saying that in communications, the conscious mind is a slower computer which has to do much work to accomplish a goal. The subconscious mind may be a very fast computer (mainframe) which takes over only when enough information has been fed to it from the conscious mind. The conscious mind has received a very efficient program which is devoted to specific subject areas. The conscious mind will concentrate on a single task, hoping to garner enough information so that it may eventually write a program which is efficient enough to be committed to its subconscious counterpart. Undoubtedly, many persons who are far more experienced in the science which explores how and why we think will attack my theory; however, most of them are not writing books on computers that talk.

Let's leave the scientific realm of thinking for now and speak specifically about programs that allow your computer to talk. All of my programs in speech mode were run on the IBM Personal computer, whose asynchronous communications adapter was connected to the Votrax Type-'N-Talk speech synthesizer. If you have another type of synthesizer most of these programs can be made to run on your system, although it may be necessary to make a few modifications with respect to the specifics of keying up your particular type of synthesizer.

Several programs in this chapter were written specifically with a speech synthesizer in mind from the beginning. Others were written more than one year before my computer was equipped for speech. When presented in this chapter, the original programs have been modified to output their information in speech form rather than on the printer or monitor screen. These conversions simply consign the output information to the synthesizer instead of either of the character displays. Other programs were left mostly intact and will output information to the monitor screen and to the synthesizer at virtually the same moment.

The point of this discussion is that with the excellent speech synthesizers available today, one does not have to program in a brand-new mode to obtain effective speech output. Think of the synthesizer in exactly the same manner as you would a monitor or printer. A List command will cause the program lines to be printed on the IBM monitor screen. A List command will cause the same lines to be displayed on printer forms. The two commands are slightly different, and accomplish completely different results with the IBM system, but each is a single command that accesses a different output device. The same idea is associated with the speech synthesizer. For instance, a PRINT "HELLO" input at the keyboard will cause the screen to display the word "HELLO". Once you have opened the communications interface, a PRINT #1,"HELLO" will cause the speech synthesizer to output this word verbally. To modify a program which formerly printed all information on the screen, use the IBM edit feature to tack a "#1," after each Print statement. This assumes that the program lines which open the communications interface have already been executed. Writing programs for voice output is entirely a text mode function. It is not nearly as difficult as making the transition from text mode to graphics mode. Generally, programs are run just as if the output would be on the monitor; only a few statements are altered to access the voice capability.

Figure 8-1 allows the computer and synthesizer to verbally count from zero to ten and then from ten to zero in increments of one. The first few lines open the communications interface (#1). Then, the first For-Next loop is entered. This loop counts from 0 to 9. Inside the loop is a synthesizer activation statement, "PRINT #1,X". The variable X is used by the synthesizer, which will state its value as it changes with every loop cycle. When the loop times out, there is a time delay line which allows for the proper spacing between the pronunciation of the nine and verbally outputing the word "TEN." Another time delay loop provides proper spacing between the pronunciation of this word and the pronunciation of the number "9". The latter number is accessed at the start of the second For-Next loop, which counts from nine to zero in steps of −1. When the program is run your computer will count from zero to ten and from ten to zero, and the synthesizer will pronounce every number.

Notice that the number ten is spelled out. If I had allowed the first loop to count to the number

```
10 REM "TALKING COUNT PROGRAM"
20 CLS
30 Z$="COM1:9600,N,8,1"
40 OPEN Z$ AS #1
50 FOR X=0 TO 9
60 PRINT #1,X
70 NEXT X
80 PRINT #1,"TEN"
90 FOR Z=0 TO 7000:NEXT Z
100 PRINT #1,"TEN"
110 FOR Z=1 TO 600:NEXT Z
120 FOR X=9 TO 0 STEP -1
130 PRINT #1,X
140 NEXT X
```

Fig. 8-1. Talking Count program.

ten, the synthesizer would have stated "ONE ZERO" instead of saying "TEN". The Votrax synthesizer is capable of pronouncing the words that denote the numbers zero through nine, but it is not equipped to go beyond this point using numbers alone. Some synthesizers may already have the capability of counting to 100 or higher based upon numbers input at the computer alone. The IBM cannot, but this is of little practical consequence.

You can modify this program to get a monitor printout as well. Following the "PRINT #1,X" line, simply input another line which contains "PRINT X;". The screen will now display the numbers zero through nine at the same time the synthesizer is uttering them. Similar additions will be necessary at the section of the program which causes the synthesizer to say "TEN" and in the last For-Next loop.

Conversely, any For-Next loop within a present program not currently designed for speech output which counts no higher than nine may be "vocalized" by adding "PRINT #1," statements. The program shown in Fig. 8-1 may not have much practical use, but it is a nice demonstration of the simplicity by which synthesizer output is obtained.

You can expand on the count range of this program by lengthening the quoted text information in lines 80 and 100. For example, to expand the count from zero to 20 and then from 20 to zero, line 80 would read:

80 PRINT #1,"TEN ELEVEN TWELVE THIRTEEN . . . TWENTY"

Line 100 would be the reverse of this, as in:

100 PRINT #1,"TWENTY NINETEEN EIGHTEEN . . . TEN"

This program mixes numbers and text, but you could do the whole program in text mode at the expense of more keyboard input time by using PRINT #1, statements throughout. You would spell out each number in alphabetic form (ONE, TWO, THREE, etc.). This would allow you to omit the For-Next loop. This is mentioned only for the sake of discussion, since the program in its present form is the most efficient method of arriving at the desired count. You will want to take advantage of the zero to nine numeral pronunciation this particular synthesizer offers, as it is far easier to input these on a numeric basis than to spell out the actual words.

Technically, the synthesizer can output any number to which the computer is capable of counting. This can become confusing for numbers ten and above. Picking up the count at this stage, the synthesizer would say "ONE ZERO, ONE ONE, ONE TWO", etc. This can be quite confusing, but only because of the quantity of numbers involved.

For single mathematical applications you can use numbers only, without the confusion noted above. For example, if you wanted the synthesizer to verbally state the answer to a mathematical problem, you would input the formula (as you would in any other mathematical program) and use PRINT #1 statements to output the answer. Let's assume the correct answer is nine. The synthesizer will then say "NINE". As another example, assume that the answer is 1,048. In this case the synthesizer will output "ONE ZERO FOUR EIGHT". Once you understand how numeric answers are given, you should have no problem in readily accepting the output answers.

What about decimal points? Fortunately, the Votrax synthesizer commits this numerical character to an internally stored word, which is "POINT".

Using the same sample program discussed above, let's assume that the answer is 139.685. The synthesizer will output "ONE THREE NINE POINT SIX EIGHT FIVE". This is not exactly the same as a human might express it. We would probably say "ONE HUNDRED THIRTY-NINE POINT SIX EIGHT FIVE". The synthesizer output is readily understandable, and can be quite useful when calculations are run for a small group of persons, some of whom may not have a direct view of the monitor screen.

The program in Fig. 8-2 will allow you to add, subtract, multiply or divide two numbers; the correct answer will be output from the speech synthesizer. This is a simple program, but it has been completely debugged (for correct synthesizer output) and serves a useful purpose. Line 40 commits the asynchronous communications adapter information to Z$. Line 50 opens the adapter and is assigned the #1 designation. Line 60 allows the user to input the mathematical function desired. The first letter of each function commits the mathematical procedure to another portion of the program. For example, if you input A here the next two numbers input will be added. An M will cause them to be multiplied. Line 70 tests for an improper keyboard input regarding the mathematical function. If you do not input an A, S, M or D, there is a branch back to line 60, and you are asked to input the mathematical function again.

At this point the screen is cleared and you are prompted on the monitor to input the value of X. This will be the number which the second number will be added to, subtracted from, multiplied by or divided into. The second number is input in line 100. This is assigned to the variable Y.

Lines 110 through 140 determine the mathematical function based upon the input at line 60. For example, if you input A, then A will be equal to X + Y. The functions for subtraction, multiplication

```
10 REM TALKING MATHEMATICAL PROGRAM
20 REM COPYRIGHT ROBERT J. TRAISTER AND
ASSOCIATES 12/1/82
30 CLS
40 Z$="COM1:9600,N,8,1"
50 OPEN Z$ AS #1
60 INPUT"ADD, SUBTRACT, MULTIPLY OR DIVI
DE?",A$
70 IF A$<>"A" AND A$<>"S" AND A$<>"M" AN
D A$<>"D" THEN 60
80 CLS
90 INPUT"WHAT IS THE VALUE OF X";X
100 INPUT"WHAT IS THE VALUE OF Y";Y
110 IF A$="A" THEN A=X+Y:GOTO 150
120 IF A$="S" THEN A=X-Y:GOTO 150
130 IF A$="M" THEN A=X*Y:GOTO 150
140 IF A$="D" THEN A=X/Y: GOTO 150
150 CLS
160 PRINT A
170 IF A<0 THEN PRINT #1,"MYNUS"
180 PRINT #1,A
190 GOTO 60
```

Fig. 8-2. Talking Mathematical program.

and division are set up in lines 120 through 140. The branch at the end of each of these lines causes the screen to be cleared, and line 60 then causes the correct answer to be printed on the screen. Line 180 outputs this same information to the communications adapter and thus to the speech synthesizer, so the numbers on the screen are then expressed verbally.

Line 170 is necessary to allow for negative answers. The minus sign (–) will not be responded to by the speech synthesizer. It will be ignored completely. Line 170, however, tests for the condition of A being equal to a value which is less than zero. If this is the case, the word "MYNUS" is committed to the communications adapter and is verbally output by the synthesizer. Immediately following this word, the numeric information is verbally output. This is set up in line 180. If the answer is positive, then A is not equal to a value of less than zero and line 170 is effectively bypassed.

It was necessary to output the word "MYNUS" to the speech synthesizer. This is a phonetic spelling of "MINUS". If you spell it the correct way, the synthesizer will pronounce it as "MEN US". Throughout this chapter you will see a large number of phonetic spellings; this is part of the debug operation. As you become more familiar with your synthesizer, you will begin to anticipate the words which must be altered from their normal English spellings to be pronounced most accurately. When you write your own original speech programs, you may wish to input all text with the standard spellings and then make changes after the initial test run. You will quickly learn the synthesizer's pronunciation traits (in regard to certain letter combinations).

While the program in Fig. 8-2 is quite simple, it does serve a useful purpose and demonstrates how the synthesizer can be put to good use in expressing mathematical quantities. This program has allowed the user to select from four different mathematical formulas (lines 110 through 140), but the same method can be used with a single fixed formula which may be far more complex. Merely insert the variable to which the correct answer will be assigned at the end of a PRINT #1, statement. Therefore this program may be used as a basis for building every other type of mathematical program with a numerical output.

Figure 8-3 is a partial repeat of a program presented earlier in this book. This is the ticking electronic alarm clock which displays time digitally. When the input alarm time is reached, a subroutine is activated. Originally this was a whooper siren. A discussion in the previous chapter suggested replacing the siren subroutine with wakeup music. I've gone one step further to allow the speech synthesizer to verbally tell you to get up.

Since this program has been discussed previously, I will concentrate on the modification lines which allow for synthesizer output. These are executed only when the alarm time has been reached. This condition is tested in line 110 and results in a branch to line 150, which starts the synthesizer routine. Lines 150 and 160 open the communications interface. Line 170 commits text to the variable A$. Line 180 verbally outputs the text. When this subroutine is accessed, the synthesizer will output "WAKE UP. IT'S TIME TO RISE AND SHINE". Line 190 is a delay loop, which allows for a second or so of spacing between the final word in line 170 and the first word when this output is repeated. The synthesizer will continue to tell you to get up until you depress Soft Key F1 on the keyboard. In other words your computer system is going to nag you until you finally get out of bed. Unlike standard alarm clocks, it won't do you any good to throw a pillow at the keyboard to shut off the alarm. Rather, you're going to have to drag yourself out of bed and focus long enough to find Soft Key F1.

Naturally you can alter the wakeup method in any way you like ("WAKE UP YOU GOOD FOR NOTHING . . ."). This program simply makes use of the speech synthesizer as a replacement for the whooper siren, music or other audible indicator.

You can go one step further with this program and emulate some of the very expensive verbal time clocks that have been on the market for a number of years. These tell you the time verbally whenever a switch is depressed, usually on the top of the case. The same program shown in Fig. 8-3 simply gains a few lines and is shown in Fig. 8-4.

```
10 REM ALARM CLOCK
20 REM COPYRIGHT 9/22/82 ROBERT J. TRAIS
TER AND ASSOCIATES
30 CLS
40 KEY OFF
50 INPUT"TYPE IN THE ALARM TRIGGER TIME
(EXAMPLE:01:30:00) ";A$
60 CLS
70 LOCATE 2,30
80 PRINT "ALARM TIME="A$
90 LOCATE 14,37
100 PRINT TIME$
110 IF TIME$=A$ THEN 150
120 FOR X=1 TO 600:NEXT
130 SOUND 12500,.35
140 GOTO 90
150 Z$="COM1:9600,N,8,1"
160 OPEN Z$ AS #1
170 A$="WAKE UP. ITS TIME TO RISE AND SH
INE"
180 PRINT #1,A$
190 FOR X=1 TO 5000:NEXT X
200 KEY(1) ON
210 ON KEY(1) GOSUB 230
220 GOTO 170
230 CLS
240 GOTO 90
```

Fig. 8-3. Alarm Clock.

Line 102 activates Soft Key F2. When this key is depressed, line 105 detects this condition and branches to line 1000. This line commits the current time to the variable B$. Lines 1010 and 1020 open the asynchronous communications adapter to the synthesizer, and line 1030 causes the time numbers to be output to the communications adapter. The synthesizer will verbally state the time. Line 1040 closes the asynchronous communications adapter, and line 1050 branches back to the timekeeping portion of the program.

The Close statement in line 1040 is necessary to avoid an error message after the return. This will occur when the alarm time is reached or when you depress F2 again, since the communications adapter was originally opened in line 160. The Close simply shuts down the synthesizer until this mode is reopened again. You may wish to insert some text in this program addition, namely, the word "O CLOCK". I didn't include it because the time will be given in hours, minutes and seconds, as in "ZERO ONE THREE TWO ZERO FOUR" for the equivalent time "01:32:04". The synthesizer is telling you that the time is approximately one thirty-two, although it gives its answer to the nearest second.

Figure 8-5 is the speech version of a program that was originally designed to calculate electronic values. Those readers who have an electronic background will understand what resonant frequency pertains to; if you are not one of these it does not matter, since the method used to develop this program can be put to many other uses.

This program calculates the resonant frequency of an LC circuit, with L standing for inductance and C for capacitance. At the beginning of the program a communications file is opened with the lines used for all previous programs (30 and 40). Lines 60, 70 and 80 explain the nature of the program by means of a monitor screen write. Lines 130 and 140 allow your computer system to output a request, both on the screen and from the speech synthesizer. Looking at line 140 first, the screen will prompt the user to input the capacitance value in picofarads. Line 130 does the same thing, but the prompt is from the speech synthesizer. I have resorted to phonetic spelling to get the pronunciation desired. Notice that the word "VALUE" is input as "VAL U". "CAPACITOR" is phonetically spelled "COPASSETTORE". "PICOFARADS" also has its own phonetic spelling. You will see the prompt line on the screen and hear it spoken at approximately the same time.

When the capacitance value is input, lines 170 and 180 perform the same function as lines 130 and 140, but now for the value of inductance. I originally input the word "MICROHENRYS" to the speech

```
102  KEY (2) ON

105  ON KEY (2) GOSUB 1000

1000 B$ = TIME$

1010  Z$ = "COM1:9600,N,8,1"

1020  OPEN Z$ AS #1

1030  PRINT #1,B$

1040  CLOSE

1050  RETURN
```

Fig. 8-4. Additional program lines for Alarm Clock program.

line but the pronunciation was horrible, so I spelled it phonetically as "MY CROW HENRYS". There are probably several other phonetic spellings which will work just as well, many perhaps shorter than mine. After some practice with the synthesizer you will develop your own methods for phonetic spellings; as long as you get the pronunciation desired, it doesn't make any difference what is used.

When the inductance value is input via the keyboard, the screen is cleared and will then display the two values you have inserted. Line 240 is the mathematical formula for determining resonant frequency from the values given. Lines 270 and 280 act in conjunction with each other to output the answer, both on the screen and from the speech synthesizer. In each case the correct answer is assigned to the variable F. The phonetic spelling in line 270 will cause the synthesizer to output "THE RESONANT FREQUENCY IS . . . ". The actual value is specified by the variable F in this same line. F falls outside the two sets of quotation marks which surround the opening phrase and the final phrase, which is "KILOHERTZ". The screen displays the same message.

Following the outputting of the answer, there is a For-Next time delay loop in line 310. After this pause the synthesizer asks if you would like to input other values and instructs you to press the Enter key to rerun the program. This last statement is an audio prompt. There is no screen version on the monitor.

The entire program could be treated in speech mode without a single screen prompt. This could be done by changing all Print statements followed by text to PRINT #1, statements. The Print statements which are not followed by text are used to space text lines on the screen and could be deleted. The main reason for using text and speech prompts is the human operator. The screen prompts are present as backups in case the operator becomes confused and is unable to recall the information in the speech prompt. Moreover, most of us are more accustomed to screen prompts than to audio prompts, so it may be some time before audio prompts are used alone in most computer programs. Currently, such prompts are used mostly as

```
10 REM "VERBAL RESONANT FREQUENCY CALCUL
ATOR"
20 REM COPYRIGHT ROBERT J. TRAISTER AND
ASSOCIATES 12/2/82
30 Z$="COM1:9600,N,8,1"
40 OPEN Z$ AS #1
50 CLS
60 PRINT"THIS PROGRAM WILL ALLOW YOU TO
FIGURE THE RESONANT FREQUENCY FOR"
70 PRINT"AN LC CIRCUIT WHEN THE VALUES O
F INDUCTANCE(L) AND CAPACITANCE(C)
80 PRINT"ARE GIVEN."
90 PRINT
100 PRINT
110 INPUT"PRESS 'ENTER' TO BEGIN",A$
120 CLS
130 PRINT #1,"WHAT IS THE VAL U OF THE K
OPASSETTORE IN PEEKO FAIREDS"
140 INPUT"WHAT IS THE VALUE OF THE CAPAC
ITOR IN PICOFARADS  ";C
150 PRINT
160 PRINT
170 PRINT #1,"WHAT IS THEE VALUE OF INDU
CTANCE IN MY CROW HENRYS"
180 INPUT"WHAT IS THE VALUE OF INDUCTANC
E IN MICROHENRYS  ";L
190 CLS
200 PRINT"THE VALUE OF CAPACITANCE IS",C
 "PICOFARADS"
210 PRINT
220 PRINT
230 PRINT"THE VALUE OF INDUCTANCE IS ",L
 "MICROHENRYS"
240 F=10^6/(6.28*SQR(L*C))
250 PRINT
260 PRINT
270 PRINT #1,"THE RESSONANT FREEQUENCY I
S"F" KILLO HURTS"
280 PRINT"THE RESONANT FREQUENCY IS ",F "
KILOHERTZ
290 PRINT
300 PRINT
310 FOR X=1 TO 6000:NEXT X
320 PRINT #1,"IF YOU WOULD LIKE TO INPUT
 OTHER VALUES, PRESS THEE ENTER KEY"
330 INPUT A$
340 GOTO 120
```

Fig. 8-5. Verbal Resonant Frequency Calculator.

program enhancements. This trend is slowly changing; it is conceivable that in the near future many computers will normally be equipped with on-board speech synthesizers, and programs will be written to take advantage of this feature. For example, the computer screen may be used to display basic information, prompts and so forth. A full explanation may be simultaneously offered by a speech subroutine. This would be ideal for educational as well as general purpose use. For now, the use of computer speech is still only midway through its infancy.

ANOTHER TALKING CLOCK PROGRAM

A previous program in this chapter produced a digital clock with an alarm that operated in the speech mode. It is quite easy to commit the time information to the synthesizer for an output which would verbally tell you the time. Of course the simple conversion discussed only allowed the synthesizer to repeat the numbers which make up the time string. For example if the time was 11:32:46, the output would be "ONE ONE THREE TWO FOUR SIX". From a communications standpoint, this type of output would certainly be adequate to inform you of the correct time. But if a person was not aware of how the computer expresses time, there would be much confusion until the format was learned. There is nothing unusual about verbal clocks, although most use an actual recording of the human voice rather than speech synthesizers. These clocks usually express time the way humans do (i.e., "IT'S ELEVEN FORTY-SIX").

In an effort to arrive at a more easily understood verbal clock, the program shown in Fig. 8-6 was developed. The debugging routine was slowed considerably because it was necessary to input different values of time (TIME$ =). I thought the program was completed several times, but then a new combination of numbers which made up the TIME$ would indicate that more lines were necessary.

The program is not exceptionally long, and you should be able to input it in quickly on your IBM Personal computer. This program will set up your machine as an alarm clock which gives a verbal wakeup call, and it will tell you the time whenever Soft Key F2 is depressed. This latter feature is what took so long to debug. Additionally, the program is set up to automatically announce the time on the hour and on the half-hour. This is an optional feature and may be removed.

You can see that the first ten lines are nearly identical to other clock programs in this book. A subroutine produces the clicking sound of a windup alarm clock, but this is optional and may be removed. As before, you can input the alarm trigger time; when this occurs, there will be a branch to line 200 which opens the communications channel and outputs the alarm information to the speech synthesizer. When you depress Soft Key F1 the alarm switches off.

The most interesting aspect of this program begins in line 310. This is the point in the program to which a branch occurs whenever you depress Soft Key F2. This key is brought to the active state by lines 140 and 150. When the branch occurs, there are many test lines which check for certain numbers within the TIME$. Separate portions of the TIME$ are treated differently. Line 310 effectively reads the first two digits in the TIME$. One must remember that time is displayed on this computer with eight characters. Six of these are numbers, and the remaining two are separating colons as in "01:22:46". The first group of numbers indicate hours, the second minutes and the third seconds. Therefore line 310 accesses the first two characters from the left-hand side of the time string. In the above example this would be "01".

Since the speech synthesizer will output "ONE" when it receives the number one, there is no real conversion problem. This applies to all numbers from zero to nine. However, acting upon this information alone the synthesizer will announce "ZERO ONE". This is not desirable since we don't say "IT'S ZERO ONE O'CLOCK". When the hours portion of the TIME$ is less than ten, it is most desirable to drop the leading zero, which is done by line 320. When B$ (the first two digits of TIME$) is less than one, the value of B$ is reassigned. I used a MID$ function applied to TIME$. However, B$ is assigned the value of the second

```
10 REM TIME VOICE
20 REM COPYRIGHT 9/22/82 ROBERT J. TRAIS
TER AND ASSOCIATES
30 CLS
40 KEY OFF
50 INPUT"TYPE IN THE ALARM TRIGGER TIME
(EXAMPLE:01:30:00) ";A$
60 CLS
70 LOCATE 2,30
80 PRINT "ALARM TIME="A$
90 LOCATE 14,37
100 PRINT TIME$
110 TOH$=MID$(TIME$,4,5) 'optional line
for automatic time announcement
120 IF TOH$="00:00" THEN BEEP:FOR H=1 TO
 400:NEXT H:BEEP:GOSUB 310 'optional lin
e for time on the hour
130 IF TOH$="30:00" THEN BEEP:GOSUB 640
'optional line for time on the half hour

140 KEY(2) ON
150 ON KEY(2) GOSUB 310
160 IF TIME$=A$ THEN 200
170 FOR X=1 TO 600:NEXT
180 SOUND 12500,.35
190 GOTO 90
200 Z$="COM1:9600,N,8,1"
210 OPEN Z$ AS #1
220 A$="WAKE UP. ITS TIME TO RISE AND SH
INE"
230 PRINT #1,A$
240 FOR X=1 TO 5000:NEXT X
250 KEY(1) ON
260 ON KEY(1) GOSUB 280
270 GOTO 220
280 CLS
290 CLOSE
300 GOTO 90
310 B$=LEFT$(TIME$,2)
320 IF B$<"1" THEN B$=MID$(TIME$,2,1)
330 IF B$="10" THEN B$="TEN"
340 IF B$="11" THEN B$="EE LEVEN"
350 IF B$="12" THEN B$="TWELVE"
360 C$=MID$(TIME$,4,2)
```

Fig. 8-6. Time Voice.

```
370 IF C$<"10" THEN C$="O  "
380 IF C$="10" THEN C$="TEN"
390 IF C$="11" THEN C$="EE LEVEN"
400 IF C$="12" THEN C$="TWELVE"
410 IF C$="13" THEN C$="THIRT TEEN"
420 IF C$="14" THEN C$="FORT TEEN"
430 IF C$="15" THEN C$="FIF TEEN"
440 IF C$="16" THEN C$="6TEEN"
450 IF C$="17" THEN C$="7TEEN"
460 IF C$="18" THEN C$="EIGHTEEN"
470 IF C$="19" THEN C$="9TEEN"
480 IF C$="20" THEN C$="TWENTY"
490 IF C$>"20" AND C$<"30" THEN C$="TWEN
TY"
500 IF C$=>"30" AND C$<"40" THEN C$="THI
RDEE"
510 IF C$=>"40" AND C$<"50" THEN C$="4D"

520 IF C$=>"50" AND C$<"60" THEN C$="FIF
TEE"
530 D$=MID$(TIME$,5,1)
540 IF MID$(TIME$,4,2)=>"10" AND MID$(TI
ME$,4,2)<"20" THEN D$=""
550 IF MID$(TIME$,4,2)="00" THEN D$="CLO
CK"
560 Z$="COM1:9600,N,8,1"
570 OPEN Z$ AS #1
580 PRINT #1,"THE KUHRECT TIME IS"B$
590 FOR TD=1 TO 1000:NEXT TD
600 IF D$="O" THEN D$=" "
610 PRINT #1,C$D$
620 CLOSE
630 RETURN
640 Z$="COM1:9600,N,8,1"
650 OPEN Z$ AS #1
660 F$=MID$(TIME$,1,2)
670 IF LEFT$(TIME$,1)="O" THEN F$=MID$(T
IME$,2,1)
680 IF F$="10" THEN F$="TEN"
690 IF F$="11" THEN F$="EE LEVEN"
700 IF F$="12" THEN F$="TWELVE"
710 PRINT #1,"IT IS HALF PAST THE  OUR O
F" F$ " O CLOCK"
720 CLOSE
730 RETURN
```

character only in the TIME$ (TIME$,2,1). The computer reads any TIME$ hour group which begins with zero as a value of less than one, so line 320 allows the zero to be effectively dropped and the second character is the only one that is read. This means that in the above example the synthesizer would output only the number one.

When the hour numbers rise to ten or above, it is necessary to output the proper text information to the synthesizer. The variable B$ is assigned the value of any number from one to 12, which is adequate to take care of the hour segment of TIME$. This assumes, of course, that you stay with 12-hour time and do not switch to military or 24-hour timekeeping.

Lines 330 through 350 reassign B$ when the hour numbers are 01, 11 or 12. Notice the phonetic spelling of 11 in line 340. Line 580 causes the synthesizer to output "THE CORRECT TIME IS" and then output B$. The phonetic spelling of "CORRECT" used in line 580 produces the most understandable pronunciation.

So far, only the lines which will read and output the proper characters to the speech synthesizer for the hour portion of the TIME$ has been covered. This portion is quite simple because we are only dealing with twelve different numbers, nine of which do not require text spellings. Unfortunately, the difficulty factor increases when we treat the minutes portion of TIME$.

The minute elements are assigned to the variables C$ and D$. Let's begin with C$. In line 360 this variable is assigned to the value of the fourth and fifth digits in TIME$. These are the digits which display minutes. Most of us don't say "The correct time is ten zero nine (10:09)". We would probably express it as "The correct time is ten oh nine". This has been taken into account by line 370. When C$ is equal to a value of less than 10, C$ equals the letter O. The other variable, D$, will be for the actual number of minutes and will be discussed shortly. Lines 380 through 480 make the proper assignment when C$ is equal to a value of 10 or more. Note that each number from 10 to 20 is spelled out in text form, often phonetically using combinations of letters and text, as in "6TEEN" for "sixteen". Lines 380 through 480 are used to directly output minutes which fall between 10 and 20 past the hour. When the actual time exceeds twenty minutes past the hour, it is necessary to use another string variable (D$) for expression. This will be discussed later.

Line 490 tests for the condition of the numbers portion of TIME$ falling between 20 and 30. If this portion is equal to or greater than 21 and is less than 30, C$ retains the value of "twenty". Line 500 performs the same function for values between 30 and 40, wherein C$ is assigned the value of "thirty". This sequence continues up to a maximum value of "fifty".

Our next string variable, D$, is assigned in line 530. This allows D$ to be equal to the fifth character in TIME$. Let's assume that the time which we wish to output to the synthesizer is "10:23". B$ is assigned the value of "TEN" in line 330. Since the minutes portion is between 20 and 30, C$ will have a value of "TWENTY". D$ is equal to the last character in the minutes portion only, which is a three. The synthesizer can pronounce this without a text spelling; when the Print statements in lines 580 and 610 are executed, the time is specified as "TEN-TWENTY-THREE". B$ equals "TEN", C$ equals "TWENTY", and D$ equals "THREE". This works very well for minutes portions that are not of even values in increments of 10, such as "10:20, 10:30, 10:40" and so forth. This sounds confusing, since the situation is apparently accounted for in lines 490 through 520 with the assignment of C$. However, remember that D$ is still going to be output, and it reads the last character in the minutes portion. If we left the program as it now is, when 6:20 occurred the synthesizer would output "THE CORRECT TIME IS SIX TWENTY ZERO". The zero is added because D$ equals the last character in the minutes portion. In this case we don't want the last character to be read, so line 600 tests for this condition. If D$ equals zero D$ is assigned a value of one space, which is the null character with respect to the synthesizer.

The same situation occurs when the value of the minutes portion of TIME$ is equal to or less than 20. The D$ is still present and will be read by the synthesizer unless something is done. Line 540 tests for the condition of the minutes segment being between 10 and 20 inclusive. When this occurs, D$ is again assigned a null value.

The seconds are not read out by the synthesizer, although this would be possible using the same type of programming. In normal practice we are concerned with time to the minute and not to the second. While seconds will be shown on the screen, the synthesizer will not verbally output this information.

There is one more factor to consider when developing a practical voiced timekeeping program. Assume that the time is two o'clock. The program will cause the synthesizer to output "THE CORRECT TIME IS TWO OH" because of line 370, which tests for a condition of the minutes portion of the string being less than 10. This is what causes a time readout such as "TWO *OH* NINE". Line 550 acts in conjunction with line 370, however, and tests for a condition of the minutes portion of the string being equal to 00. If this is the case, then D$ equals "CLOCK". Two conditions are met: In line 370, the minutes portion is less than 10; therefore, the synthesizer will output the word "OH" when C$ is executed. Line 550 causes the synthesizer to output the word "CLOCK" when minutes are equal to 00. This combination yields "OH CLOCK". Thus when the top of the hour is reached, the synthesizer will output the hours number followed by "OH CLOCK", or "TWO OH CLOCK" for instance.

When you depress Soft Key F2 the entire portion of the program under discussion is entered. Line 570 opens the communications channel, line 580 prints the first portion of the phrase and the hours figure. Then there is a time delay loop which provides pleasing spacing between the output of the hours and the following minutes output in line 610. The communications adapter has been closed out, and the Return statement in line 630 creates a branch back to line 160, where the timekeeping sequence and the tick are again output. When you depress Soft Key F2 the time numerals will be frozen on the screen, and the time output from the synthesizer reflects this. It takes a few seconds for the time to be verbally output, so when you return from the speech subroutine the clock will automatically skip over the seconds lost during the speech output. This means that the clock will always show the correct time when the numerals are advancing. In other words, the seconds required for the speech output do not cause the clock to slow by the same amount. Time is kept internally within the computer and is not affected by branches to subroutines that temporarily stop the advancing numerals on the screen.

I was quite pleased with this program, but decided to go a few steps further by offering the automatic verbal output of time on the hour and on the half-hour. Lines 110 through 130 cause these optional program functions. In line 110 the last four digits of the TIME$ are sampled. This value is assigned to the string variable TOH$ in line 120. When TOH$ is equal to "00:00" a beep will occur. A time delay loop is entered and another beep is output. Then there is a GOSUB branch to line 310, which is the same routine entered by depressing Soft Key F2. This branch is automatic and occurs only when the last four digits of the TIME$ are given values of zero. These four digits represent the minutes and seconds portions of TIME$. Therefore when this automatic entry procedure is executed, it will always be when the clock reads the beginning of a new hour.

In writing this program I originally keyed on only the minutes portion of TIME$, leaving the seconds alone. I immediately met problems since it takes a full sixty seconds for the "00" minutes portion to advance to "01". It takes only about five seconds for the time to be verbally output. Therefore when the Return statement branched back, minutes were still equal to "00". By keying on the seconds, as shown in this program, you will not get a constant repeat of the time on the hour for the full sixty-second duration. Originally the automatic branch simply caused the synthesizer to read, for example, "TWO OH CLOCK" again and again until the time advanced to "2.01".

Line 130 causes the synthesizer to announce time on the half-hour. TOH$ is used, but now the branch occurs when TIME$ equals "30:00". This is the half-hour point which causes the machine to output a single beep. There is then a Gosub to line 640. Additional lines have been added to the end of the program. It would have been quite possible to use the original lines as was the case with the hourly output, but I wanted a slightly different verbal prompt. Lines 640 and 650 open the communications channel. Line 660 assigns the hourly value to the variable F$. Line 670 tests for a condition of the first numeral being equal to zero, as in "03:30". When that occurs the zero is dropped, as before, and the synthesizer is fed only the second character in the hour portion. Lines 680 through 700 are repeats of lines 330 through 350, except they are assigned to the new variable F$. This results in the pronunciation in text mode of the numbers 10, 11 or 12. Line 710 causes the synthesizer to output the phrase "IT IS HALF PAST THE HOUR OF". Then F$ is output, followed by "O CLOCK". At 2:30 the synthesizer will output "IT IS HALF PAST THE HOUR OF TWO O CLOCK". Line 720 closes the communications channel, and there is a branch back to the main timekeeping routine.

There you have it - a complete digital electronic clock with simulated ticking sounds, automatic time announcements on the hour and half-hour, and verbal time readout at the press of a button. Those persons who have the new version of IBM DOS may input the correct time before entering BASIC. Of course those without the new DOS will simply enter BASIC, load the program and then type TIME$ = "correct time". The program may now be run and the new input time will be reflected. In the latest DOS version it is not necessary to return to "SYSTEM" to change the time. You would use the above precedure for time changes while in BASIC.

Phonetic spellings are used throughout this program in an attempt to obtain the most understandable output from the synthesizer. If you are not careful, "THIRTEEN" may sound very much like "THIRTY". Notice that I spelled the number "13" as "THIRT TEEN". The same procedure was used for numbers 14 and 15, which might sound like "FORTY" or "FIFTY" without the phonetic emphasis given. You probably will want to experiment with these and other phonetic spellings, but I think you will find the program as shown in these pages to be quite satisfactory.

If you wish to have verbal output of seconds as well as hours and minutes, follow the same procedure used in lines 310 through 520. You will have to add additional MID$ functions to read the seconds portion, as was partially done in lines 110 through 130. Few people will want to go to such trouble. If you want to get rid of the tick, remove lines 170 and 180. Some readers may feel that a ticking sound for an electronic clock with all of these features is inappropriate.

DAY OF THE WEEK

The program in Fig. 8-7 will allow you to input any date in the 20th century and will then tell you on what day of the week that date did or will fall. These programs are quite common and you will see them in many different forms. This one uses the speech synthesizer to output the day of the week rather than restoring to a monitor screen or printer.

Lines 30 through 90 assign the seven days of the week to string variables. Notice that each day is spelled phonetically where necessary. Line 100 prompts the user to input the month, day and year and shows an example of the form which is to be used for input. Each input figure must be separated from the others by a comma. Notice that only the last two digits of the year are necessary, since the program assumes the 20th century. Lines 120 and 130 check for an improper date input. A branch to line 100 occurs if the date is not input in the correct format. Lines 150 through 240 make up the complex mathematical formula that will calculate the correct day. Notice in line 160 that 1900 is added to Y. This latter variable is assigned the last two digits of the year in which the day occurred. The communications channel is opened between the computer and the synthesizer in lines 250 and 260. Line 270 then causes the synthesizer to output the day of the week. The variable D$X represents the day.

To input another date, rerun the program. If you wish you can input a branch line at the end of this program to return to line 100 after the first day has been output. If you elect to do this, be sure to

```
10  REM DAY OF WEEK
20  CLS
30  D$(1) = "SUNDAY"
40  D$(2) = "MONDAY"
50  D$(3) = "TEWSDAY"
60  D$(4) = "WENSDAY"
70  D$(5) = "THURZE DAY"
80  D$(6) = "FRY DAY"
90  D$(7) = "SATURDAY"
100  PRINT "ENTER MONTH(M), DAY(D) AND Y
EAR(Y) (EXAMPLE:3,15,83)"
110  INPUT M,D,Y
120  IF D < 1 OR D > 31 THEN 100
130  IF M < 1 OR M > 12 THEN 100
140  GOTO 150
150  AA = INT(.6 + (1/M))
160  BB = (Y+1900)-AA
170  CC = M + 12*AA
180  DD = BB/100
190  X1 = INT(DD/4)
200  X2 = INT(DD)
210  X3=INT((5*BB)/4)
220  X4=INT(13*(CC+1)/5)
230  X=X4+X3-X2+X1+D-1
240  X=X-(INT(X/7)*7)+1
250 Z$="COM1:9600,N,8,1"
260 OPEN Z$ AS #1
270  PRINT #1,"THE DAY OF THE WEEK IS ";
D$(X)
```

Fig. 8-7. Day of the Week.

add a Close statement in line 280 or the screen will display an error message during the next run.

The synthesizer's pronunciation of the seven days of the week is quite good when outputing Sunday, Monday and Saturday. The remaining days, however, are phonetically spelled to arrive at a pronunciation which is quite accurate. While it is not done in this program, it would be quite easy to open the communications channel preceding line 100, changing the prompt in this line to an output from the voice synthesizer. This program takes leap year into account, and you will find it capable of faithfully outputing the day on which a specific date occurred anytime in the 20th century.

FORTUNE TELLER

This is a simple game program (Fig. 8-8) that I call Fortune Teller. You may ask the computer any question you desire, as long as it may be answered by yes or no. The computer will then output its answer through the speech synthesizer. Questions are restricted to a yes or no answer format in order to prompt the human not to ask a question that lies outside the computer's thirteen possible re-

```
10 REM FORTUNE TELLER
20 REM COPYRIGHT ROBERT J. TRAISTER AND
ASSOCIATES  12/7/82
30 CLS
40 KEY OFF
50 WIDTH 80
60 PRINT"ASK THE COMPUTER ANY QUESTION W
HICH CAN BE ANSWERED"
70 PRINT
80 PRINT"WITH A YES OR NO. IT WILL TELL
YOU WHAT YOU NEED TO KNOW.
90 PRINT
100 INPUT"PRESS <ENTER> TO ACCESS THE CO
MPUTER FORTUNE TELLER." ;A$
110 CLS
120 PRINT"WHAT IS IT YOU WISH TO ASK THE
 ALL-SEEING, ALL-KNOWING"
130 PRINT
140 PRINT"COMPUTER NOW?"
150 PRINT
160 INPUT B$
170 C$=MID$(TIME$,7,2)
180 R=VAL(C$)
190 RANDOMIZE R
200 X=INT(RND*13)+1
```

Fig. 8-8. Fortune Teller.

sponses. The machine may indeed respond with a yes or no answer, but it may also answer "POSSIBLY", "I WILL NOT ANSWER THAT", or a number of others included in the program.

Lines 30, 40 and 50 set up the screen; lines 60 through 100 provide screen prompts for the user. As soon as the user understands how the game is played, the screen is cleared and line 120 asks for the player to input his question. It is not necessary to type a question, as the computer will respond with one of the thirteen answers anyway. The input instruction is for the psychological benefit of the player only.

This program acts on random numbers (1-13); in order to obtain a different pattern during each run, I have used the Randomize function in line 190. If you use Randomize alone, execution will automatically halt at this line and you will be prompted to input a random number. The random number generator then acts on your input number to produce a continuous series of truly random numbers. This is sometimes unpleasant and can detract from the enjoyment of the game. You can also use a number with the Randomize statement, but that leads nowhere since the number will always be the same. Therefore the same pattern of random numbers comes up every time.

To overcome this difficulty I elected to randomize a portion of the TIME$ readout. In line 170 I have assigned to the variable C$ the seconds portion of the TIME$. The MID$ function is used to extract the seventh and eighth digits from TIME$.

```
210 IF X=1 THEN Q$="YES"
220 IF X=2 THEN Q$="NO"
230 IF X=3 THEN Q$="POSSIBLY"
240 IF X=4 THEN Q$="ABSOLUTELY NOT"
250 IF X=5 THEN Q$="MOST DEFNITLY"
260 IF X=6 THEN Q$="THERE IS A SLIGHT PO
SSIBILITY"
270 IF X=7 THEN Q$="I WILL NOT AN SER TH
AT"
280 IF X=8 THEN Q$="THE SINES ARE GOOD"
290 IF X=9 THEN Q$="I MUST GIVE U A NEGE
TIVE ON THAT ONE"
300 IF X=10 THEN Q$="ASK ME AGAIN LATER"

310 IF X=11 THEN Q$="THAT QUESTION IS AN
 INSULT TO MY ARTIFICIAL INTELLIGENCE"
320 IF X=12 THEN Q$="THE SINES ARE NOT G
OOD"
330 IF X=13 THEN Q$="MOST CERTENLY"
340 Z$="COM1:9600,N,8,1"
350 OPEN Z$ AS #1
360 PRINT #1,Q$
370 CLOSE
380 CLS
390 GOTO 120
```

These correspond to the seconds. Line 180 assigns the value of these numbers to the variable R. Line 190 then randomizes R, or more accurately the value of R is used to reseed the random number generator. When you enter IBM DOS you will be prompted to input the correct time, although this is not necessary for this program to work properly. If you don't input the correct time, the TIME$ characters will advance from the last setting, and there will be some number for the Randomize statement to act upon. This assures a different pattern almost every time you run your program, so you will never be sure what answer the computer will output.

Line 200 assigns a random number to the variable X which is always an integer (INT) and which will lie between one and 13. Lines 210 through 330 test for a certain random number output, and assign an answer based on this number to the variable Q$. For example, if the value of X is 1 the output answer will be "YES". In line 340 the opening of the communications channel begins, and line 360 causes the answer to be output from the speech synthesizer. Following this the channel is again closed, the screen is cleared, and there is a branch back to line 120, which will allow you to ask another question. In testing this program I asked the computer if I was handsome. It responded with "MOST DEFINITELY". This was all the debugging I needed to do, since the answer was obviously correct.

Phonetic spellings are used in many cases throughout lines 210 through 330. Arriving at the right combinations took some time. The only answer I'm not satisfied with involves the word "NO". The synthesizer pronounces it fairly well; I could not obtain a phonetic spelling that was better, and left the word in its original form.

This program acts upon random numbers to output an answer. The computer does not care what question you ask; the answer is already determined before the question is asked. In other words, don't take this program too seriously. It is a great party program and is bound to hold audience attention for quite some time. This is one of the better programs I have written, although it serves no practical purpose. Naturally, the speech synthesizer is not mandatory to take advantage of this type of program. If you want to run in text mode only, delete lines 340 through 370 and insert a single line to replace one of these numbers, such as:

```
360   PRINT Q$
```

The program will perform exactly as before, except that the answer will be printed on the screen. If you make this modification, be sure to go back through lines 210 through 330 and change the phonetic spelling to a visually correct form.

In either form, you are encouraged to come up with your own answers to tailor the program to your audience. You can even add a few lines to allow the

```
10 REM PROGRAM TO CALCULATE S.W.R. WHEN
THE LOAD IMPEDANCE AND CHARACTERISTIC
20 REM IMPEDANCE OF THE TRANSMISSION LIN
E ARE KNOWN
30 REM COPYRIGHT ROBERT J. TRAISTER AND
ASSOCIATES-6/29/82
40 CLS
50 PRINT"WHEN A TRANSMISSION LINE IS COU
PLED TO A RESISTIVE LOAD(OR ANTENNA)"
60 PRINT"AN IMPEDANCE MISMATCH WILL OCCU
R IF THE IMPEDANCES OF THE TWO ARE"
70 PRINT"NOT IDENTICAL. THIS WILL BE EVI
DENCED BY STANDING WAVES ON THE"
80 PRINT"LINE AND AT THE TRANSMITTER. TH
IS PROGRAM WILL COMPUTE THE ACTUAL"
90 PRINT"SWR WHEN THE CHARACTERISTIC IMP
EDANCE OF THE TRANSMISSION LINE"
100 PRINT"ARE KNOWN."
110 PRINT
120 PRINT
130 PRINT
140 INPUT"PRESS ENTER WHEN READY TO BEGI
N",A$
150 CLS
160 PRINT"WHAT IS THE CHARACTERISTIC IMP
EDANCE OF THE TRANSMISSION LINE IN OHMS"
,L
170 INPUT L
180 PRINT
```

Fig. 8-9. SWR program.

name of the person asking the question to be input. The synthesizer will then say the name of the person just before providing the output answer. This is one of those programs which will rarely be run in its original form as shown here, but will be modified to reflect the audience and the desires of the programmer. Try inputting the program exactly as shown. Once you have obtained a successful run, you can make desired changes.

SWR CALCULATOR

The program shown in Fig. 8-9 was originally written to display accurately the standing wave ratio on a transmission line, based upon the characteristic impedance of the transmission line and the load impedance. This version goes a step further by outputting the answer from the synthesizer. The on-screen version is accurate to many decimal places. The synthesizer output is an approximation, rounding the ratio to the nearest whole number.

Lines 10 through 140 provide instructions to the user. Lines 160 and 200 prompt the user to input the transmission line impedance and the load impedance in ohms. Lines 230 and 250 reprint this information, and line 290 then asks whether the input values are correct. If you type in "Y", the execution advances; if you type in "N", there is a branch back to line 150 so that you may re-input the information.

```
190 PRINT
200 PRINT"WHAT IS THE IMPEDANCE OF THE L
OAD IN OHMS",T
210 INPUT T
220 CLS
230 PRINT"THE LINE IMPEDANCE IS ",L  "OH
MS"
240 PRINT
250 PRINT"THE LOAD IMPEDANCE IS ",T  "OH
MS
260 PRINT
270 PRINT
280 PRINT
290 INPUT"ARE THESE VALUES CORRECT (Y/N)
",B$
300 IF B$="Y" GOTO 320
310 IF B$="N" GOTO 150
320 CLS
330 IF L<T THEN Z=(T/L)
340 IF L>T THEN Z=L/T
350 IF L=T THEN Z=1
360 PRINT "THE STANDING WAVE RATIO IS"Z"
: 1"
370 Z=CINT(Z)
380 Z$="COM1:9600,N,8,1"
390 OPEN Z$ AS #1
400 PRINT #1,"THE STANDING WAVE RAYSHEE
O FOR THIS CONFIGURATION IS",Z"2 1"
410 END
```

This allows you to correct a typing error which might occur during input.

When the correct information has been supplied to the computer, execution advances to lines 330 through 350, which contain the formulas for calculating standing wave ratio. Line 360 prints the standing wave ratio on the screen. The second number will always be one; the first figure is represented by the variable Z and will be the determinant of the standing wave.

That takes care of the screen portion of the program. The synthesizer setup begins in line 370. The value of Z is converted to an integer by rounding the fractional portion using the Cint function. If the standing wave ratio is 1.25:1, the 1.25 is converted to one. If the ratio is 1.75:1, it is converted to two. The communications channel is opened in lines 380 and 390. Line 400 causes the synthesizer to output the standing wave value. Notice a two near the end of line 400. I have used this in preference to the word "TO", as most standing wave ratios are given as "FOUR TO ONE", for example.

Using this program you can compute standing wave ratios for citizens' band radios, amateur radios, and any other type of high-frequency communications system. An approximate answer is given by the synthesizer, whereas the exact answer is displayed on the screen. If you want the synthesizer to give the exact answer as well, omit line 370. No other changes are necessary.

The programs presented in this chapter are unusual only because a speech synthesizer has been used as an output device. Remove the synthesizer, and many are common programs. The minor changes required to obtain synthesizer output present no programming problems. You will have noticed by now that the same basic activation programs (synthesizer) have been used every time. It is no more difficult to feed an output to the synthesizer than it is to print something on the screen. You will often have to convert to phonetic spellings, but that is not very difficult. All you need for wide-range voice output from your IBM computer is the optional asynchronous communications adapter, inserted in one of the system expansion slots, and of course a compatible synthesizer. All voice programs in this book were tested using the Votrax Type-'N-Talk speech synthesizer, but any other model compatible with the IBM Personal computer should work as well. In the latter case it may be necessary to modify some of the commands to open the adapter at the proper transmission rate; these changes can be made in a few minutes.

The speech synthesizer is another output device which allows the computer system to communicate information to the human user. Treat it as this and no more . . . at least from a programming standpoint. With the synthesizer, however, you will have a completely different communications medium which will offer its own special advantages especially when coupled with the more standardized mediums such as monitors and printers. Also remember the internal tone generator and speaker in the IBM Personal computer. This is yet another medium at your command and may be used with the voice synthesizer. By writing your programs to access the various communication media at your disposal, a program run which is rather drab using the screen alone may become much more appealing.

Appendix A

Additional Programs

Here are some bonus programs for your enjoyment. The discussions in this book explain how programs of this nature are written and used. These programs involve music and sound effects.

SCHERZO

```
10  REM "SCHERZO"
20  PLAY "MF MN T130 O2A8B-8"
30  FOR X = 1 TO 2
40  PLAY "O3C4.C8C4D4C4P4"
50  PLAY "O2B-4A4P4G4F4A8B-8O3C4.C8C4F4E
4P4"
60  PLAY "O3D4C4P4O2B4O3C4"
70  IF X = 2 THEN 100
80  PLAY "O2A8B-8"
90  NEXT X
100  FOR Y = 1 TO 2
110  PLAY "O3P4C#4.C#8C#4E4C#4P4C#4.C#8C
#4E4C#4"
120  PLAY "O2A8B-8O3C4.C8C4D4C4P4O2B-4A4
P4G4F4P4"
130  NEXT Y
140  PLAY "O2G4F4P4G4P2F4"
150  END
```

BOOLA BOOLA

```
10   REM "BOOLA BOOLA"
20   PLAY "MF ML T255 O2E4.F8G2O3E2E2D4.P
64D8C2"
30   PLAY "O2G2G2A4.G8P64G2B2B2A4.G8P64G2
O3C2C2"
40   PLAY "O2E4.F8G2O3E2E2D4.P64D8C2"
50   PLAY "O2G2G2A4.G8P64G2B2B2A4.G8O3C1C
4P4C8P4"
60   END
```

GLOW WORM

```
10 REM "GLOW WORM"
20 PLAY"MF ML T170 O2 A4MSG8G8F#4G4G#4A4
O3G#4A4O2MLB4MSA8A8G#4A4"
30 PLAY"O2B4O3C4B4O4C4O3MLD4MSC4O2B4O3C4
O2MLB4MSA4G#4A4O3MLC4"
40 PLAY"MS O2B4A#4B4MLA4MSG4F#4G4"
50 PLAY"MLA4MSG8G8F#4G4G#4A4O3G#4A4O2MLB
4MSA8A8G#4A4"
60 PLAY"O2B4O3C4B4O4C4O3D4C4O2B4O3C4O2ML
B4MSA4O3D2.O2A8G4G8G8O3D4.C8C2."
70 END
```

IN THE GOOD OLD SUMMERTIME

```
10   REM "IN THE GOOD OLD SUMMERTIME"
20   PLAY "MF ML T200 O2D8E8D4O1B2O2D2G4B
2.B4"
30   PLAY "O2A4G4P64G4A2G2E4D2.D2."
40   PLAY "O1B2O2D4G2A4B2A4G2.A2B4A2B4A2.
A2D4"
50   PLAY "O1B2O2D4G2A4B2A4G2G4P64G2A4G4E
4G4D2.D2P64D4"
60   PLAY "O1B2O2D4G2A4B2A4G2D4E4G2P64G2A
4G2.G4"
70   END
```

HUNGARIAN MARCH

```
10   REM "HUNGARIAN MARCH"
20   PLAY "MF ML T150 O2A12B12O3C#12"
30   FOR X = 1 TO 2
40   PLAY "O3D4C#8E8D4C#8E8D4C#4D2P64D8C#
8D8E8F2P64F8E8D8C#8D4.F8E8D8C#8E8"
```

```
50  PLAY "O3D8O2F#8B8O3D8C#8O2B8A8O3C#8O
2B8A8G#8B8"
60  PLAY "O2P64B8MNA8MLA8MNG#8MLB8MNA8ML
A8G#8"
70  PLAY "A2O3A4"
80  IF X = 2 THEN 110
90  PLAY "O2A12B12O3C#12"
100  NEXT X
110  PLAY "O2B12A12G#12A4P4O3C#4P4E2.A4"

120  PLAY "O3E4.A8E8A8E8A8E2A2F8A8F4E8G8
E4"
130  PLAY "O3D8F8D4C#8E8C#4O2B-8O3D8O2B-
4A4.O3C#8"
140  PLAY "O2A4.O3C#8O2A8O3C#8O2A8O3C#8O
2A2O3A4"
150  PLAY "O2A12B12O3C#12D4C#8E8D4C#8E8D
4C#4D2"
160  PLAY "O3D8E8F4F8E8D4D8C#8O2B-4.A8G8
F#8G4F#8A8G4F#8A8G4F#4G2"
170  PLAY "O2G8A8B-4.A8G4G8F8E4.D8C#8D8C
#8E8A4P2D8F8A4P2"
180  PLAY "O2C#8E8C#8E8A2D8F8D8F8A2A4A2O
1B8O2C#8D4C#8E8D4"
190  PLAY "O2F#8A8"
200  FOR Y = 1 TO 2
210  PLAY "O2D2.F#8A8D4F#8A8D4O3D8MNC#8M
LC#8MNO2B8MLB8A#8"
220  PLAY "O3C#8O2MNB8MLB8A8B2.P64B8MNA8
MLA8MNG8MLG8F#8A8MNG8MLG8F#8G2.P64"
230  PLAY "O2G8B8E2.P64E8G8B4E8G8B4E8G8"

240  PLAY "O2L8F#EDF#EDC#EDF#C#ED"
250  IF Y = 2 THEN END
260  PLAY "O2F#8A8"
270  NEXT Y
280  END
```

JEUX D'ENFANTS

```
10  REM "JEUX D'ENFANTS"
20  PLAY "MF MS T100 O2D8"
30  FOR X = 1 TO 2
40  PLAY "O2A32L8GF#GABO3CDO2G"
50  PLAY "O3L8EF#GEA4.G8L8F#DGF#"
60  PLAY "O3L8ECF#EDEDEDCO2AO3D"
```

JEUX D'ENFANTS (continued from page 169).

```
70  PLAY "O2A32L8GF#GABO3CDO2GO3EF#GEA4.
G8L8F#BDFEAO2B"
80  PLAY "O3L8C#EDE64L8DC#MLD4P8O2D8MS"
90  NEXT X
100  FOR Y = 1 TO 2
110  PLAY "O2B24MSL8AG#ABO3CDEF#GABO4C"
120  IF Y = 2 THEN 150
130  PLAY "O4E4D8O2D8"
140  NEXT Y
150  PLAY "O4E4D8P8O3G8D8O1B8B8"
160  END
```

This clock program announces time on the hour by simulating a cuckoo clock. The "coo coo" sound is repeated for a number of times that corresponds to the hourly reading.

COOCOO CLOCK

```
10 REM COOCOO CLOCK
20 REM COPYRIGHT 12/8/82 ROBERT J. TRAIS
TER AND ASSOCIATES
30 CLS
40 KEY OFF
50 CLS
60 LOCATE 14,37
70 PRINT TIME$
80 IF MID$(TIME$,4,5)="00:00" THEN 120
90 FOR X=1 TO 600:NEXT
100 SOUND 12500,.35
110 GOTO 60
120 E$=MID$(TIME$,1,2)
130 IF MID$(TIME$,1,1)="0" THEN E$=MID$(
TIME$,2,1)
140 QRS=VAL(E$)
150 FOR X=1 TO QRS
160 PLAY"MF MS T47O4C16O3A16."
170 FOR Y=1 TO 600:NEXT Y
180 NEXT X
190 GOTO 60
```

TIMER SWITCH

This program acts as an electronic timer and allows you to input an on time and an off time. The Motor statement is used to activate and deactivate the cassette motor control relay, which is accessed at pins 1 and 3 on the cassette receptacle at the rear of the system unit. A Motor 1 statement activates the relay (closes the contacts). A Motor 0 statement deactivates it. Any external device may be controlled by being placed in series with the relay contacts, although current must be held to less than 1 ampere. I recommend using a 12-volt external relay whose power leads are connected in series with the internal relay in the system unit.

Input the activation time and the deactivation time and make certain the internal clock has been fed the current time of the day. When the activation time occurs, you will hear a beep and a flashing box will appear next to the activation prompt on the screen. When the deactivation time has occurred, you will hear another beep and another flashing box will appear next to this prompt on the screen. For most versatile use, resort to the 24-hour (military) timekeeping mode; i.e., 12 noon equals 1200 hours, 12 midnight equals 0000 hours. The on/off cycle is good for any 24-hour period of time.

This program is not recommended for computer users who do not have experience in connecting home-made peripherals to microcomputers.

TIMER SWITCH

```
10 REM TIMER SWITCH
20 REM COPYRIGHT 11/22/82 ROBERT J. TRAI
STER AND ASSOCIATES
30 CLS
40 KEY OFF
50 INPUT"TYPE IN THE ACTIVATION (ON) TIM
E (EXAMPLE:22:00:00) ";A$
60 CLS
70 INPUT"TYPE IN THE DEACTIVATION (OFF)
TIME ";B$
80 CLS
90 LOCATE 2,30
100 PRINT "ACTIVATION (ON) TIME="A$
110 LOCATE 4,30
120 PRINT"DEACTIVATION (OFF) TIME="B$
130 LOCATE 14,37
140 COLOR 0,2
150 KEY(1) ON
160 ON KEY(1) GOSUB 270
170 PRINT TIME$
180 IF TIME$=A$ THEN 210
190 IF TIME$=B$ THEN 270
200 GOTO 130
210 MOTOR 1
220 LOCATE 2,28
230 COLOR 16,1
240 PRINT CHR$(219)
250 BEEP
260 GOTO 130
270 MOTOR 0
280 LOCATE 4,28
290 COLOR 16,1
300 PRINT CHR$(219)
310 BEEP
320 GOTO 130
```

Appendix B

Musical Note/Frequency Chart

FREQUENCY	NOTE	FREQUENCY	NOTE
130,810	C	523,250	C (middle)
146,830	D	587,330	D
164,810	E	659,260	E
174,610	F	698,460	F
196,000	G	783,990	G
220,000	A	880,000	A
246,940	B	987,770	B
261,630	C	1046,500	C
293,660	D	1174,700	D
329,630	E	1318,500	E
349,230	F	1396,900	F
392,000	G	1568,000	G
440,000	A	1760,000	A
493,880	B	1975,500	B

Appendix C

Play Statement Commands Summary

A-G: Plays the note indicated in the current octave. When any note is followed by a plus (+) or a sharp (#) sign, this indicates the note is to be played as a sharp. A minus (–) sign causes the note to be played as a flat. Sharp and flat designations must correspond to a valid sharp or flat key (black key) on a piano. For example, C– is invalid, because a C flat is actually a B and there is no black key on the piano which plays this note.

Lx: The L sets the length of all notes which follow; x may range from 1 to 64. A "1" indicates a whole note, "2" a half note, and so forth. Length may be specified in the direct mode without using the L designator. When entering notes in a Play string, the designation C4 indicates that the note C is to be output as a quarter note.

MF: This is the command for music foreground and may be used with the Sound or Play statement. When in this mode each note is an entity unto itself, and the next note will not begin until the previous note has finished. Music foreground is the default state, and this mode will be in effect even when MF is not specified unless counteracted by one of the following commands.

MB: This stands for music background. This mode of operation places each note in a buffer, which allows the basic program to continue execution while music is played in the background. The buffer has limited capability, and a maximum of 32 notes or rests may be played in background at any one time.

ML: This stands for music legato. Each note is held for the full period of time (established by a previous L command).

MN: This stands for music normal and is the default state. Each note is held for ⅞ of the time specified in a length command (L).

MS: This stands for music staccato. Each note is held for ¾ of the time specified by the length command (L).

Nx: This command plays note x. The variable may range from 0 to 84, and N = 0 indicates a rest. This mode is very similar to the direct mode which specifies individual note letters, but each note is given a number rather than a letter designator.

Ox: This is the octave command and sets the octave for the notes which follow. On the IBM Personal computer there are seven octaves which are numbered 0 to 6. Each octave begins at C and ends at B. Middle C is specified by 03. The default octave is 04.

Px: This is the pause or rest command. The variable x may range from 1 to 64, as was the case with the length command (L). A P1 command indicates a rest for the equivalent of a whole note. P4 is a quarter note rest.

Tx: This is the tempo command. It sets the number of quarter notes which may be played in a sixty-second period. The value of x may range from 32 to 255. If tempo is not specified the default is equivalent to a T120, which would be musically classified as Moderato.

X (variable): This is the command that executes a specific string, as in PLAY "XA$;". A$ will consist of the alphabetic or numeric designators for a series of notes.

Note: Regarding the length of each note, a dot may be placed after a note designator to cause it to be played as a dotted note. This means that the specified length is multiplied by 3/2. In the case of a half-note, a dot will produce a total length of ¾ of a whole note. This follows standard music manuscript phrasing, and when transposing from manuscript to computer a dot may be inserted after any designator appears on the manuscript. This will yield the same results.

Index

Music and Speech Programs for the IBM PC®

If you are intrigued with the possibilities of the programs included in *Music and Speech Programs for the IBM PC®* (TAB Book No. 1596), you should definitely consider having the ready-to-run disk containing the software applications. This software is guaranteed free of manufacturer's defects. (If you have any problems, return the disk within 30 days and we'll send you a new one.) Not only will you save the time and effort of typing the programs, the tape or disk eliminate the possibility of errors that can prevent the programs from functioning. Interested?

Available on disk for the 48K IBM PC at $34.95 for each disk plus $1.00 each shipping and handling.

I'm interested. Send me:

______ disk for Music and Speech Programs for the IBM PC® (6607S)

______ Check/Money Order enclosed for $ ______ ($34.95 plus $1.00 shipping and handling for each disc)

______ VISA ______ MasterCard

Acct. No. ______________________ Expires ______________

Address ______________________________________

City ______________________ State __________ Zip ________

Signature ______________________________________

Mail To: **TAB BOOKS Inc.**
Blue Ridge Summit, PA 17214

(Pa. add 6% sales tax. Orders outside U.S. must be prepaid with international money orders in U.S. dollars.)

TAB 1596